BOROBUDUR
Buddha's Garden of Peace and Healing

BOROBUDUR Buddha's Garden of Peace and Healing
A spiritual journey with Lama Gangchen through the flower-fields of love, compassion, harmony and joy

© Karin Zwaan & Irene Zwaan
© 2016 Uitgeverij Aspekt

2nd edition 2017

Amersfoortsestraat 27, 3769 AD Soesterberg, the Netherlands
info@uitgeverijaspekt.nl – www.uitgeverijaspekt.nl

Editors: Laura Lau & Sarah Steines

Cover photo: Thomas Nitzsche, retouching by Denis Michael Lazaro

Design: Renata Reis & Renata Zincone

Illustrations: Matteo Calautti

Photographs: Lama Michel Rinpoche, Isthar Adler, Mr. Ashani, Maurice Bosman, Lama Caroline, Tiziana Ciasullo, Lidy Haarman, Gunawan Kartapranata, Kiran KC, O. Kurkdjian, Renata Reis, Maartje Roeterdink, Gil Souza, Rafaela Zincone Albieri, Renata Zincone, Karin Zwaan and the archive of Lama Gangchen Peace Publications

Some images are from the collections of the Tropenmuseum and the Museum Volkenkunde, The Netherlands. These images, as well as the images by Gunawan Kartapranata, are licensed under Creative Commons (creativecommons.org): CC BY-SA 3.0

ISBN: 9789463380850
NUR: 720

All rights reserved. No part of this book may be reproduced or translated in any form, by print, photo-print, microfilm, microfiche or any other means without written permission from the publisher.

Reading guide
This book consists of ten chapters, each with a general introduction followed by a number of personal stories that are grouped around the theme of the chapter. These personal interviews can also be read separately in any order.
    Tibetan and Sanskrit words are used occasionally in the text. These are explained in a glossary that appears in the appendix, and sometimes – when first used – in a footnote as well. Rinpoche is a frequently reoccurring word. It is a title used to address a high Buddhist lama, like Lama Gangchen Rinpoche. When used alone, it almost always refers to Lama Gangchen in this book.

BOROBUDUR

Buddha's Garden of Peace and Healing

A spiritual journey with Lama Gangchen
through the flower-fields of love, compassion, harmony and joy

aspekt

Table of of Contents

Foreword ———————————————————— 10
By Lama Gangchen Rinpoche

Kind words ———————————————————— 12
We blossom in a symbolic universe. By Professor Lokesh Chandra

Prologue ———————————————————— 18
Bit by bit I become a Buddha

Introduction ———————————————————— 21
The Love for Borobudur

1. Called by Borobudur ———————————————————— 25

The call for a long journey
Lama Gangchen, Lama Michel and Lama Caroline
Borobudur
NgalSo Self-Healing
A living ancient wisdom tradition (Laura Lau)
Strong desire to go to Borobudur (Jampa Drolma)
King of Bliss (Annabel Nguyen Tat)

2. The Garden of Central Java ———————————————————— 45

Working and living at Borobudur
Gratitude to the builders
Borobudur through the centuries
The rescue
Local ceremonies at Borobudur (Mr. Sucoro)
A whole life with Borobudur (Ariswara Sutomo)
About betjaks and helping from the heart (Jamal)
Stones as big as our living room (Lidy Haarman)
Many layers of religion (Laura Lau)
We come as spiritual tourists and receive something from the people who live here

(Valter Berten - Jampa Chöpel)
Sleeping and dreaming in the jungle (Liana Casagrande - Champa Tsomo)

3. Indonesia & The Netherlands ———————— 69
Collective karma
The truth on the table
Three hundred fifty years of colonial rule
Recognition and acknowledgement
Paragon of love and compassion (Toet de Best)
Following in the footsteps of my father (Thresia Flora Bernet)
The power of purification (Kitlyn Tjin A Djie)

4. The Stupa Deciphered ———————————— 81
About a wedding ring and female Buddhas
Mandala for all traditions
Theravada
Mahayana [the great vehicle]
Vajrayana [the fast vehicle]
About Tibet and Indonesia
Atisha visited Borobudur
Numerology and connection with the cosmos
Silver coins for a lama (Toet de Best)
The map to Shambala (Claudio Cipullo)
The boy with the precious key (Dominique Detchen Bock Nayir)
The vajra in the hand of Vajrapani (Leonardo Ceglie)

5. Magical Experiences Around the Sanctuary ———— 107
Energy field
NgalSo Self-Healing is the key to Borobudur
Authentic practice
A poetic miracle
The six perfections
The real miracle is transformation of the mind
The mind that can make things happen (Alen Kok)
A myriad of colors (Lola Hernandez)
Each time I reach a point where my mind is still and happy (Gabriella lo Re)
The impossible is possible (Ulrich Hüschelrath)
My mother's dream (Irene Zwaan)
The sun and moon in line with the stupa (Laura Oliveira)

6. The Feeling of Borobudur 131

Golden light
Lama Gangchen is the King of Feeling
Lama Gangchen knows what bothers you
A lotus on a lake?
A power plant that radiates cosmic energy (Daniel Calmanowitz)
Father and mother at the same time (Mieke Marchand)
Borobudur softens our rational mind (Peter Webb)
Borobudur brought me love (Bel Cesar)

7. A Place of Healing 149

Comprehend the cause
Invited by the King of Sikkim
What is healing?
Energy in motion
Positive use of the senses
Buddhist philosophy provides a missing link in science (Paola Muti)
At Borobudur I could accept myself as I was (May Heerkens)
More physical and mental stability (Moreno Sartori)
A turbo experience that gave me a boost (Rob Assmann)
Working with blessed oil and healing nectar (Janne Zevenberg)
Rinpoche saved my life (Carlotta Segre)
Our heads were shaved like monks (Claudia Rapisarda)
The woman who prays for all of us (Jose Mutsaerts)
A flower for my dog (Renata Zincone)

8. The Way of Personal Growth 177

An elephant never forgets
Hidden behind stone
The difference between Buddhism and psychology
The way out
No preaching
The five Buddhas and their qualities
Even if you don't want to change, you change (Roberto Mori)
A journey through volcanic ashes (Lotte Janssen)
Elephant's karma (Kersten Dohmen)
Sweet rice with raisins (Loes Thijssen)
I only saw a heap of stones (Maurice Bosman)
A journey with obstacles (Claudia Sobrevila)

9. In the Mandala of the Guru 201

Crazy wisdom
Cultural influence
A magical pilgrimage

Women
Child of the sun and the moon (Florence Roulleau)
Absolutely in heaven (Petrus Linnemann – Sangye Chöpel)
An ordeal (Anouk de Best)
The other end of the rainbow (Anneke Tabak)
Connecting worlds, feeling togetherness (Betty Voon)
Pia's ashes (Lidy Haarman)

10. Ocean of Mandalas _____ 227

Meditating at home
Inner science
What do we do when we practice NgalSo Self-Healing?
Channels, winds and drops in the mandala
Multi mandala
Once in your life to Borobudur
World Peace Stupa
Scientific research into NgalSo Self-Healing (Paola Muti)
An appointment with the five Dhyani Buddhas (Mathias Nguyen Tat)
An intense sensation of warmth (Lidy Haarman)
Emptiness is something so beautiful! (Nico Smith)
In the mandala of the Medicine Buddha (Kiran KC)
Dharma Singer (Tiziana Ciasullo)

Epilogue _____ 253
The rainbow picture

Biographies _____ 255
Lama Gangchen Rinpoche
Lama Michel Rinpoche
Lama Caroline

Glossary _____ 260

Literature and other sources _____ 269

Acknowledgements _____ 272
Together we can

Foreword

by Lama Gangchen Rinpoche

It is with pleasure that I learn about the publication of the second edition of this book by Karin Zwaan and Irene Zwaan.

Since many years I have encouraged my friends and disciples to write down their experiences, feelings, dreams and impressions of encounters and travels with me to many places. So I am very happy that Karin and Irene have made this collection of many people's experiences, especially of their journeys with me to Borobudur, and that this book in turn has become beneficial to many.

These personal testimonies bear witness to the validity of an ancient spiritual tradition in these modern times. It is through these experiences that we can learn of the benefits of spiritual practice, although we cannot easily quantify and measure such results by today's highly respected scientific means.

As almost all of us, most likely, sooner or later encounter difficulties, other's experiences like those revealed in this book, may encourage us to turn towards spiritual practice to find solutions and the strength to overcome the straits and abysses of our common life.

I rejoice in the second edition of this book and hope that it may be an inspiration to many more readers to integrate spiritual practice into their daily lives.

T.Y.S. Lama Gangchen
Albagnano Healing Meditation Centre, Italy
13 June 2017

Kind words

We blossom in a symbolic universe

Professor Lokesh Chandra (1927) from India is known worldwide as one of the greatest scholars of Buddhism. Lokesh Chandra has over 360 publications to his name and he speaks 24 languages. As a member of the Indian parliament he played a crucial role in the realization of Borobudur's restoration by UNESCO. After this restoration (1973-1984), Borobudur was placed on the UNESCO World Heritage Site list in 1991.

We are very much honored with the letter we received from this great scholar after publication of the first edition of this book in October 2016. The letter happened to arrive at a very auspicious moment, during a *Rabne Chenmo* ritual in Lama Gangchen Rinpoche's house. The letter was read at this event and Lama Gangchen deeply rejoiced in the words of his well-respected friend. As requested by Lama Gangchen, we share the precious words of the great professor here in various languages.

New Delhi, 24 December 2016

Dear friends in Dharma,

Thanks for two copies of the lovely book on Borobudur,
so different from what we are accustomed to.
What experiences and how they have changed lives.
We blossom in a symbolic universe.

Yours in Dharma,
Lokesh Chandra

Tibetan

ཆོས་གྲོགས་རྣམས་ལགས།

བྱོ་རོ་བུ་ཌཱུར་མཆོད་རྟེན་ཆེན་པོའི་སྐོར་གྱི་དེབ་གཉིས་རང་ལ་སྤྲོར་བ་བགའ་ཇིན་ཆེ། དེ་བ་དེ་ཡང་འཁར་ཅན་གྱི་དེབ་དང་འདྲ་བ་མི་འདུག དེ་ནང་ཡང་མཆོད་རྟེན་ཆེན་པོ་མི་ཁག་གི་ཉམས་སྦྱོང་གི་འགྱུར་དང་སོ་སོའི་མི་ཚེ་ལ་གྱུར་བ་ཆེན་པོ་བྱུང་བའི་འགྱུར་གྱི་མི་ཐོག་ཕར་བ་བཞིན་གྱི་ཧགས་མཚོ་རེད།

ཆོས་དད་ཀྱི་ཐོག་ནས།

ལོ་ཀེ་ཙན་དྲ་

Dutch

Beste Dharmavrienden,
Dank voor twee exemplaren van het prachtige boek over de Borobudur,
zo anders dan wat we gewend zijn.
Wat een ervaringen en hoe deze levens hebben veranderd.
We bloeien in een symbolisch universum,

De Uwe in Dharma,
Lokesh Chandra

German

Liebe Freunde im Dharma,
Vielen Dank für zwei Exemplare des schönen Buches über Borobudur,
so anders als das, was wir gewohnt sind.
Welche Erfahrungen und wie diese das Leben verändert haben!
Wir blühen in einem symbolischen Universum.

Im Dharma Ihr,
Lokesh Chandra

Portuguese

Queridos amigos do Dharma,
Obrigado pelas cópias do adorável livro das histórias de Borobudur,
muito diferente do que estamos acostumados a ver.
Que experiências! E como mudaram a vida de tantas pessoas!
Nós florescemos em um universo simbólico.

Seu amigo do Dharma,
Lokesh Chandra

French
Chers amis du Dharma,
Merci pour les deux exemplaires du merveilleux livre de Borobudur,
si différent de ce qu'on lit habituellement à ce sujet.
Que d'expériences qui ont transformées des vies entières.
Nous nous épanouissons dans un univers symbolique.

Avec vous dans le Dharma,
Lokesh Chandra

Spanish
Queridos amigos del Dharma,
Gracias por las dos copias del libro tan bonito sobre Borobudur,
tan diferente a lo que acostumbramos.
¡Que experiencias y como ha cambiado vidas!
Florecemos en un universo simbolico.

Vuestro en el Dharma,
Lokesh Chandra

Italian
Cari amici di dharma,
Grazie per le due copie del delizioso libro su Borobodur,
così diverso da quello a cui siamo abituati.
Che esperienze e come hanno cambiato le vite.
Sbocciamo in un universo simbolico.

Vostro sinceramente in dharma,
Lokesh Chandra

Chinese
亲爱的佛友们，
感谢你们寄给我有关婆羅浮屠的如此风格独特的书籍。在这本书里我很欣慰地看到这么多的人在朝圣中受益匪浅。愿我们像百卉一样怒放在宇宙之中。

祝福你们。
Lokesh Chandra

Nepalese Phonetics
Pyara Dharma mitra haru,
Borobudur ko bishaye ma duie pratilipi sundar pustak ko lagi dhanyebad.
Hamro anuvab bhanda kati bhinnata cha!
Kasto anuvab ra kasari bivinna bekti haru ley afno jivan pariwartan garey.
Hami sabai pratikatmak brahmand ma fullaun.

Dharma ma tapaiko,
Lokesh Chandra

Prologue

Bit by bit

I become a Buddha

Bit by bit, I become a Buddha.
   Not by a single, earth-moving leap from samsara to omniscience
   while meditating at the Mother Stupa
   but rather – piecemeal – my colors gradually brighten.

   Seed syllables sprout in the Buddha Garden at Borobudur.
   Every day they grow to be a little more like their symbols.
   Every day the symbols resemble their Dhyani Buddhas a little more;
   till one day – one life – I will become more Buddha than not.

Bit by bit I become a Buddha.
   Each of us a pot pourri of habits
   and karma, gathered over lifetimes.
   Each a rainbow of wise and reckless habits;
   shining in some directions, still hampered in others.
   Everyone unique.

   All lovingly supported and guided by one Master –
   Lama Gangchen Rinpoche.

Bit by bit I become a Buddha.
   We come from different backgrounds,
   different cultures, different countries,
   of different ages and attitudes.
   Each of us with our own blind spots
   Each requiring individual handling
   by our one skilled Master –
   Lama Gangchen Rinpoche.

Bit by bit I become a Buddha.
   Only through constancy will I grow towards the light.
   Practice makes perfect.
   A lifetime of unsurprising rainy Tuesdays
   inching forward towards perfection.

Bit by bit I become a Buddha.
   NgalSo: I accept myself more than before
   NgalSo: I accept my light ... and my shadow too.
   Gradually I relax with who I am,
   with where I have come from and
   with the path I need to follow
   in the Buddha Garden of Borobudur.

Bit by bit I become a Buddha.

Sarah Steines (1961) England
Borobudur, March 2016

Introduction

The Love

for Borobudur

Why do around two hundred pilgrims from all corners of the world travel to Borobudur in Indonesia year after year to climb the temple together at the crack of dawn, performing mudras, mantras and meditations? What motivates them to accomplish this nearly seven-kilometer long 'spiritual marathon' every morning for two weeks? What is it that they experience at this ancient Buddhist sanctuary?

When Karin first joined a Borobudur retreat with the Tibetan Lama Gangchen Rinpoche in 2009, her journalist heart started beating faster. This was worth a story; she could feel it. But just then the time wasn't yet ripe. She had to have her own experience first. A year later she carefully started to think about a book, inspired also by Lama Gangchen's frequent requests to his followers to write down their experiences. However, it was not until she had finished another book, the life story of Toet de Best, another disciple of Lama Gangchen, that the idea of writing about Borobudur really started to take shape. In April 2013 Karin went with her sister Irene to see Lama Gangchen to present her ideas.

During this meeting, he advised us, Karin and Irene, to write together and in two languages: Dutch and English. He also requested us to pay attention to the various connections between Indonesia, The Netherlands and Tibet. Lama Gangchen often stresses the fact that Tibet is the highest country in the world whilst Holland – 'Holy Land' – is the lowest, and that The Netherlands have played an important role in the rescue of Borobudur. Due to the efforts of the Dutch in Indonesia, the ancient Tibetan wisdom mandala has been preserved for current and future generations.

Following our meeting, Lama Gangchen allowed us the space to write about anything that we have learnt about Borobudur and also about the extraordinary phenomena that people see or experience.

We also received the valuable instruction that the book should be about the love for Borobudur – genuine and transcending love.

For both of us, Lama Gangchen is very important in our lives and we rely upon his advice and direction. Karin got in touch with Lama Gangchen two years after her partner Hans suddenly died at the age of forty-two. During a moment of deep pain she prayed aloud to the Buddhas, Jesus, God and the starry sky above her garden, asking for help. The next day, unasked, a colleague gave her a telephone number of someone who might be able to help. Karin knew, "This is the help I have been asking for." She made an appointment and she saw a photo of Lama Gangchen in the meditation room of this Buddhist healer. In late 2004 she met Lama Gangchen for the first time in person and she knew she had come home.

Irene had moved in with Karin after Hans passed away, but like so many Westerners, she was rather skeptical about following a guru or a religion.

However, she started to have dreams about Lama Gangchen. On holiday and unaware of the connection, she went to the place on Lesbos where Lama Gangchen had established his first center in Europe. During a subsequent holiday on Naxos, also in Greece, she heard the music of Lama Gangchen's NgalSo Self-Healing meditation from the speakers of a beach bar, like at Karin's house. For all that, it took a couple of years. Then, she had a dream where Lama Gangchen appeared as a construction worker with rolled-up sleeves. He started to demolish her barn. Irene exclaimed, "I need to know the price first!" "But I have already put you on my schedule," the lama objected. Not much later, Irene also took refuge in Buddha, dharma and sangha.

Nowadays there is an increasing number of people who, like us, find spiritual fulfillment in Buddhism. According to Tibetan Buddhism, we live in a Kaliyuga time. This means we find ourselves in a period of degeneration of our existence. There are five points that show this clearly:

● Degeneration of Health: New diseases arise, like AIDS and cancer;

● Degeneration of Medication: Effectiveness of medicine diminishes or medication is insufficiently available;

● Degeneration of Food: Foods are less nutritious due to pollution and production methods;

* Degeneration of Time: Time becomes less valuable - many of us recognize the feeling that time goes faster. This degeneration started in the 1980s. It is said that what we used to experience as 24 hours has now contracted to 16 hours;

* Degeneration of Sentient Beings: Negative characteristics like anger, hatred, fear, jealousy, attachment, miserliness and arrogance are increasing.[1]

Living in this timeframe of degeneration probably makes our need for meaning in the form of spirituality and philosophy greater. An interesting aspect of Tibetan Buddhism is the fact that it doesn't only provide meaning; it also uses and works with these five points of degeneration in order to create a positive transformation.

For this book we interviewed over fifty disciples and friends of Lama Gangchen about their experiences in relation to Borobudur. They opened their hearts. For some it wasn't easy or obvious to share their very personal stories. But they were convinced by the frequently-expressed wish of Lama Gangchen for practitioners of NgalSo Self-Healing to share their experiences or write them down.

Together their stories tell the story of Borobudur in relation to the NgalSo Self-Healing and Lama Gangchen.

During the 27th retreat at Borobudur, on March 1 2016, Lama Gangchen Rinpoche blessed this book on top of the stupa with prayers, together with a group of monks. May this book contribute to the wellbeing of all sentient beings.

Karin and Irene

---

[1] Lama Michel, February 12th 2016, Teaching: Seven Point Mind Training Part 1, AHMC, Albagnano, Italy

View of Merapi volcano

Chapter 1

Called by Borobudur

The call for a long journey

"Around 1986 and 1987, shortly after Lama Gangchen had moved to Italy, I used to spend a lot of time with him. It was before he had established his own center in Milan and he was not nearly as busy as he is nowadays. We often used to watch TV together. One day, I showed him a video about Borobudur. It was a travel show with tourist information I had recorded from the TV. I am not sure if Lama Gangchen already knew about Borobudur back then, but after having seen the video he said: 'That is the place where we have to go!'" Francesco Prevosti (1956, Italy), Lama Gangchen's translator.

In the late 1980s, Lama Gangchen visited the world's largest Buddhist *stupa*,[1] Borobudur in Indonesia for the first time. Inspired by the ancient temple, he soon began teaching a simple meditation method, based on profound *sutras*[2] and *tantras*[3] from Tibetan Buddhism. Lama Gangchen named this practice, *NgalSo Self-Healing, a method to relax body and mind.*

Ever since, Lama Gangchen – together with Lama Caroline, who is educated academically in Buddhism and is also a Buddhist practitioner – conducts research on Borobudur. They continue to discover more and more indications that this ancient sanctuary is a three-dimensional stupa-mandala,[4] suitable for numerous practices in Tibetan *Vajrayana* Buddhism. Among academics, this position is currently under debate and discussion.

---

1 Originally a tomb for a highly-realized person. A stupa often contains relics and sacred objects. The stupa also symbolizes the enlightened mind of a Buddha.
2 Sutras are all Buddha's publicly transmitted teachings and methods.
3 Tantras are the esoteric or 'secret' teachings of the Buddha that are followed in Vajrayana Buddhism, besides the sutras.
4 In Vajrayana Buddhism, a mandala forms an energetically pure environment in which one or more Buddhas reside.

Lama Michel, Lama Gangchen and Lama Caroline

Meanwhile, around two hundred people from all corners of the world travel with Lama Gangchen to Borobudur annually. At the crack of dawn, they climb the stupa each day, performing *NgalSo Self-Healing*. Many of these disciples and friends of Lama Gangchen share their experiences, insights and feelings in this book. In this way, they tell the story of Borobudur together in relation to Lama Gangchen and NgalSo Self-Healing, which are the three pillars of this book's contents.

Lama Gangchen, Lama Michel and Lama Caroline[5]

Lama Gangchen (1941) is a Tibetan Buddhist lama from the *Gelugpa* tradition, who had to flee from Tibet in the 1960s, due to the political situation. After having lived in India for a while, he came to the West. Since then, he has travelled the world and spreads his peace message everywhere, 'Inner peace is the most solid foundation for world peace.' Since 1998, his home and one of his study centers is situated in Albagnano, Italy.

In 1989, Lama Gangchen visited Borobudur for the first time with five disciples. Nowadays, more than two hundred friends and adepts come along for an annual spiritual gathering at the stupa.

Lama Gangchen is the holder of an ancient uninterrupted *lineage* of tantric masters that goes back to the time of Buddha *Shakyamuni*[6] around two thousand five hundred years ago.

Lama Michel and Lama Caroline have a special connection with Lama Gangchen and they are holders of the NgalSo lineage.

Lama Michel (1981) was born in Brazil into a Christian-Jewish family. When he was five years old, Lama Gangchen recognized him as a *tulku*, a reincarnation of an important Tibetan master. At the age of twelve, he moved on his own initiative into a Tibetan monastery in India. To date, he studies and teaches Buddhist philosophy according to the Gelugpa tradition.

Lama Caroline (1965) is from England. During her studies, she found that Western science was too conceptual and insufficient to explain reality. She was introduced to Gelugpa Buddhism and met

---

5 Refer to the appendix for biographies.
6 The historical Buddha, who was born around 560 years B.C. as the king's son Siddhartha Gautama, in Lumbini (currently in Nepal bordering India).

Lama Gangchen. In 2000, she was recognized by Lama Gangchen as Lama Dorje Khanyen Lhamo. She works intensively with Lama Gangchen and has written books with him. She also conducts historical research and teaches about Vajrayana Buddhism.

Borobudur

Borobudur is a Buddhist sanctuary in Central Java, Indonesia. Since antiquity, the temple was shrouded by all kinds of mysteries about its origin, the way it was constructed and its meaning. Numerous antiquarians from the nineteenth and twentieth century examine what can be called 'the miracle of Borobudur'. Nowhere in the world does another temple of this size and shape exist.

Borobudur was built in the eighth century by the kings of the Buddhist Sailendra Dynasty (circa 750 - 850 AD) that then ruled Java. It was a huge construction job. The temple was built with fifty-five thousand square meters of stones that were hewn, piece by piece, from river rocks. The construction measures 123 by 123 meters and is 35 meters high. Two and a half kilometers of detailed bas-relief carvings with detailed scenes of Buddhist stories were carved into the walls of the galleries of the temple. There are hundreds of Buddha statues, stupas, ornaments, decorations, alcoves, lotuses, animals, *etc*. Borobudur was built over a hill, which didn't make the work easier. It must have taken several generations to finish the job, with the effort of hundreds of craftsmen. Estimates for its construction period vary from seventy to one hundred years.

Probably only one hundred fifty years later, things went quiet around Borobudur, presumably because Buddhism gradually disappeared from the region. Meanwhile, a rain of volcanic ash and bountiful vegetation covered the sanctuary, which steadily vanished into the jungle. It was due to this natural conservation that the temple was preserved for the future. In early 1800s, the British and Dutch colonialists in Indonesia excavated the stupa. Later Borobudur was restored in phases.

Borobudur not only captures your imagination, it also plays with your imagination. When you look at it from a distance you see a round dome construction but on getting nearer, it becomes clear that it is square. The light on the stupa during the daytime is magnificent. Sometimes the stone of the temple almost looks black, then it shines in bright golden light or appears warm gold in the mists of dawn.

Borobudur is constructed as a pyramid. Four staircases lead to the top, one in the middle of each side. From above, the staircases lie over the stupa like a cross.

Over the foundation, there are five ascending terraces with four narrow galleries that can be circumambulated. There is no space inside Borobudur, apart from the hidden chamber in the top stupa. Both the left and right walls of the galleries are adorned with stone bas-reliefs; these panels show pictorial stories from important Buddhist texts, for example the life story of the historical Buddha Shakyamuni.

Above the square tiers there are three levels where light and space play freely. Here the shapes become round and open. On these three round levels are 72 stupas and resting on the top of these levels is a very large stone lotus cushion for the great mother stupa. From the top, the view over the green and fertile Plain of Kedu is breathtaking. Borobudur is surrounded by mountains and volcanoes, of which the active Merapi erupted and rained its ashes only recently. Along the rim of the nearby Menoreh mountains one can see the profile of a sleeping figure said to be Gunadharma, the architect who designed and constructed Borobudur.

These days, Lama Gangchen shines a new light on Borobudur and unveils the temple by applying his knowledge of Tibetan Vajrayana Buddhism.

NgalSo Self-Healing

The hundreds of Buddha statues on the five levels with galleries are most striking. They sit serene in their alcoves and watch over the beautiful landscape. These are statues of the five *Dhyani Buddhas*[7] or meditation Buddhas, which are also found in Nepal and Tibet. In the early years of visiting Borobudur, Lama Gangchen was inspired at the temple to begin teaching *NgalSo Self-Healing*, a traditional meditation for modern people.

Self-Healing is a meditation method in which the five Dhyani Buddhas play a big part. The practice helps you to develop your qualities and to diminish your negative emotions. NgalSo Self-Healing is based on the teachings of the Buddha and can be

---

7 Archetypical meditation Buddhas who represent the *five wisdoms* in their perfected state.

practiced by anyone; Buddhists and non-Buddhists alike. Lama Gangchen says, "It is suitable for modern people who are occupied with their individuality and personal freedom; people who can only be controlled by their own inner positive or negative decisions and not by a god, priest, lama, king or politician."[8]

Many people in today's world are looking for spirituality and meaning in their lives. They are no longer satisfied by the traditions and religions of their own cultures. In modern society, people often have difficulties committing themselves to a religion. Their autonomous mind is skeptical. However, Buddhism does seem to appeal to a lot of people nowadays.

It is remarkable that Westerners usually embrace Buddhism with a lot of enthusiasm as a philosophy. Not taken as a religion, Buddhism is a philosophy indeed. But it is more than just a philosophy; it is also a religion.

The spiritual path, says Lama Michel, Heart-Son of Lama Gangchen, means inner growth. It is about developing one's qualities, like love, compassion, patience, stability, humility, generosity and wisdom. At the same time, it aims to steadily diminish our negative aspects, like hatred, anger, jealousy, miserliness and arrogance. A religion is a method, transferred from generation to generation, from master to disciple, to fulfil this spiritual path. The institution is the organization that supports and carries out the religion. The spiritual path, the inner process, is the essence; the religion and institution are supportive to this goal. Coming from whatever tradition, this personal learning process is the ultimate objective of any religion, as well as the institution. If this is not the case, then they are of no use, says Lama Michel.[9]

Relative to Borobudur, in the three stories that follow, we read about the journey of Laura Lau, Jampa Drolma and Annabel Nguyen Tat. All three are consciously or unconsciously longing for spirituality and looking for a method to give shape to this path. Laura is a woman from Singapore, Jampa Drolma is a Dutch woman and Annabel is French with French-Vietnamese heritage. What connects these women from different parts of the world is that all three of

---

8 Lama Gangchen, T.Y.S. (1994), *NgalSo Tantric Self-Healing III*, p. 35, Lama Gangchen Peace Publications
9 Lama Michel, Sept 13th 2015, Teaching: *Introduction to Buddhist Philosophy* Part 4, AHMC, Albagnano, Italy

them felt a strong impulse to go to Borobudur. They were 'called' by the temple, before they were familiar with Lama Gangchen or NgalSo Self-Healing.

A living ancient wisdom tradition
Laura Lau (1975) Singapore

Laura Lau feels a strong need for guidance and structure on her spiritual path. When an inner sign indicates her to start looking she ends up with Lama Gangchen and Borobudur in a miraculous way.

Looking for a clear format

"At the end of 2008, I gradually came to realize that there was an urgent need in my life to create more structure in my spiritual path and to find a proper and qualified teacher. I simply didn't want to get lost for any longer in the marketplace of many spiritual practices. I needed a clear format and I wanted it to be secured on valid principles that had stood the test of time. Out of the blue an idea came to me, 'Look at tantra!' So that moved me to find out about tantric Buddhism. I discovered that the ancient methods of tantric or Vajrayana Buddhism are still in practice, so it is a living tradition of ancient wisdom. In the contemporary world of the 21st century, it is one of the only means of access that we have to the spiritual sublime, so it was easy to decide to find out more!

Soon after, I decided to organize a holiday and I planned to visit Borobudur during the *Vesak*[10] festival. Just before Christmas, I booked my flight and two hotel rooms for the festival in May, without even knowing if anyone would join me there. But again, the impulse was strong, as if I was guided: 'Don't worry about the two rooms; some people will join you, even though you don't know who they are yet'."

Meeting the master

"Meanwhile, something very auspicious and significant was also about to take place. During the Christmas and New Year season,

---

[10] The yearly commemoration of the birth, enlightenment and death of Buddha Shakyamuni.

Laura Lau
during her first visit

I met somebody who I spoke to for hours about Vajrayana and Tibetan Buddhism, who knew Lama Gangchen and who offered to bring me to the teachers directly. So in early 2009, during *Losar*, the Tibetan New Year festival, I flew to Nepal for the first time and met Lama Gangchen Rinpoche in Kathmandu. I was struck by his strong energy and felt awed in his presence. I had met my master!

I spent almost a week in Kathmandu and it rocked my mind, it really shook me up. I knew I needed to understand what I experienced; I needed to learn about the rituals, prayers and also the teachings of the Buddha. I knew that I was experiencing many things directly with great impact but still I wasn't quite aware exactly analytically what was going on – it was like being suddenly in the deep end of a swimming pool when you have to do something, otherwise you will drown."

A beautiful situation

"Then, I was completely amazed and elated to find out about Lama Gangchen's close connection to Borobudur because I had already planned on going there even before I met him. It was such a beautiful situation. Whilst in Kathmandu, I also managed to lay my hands on a copy of Lama Gangchen's prayers for practice at Borobudur. In this way, I simply just got the instruction manual for what I needed to do at Borobudur. It all made me very happy: something was coming together for me in some clear pattern for my apparently impulsive crazy trip to Borobudur. I was delighted and comforted to have a proper practice to do there, specifically because I wanted a spiritual system for making personal development safe and free from all kinds of serious problems.

So in May I arrived at Borobudur, indeed accompanied by three friends. I went to the stupa with the *sadhana*[11] prayer book from Lama Gangchen, which guided me very clearly in how and where to pray. It was precisely integrated with the stupa. I did the whole practice for the first time as best I could on my own, reciting the *mantras*[12] and performing the *mudras*[13] according to the level and the direction, without Lama Gangchen or anyone else by my side. I was just alone guided by the stupa. The reliefs on the walls of the galleries and the Buddha statues showed me what was going on and which mudra to do. It was easy to concentrate and it was especially meaningful to have a proper coherent set of prayers to offer at the great stupa. I felt very blessed and fortunate indeed.

After this experience at Borobudur, I started to study the Self-Healing. I read and did a lot of preliminary practices by myself, as there was no one else in Singapore to share fellowship with me. These events led to the dramatic changes I decided to make in my life. I felt there were things in my life that were, in perspective, no longer important to me and after a while I didn't feel the need to hang on to them. I simply knew from my heart and experiences that this lineage of Vajrayana Buddhism was right for me. Since then I have spent time with Lama Gangchen in Borobudur, where I have witnessed beautiful phenomena around the prayers and practices that he offers there."

---

11 Literal meaning: 'method to accomplish'. Sadhana usually refers to the guidelines for a religious practice. A sadhana comprises the instructions for meditation, recitation and visualization.
12 Literal meaning: 'mind protector'. A mantra is a series of sacred syllables with a deep meaning. Different Buddhas each have their own mantra. Reciting a mantra helps you to concentrate, to relax and to be protected. It brings you closer to the specific quality of the Buddha concerned.
13 Powerful hand gesture that helps to navigate the inner energies.

Yantra, astrology and more

"Since then, I have learnt a lot about the stupa as well. Today, it is one of the unique places where many cultures and religions come together. I would call it a thought-provoking place – a conjunction of monument, philosophy and intention. The message of Borobudur is captured in its stones and statues, while the architecture of the mandala is aligned with astronomical constellations. I am told there are parallels with Hindu mandalas; I heard that the structure of *Shri Yantra*[14] is similar to the levels and faces of Borobudur. It reflects a truth that is universal: the message of Borobudur includes the balance between the elements that you can also find in Chinese astrology. Perhaps the great stupa is actually a composite of many different pathways, which could be recognized in various spiritual traditions. Perhaps there is truly so much wisdom that we don't know about yet."

Strong desire to go to Borobudur
Jampa Drolma (1976) The Netherlands

Jampa Drolma is a hard working medical student who has some intense experiences in Indonesia. After this her life changes dramatically.

Traineeship in a nuns' hospital

"Being a poor student, I subscribed for a sponsored vacation-traineeship overseas. I dreamed of a beautiful place in Africa where I could do something with plant medicine related to my studies in biology and medicine. From hundreds of students, I won one of the few tickets! However, the journey wasn't going to Africa but to Indonesia, where I would have to work in a hospital in busy Jakarta. I gave the ticket back because that was absolutely not what I had wished for; I really wanted something where I could combine biology with medicine. Medicine had my preference, but I also loved botany and plant medicine.

In the pub where I worked in the evening I told the whole story to

---

[14] The Shri Yantra consists of an interweaving matrix of geometric figures. A yantra is a symbolic representation of various aspects of a god or deity.

somebody. This man said he knew a travel guide who would probably be able to help me. Not even one hour later, this woman entered the bar and again, very much by chance, she knew a nuns' hospital on the island of Flores in Indonesia. These nuns kept a herbal garden of six hectares!

With some effort I managed to get in touch with them. Initially, they didn't respond to my letter so I tried to phone them. Exactly at the moment that I picked up the phone to ring, a roommate entered with her Indonesian cousin. She helped me call them. And that is how I could get started on the island of Flores. I still had to look for sponsors because I had given back my ticket but that also turned out to be quite easy in the end.

After the traineeship, I would take a holiday with a friend on Java, where we also planned to visit Borobudur. Because I had taken a language course in Bahasa Indonesia in Yogyakarta first, I already had the idea to visit Borobudur on my own. The place appealed to me strongly. But when I told this to my friend, she reacted with disappointment; she wished us to experience the first impression of this special temple together; so I promised her I would wait."

A meditative state

"But I was overwhelmed by such a deep desire to go to Borobudur that I found it hard to keep my promise. Finally I came up with an alternative: I would go to the nearby volcano Merapi. From there I expected at least to be able to see Borobudur from a distance. It turned out not to be the case but I did have a special experience. By being at Merapi during the sunset, I entered without noticing into a state of deep contemplation. Only afterwards did I recognize it as a deep meditation.

It was there and at that moment that I realized which direction I had to take regarding my two studies. 'I will continue medicine, I will quit biology and I will develop myself in integrative care, as in Western and natural medicine.' This message came to me as a kind of vision, or a clear insight. I was not familiar with the concept of integrative care yet. Neither was I into meditation. However, I did bring the book The Quest on this journey, about finding one's life path. That intrigued me.

In the nuns' clinic I had a wonderful time. There, I formed the base for my interest in integrative medicine, which is what I am doing now. Next, I went backpacking around Java with my friend. We were full of expectation when we arrived at Borobudur. I was very much excited: something special was about to happen! But when we climbed the temple and arrived at the highest levels ... not much happened actually. In our travel-bible The Lonely Planet, we read that one could make a wish on the round daises on top of the temple and that then one should touch the hand of the Buddha inside one of the 72 bell-stupas. I found it pretty much baloney that they had built this huge temple only for this. I didn't even make the effort anymore to continue the climb to the highest point. What a disappointment ... this was certainly not what I had hoped for."

On the verge of death

"Back home in Holland, I collected money for the nuns' clinic. They were in urgent need of a generator, because the tuberculosis patients on artificial respiration died if there was a power cut, which happened not seldom. That was awful. My initiative was picked up and we collected sixty thousand guilders. Some years later, in 2004, I returned to Indonesia to see and monitor the use of this money. Again, I combined the trip with a traineeship and a holiday in Bali with a friend.

At that time I was not feeling very well because a year earlier my father had passed away. Therefore I visited an acupuncturist on Bali. Initially everything seemed to be okay but that night I felt I couldn't breathe, I felt miserable. The next morning in the hospital, it turned out to be what I already feared. I had a pneumothorax; my lung had been punctured during the acupuncture. They would rather not operate on me in Bali because of the risk of an infection, so they sent me to Surabaya in Java, a journey of eight hours.

The hospital organized transport by minivan and assured me that, with such a tiny hole in my lung, I could easily make it to Surabaya. But it turned out to be the opposite; I started a real death journey. I could breathe less and less, the pain got worse and the pleural came loose. I knew that the pressure in your chest could increase so much that your heart could simply stop. 'How terrible for my mother, brothers and sisters,' I thought. 'Now I will also die.' Then suddenly a passage from a book of the Dalai Lama that I had recently bought popped up in my mind. It was about yogic breathing and how you can reduce your breathing in such a way that one gulp is sufficient for quite a while. 'This is my rescue,' I thought.

I concentrated on slow breathing and started praying intensely. I was one of six in a Catholic family and went to church regularly. I also liked to pray the rosary, being the only one amongst us. However, I had left my rosary at home on this journey. While I was lying as still as possible in the van, I took some important decisions about my life: if I survived this, I wanted to learn all about meditation.

Also, I wanted to change the direction of my life completely. Those days I led a rather wild student life. I had many friends, was quite popular, there wasn't a party where I couldn't be found from beginning to end. But deep inside I felt unhappy. I had a heavy feeling, aroused by the death of my father when I was only twenty-five. Facing the fact that life could simply end, just like that, was very intense. And at that moment, looking death in the face myself, I knew I wanted changes."

An apron filled with rosaries

"Despite several obstacles, including trees blocking the road and drivers demanding more money, we reached the hospital in Surabaya that night and I could get treatment. The next morning somebody knocked on my door. It was a nun; I knew her. It was the nun that I had handed the symbolic cheque of sixty thousand guilders to four years earlier for the generator on Flores! We looked at each other in disbelief. She told me that she had been residing in this hospital for a couple of months to recover from a shoulder fracture caused in a motor accident.

She had heard that two Dutch women were being admitted that night and came on behalf of the staff to ask if she could be of any help. I asked her, 'Do you have, by any chance, a rosary for me?' She laughed while opening the front pocket of her apron. There were around fifty beautiful hand-made rosaries lying in there! 'Well ... I need to do something to pass time here, don't I,' she explained. She gave me a roguish wink and said, 'Pick one out!'

Eventually, everything turned out to be okay and once at home, I immediately started to work on myself; I started with processing the loss of my father, I made a first attempt to meditate and I moved to another city.

That same year I met the man who is now my husband, lecturing in a congress for natural remedies. I was moved by his presence. 'I need to speak with this man', I knew, and I approached him through my interest in plant medicine. We exchanged email addresses and I sent him a rather formal message next. He replied with a long personal letter in which he told me how he, after a difficult period, had ended up with the Tibetan Lama Healer, Lama Gangchen Rinpoche.

This fascinated me; also because of the experience I had had with the yogic breathing. Ever since that time, we have made many journeys together with Rinpoche to Italy, Spain, Tibet, Thailand, Vietnam, and so on. Up until now, we have been to Borobudur with Lama Gangchen nine times. Over the last few years I have learnt so much about NgalSo Self-Healing, the *dharma*[15] and the spiritual depth of Borobudur. Lama Gangchen has the capacity to bring this stone temple complex to life. For me, the lessons that are contained in Borobudur have become very important for my own spiritual development, and are also a source of inspiration for my daily life and work as a general practitioner helping people in an integrative way."

King of Bliss
Annabel Nguyen Tat (1970) France

An inner voice tells Annabel to go to Borobudur. With her eyes closed she sits on the stupa and starts meditating. When she opens her eyes again, she has an experience that will change her life forever.

A voice in my head

"In 1999, I worked in Bali as a scuba-diving instructor. I was looking for spiritual answers, doing a lot of meditation and yoga, without following any religious path. I practiced yoga and meditation every morning to relax my mind because my working conditions were quite difficult. By then, I already knew that I actually needed a teacher to help me further on my way and I was praying to meet one.

In order to extend my work visa I had to leave the country, so

---

15 Spiritual 'medicine' that heals the suffering of body and mind. In Buddhism, it refers to the teachings and the inner realizations and experiences that are achieved.

I planned a trip to Thailand, and thought I would combine it with a *Vipassana*[16] retreat there. During my morning meditation I heard a voice in my head, which was rather strange. 'Go to Borobudur!' I never had experienced anything like this and I didn't know what Borobudur meant. I didn't change my plans but the next day I heard the voice again. 'Go to Borobudur!' Then I remembered that, before going to Bali, I had actually planned to go work in Egypt as a scuba-diving teacher but a friend advised me to go to Indonesia, because of my Asian blood – as my father is Vietnamese – and she also showed me a picture of Borobudur. Due to this friend's advice, I chose Bali, but I forgot about Borobudur.

Anyway, I left for Thailand via Singapore, where I collected my visa and then the voice came for the third time. 'Go to Borobudur!' This time I decided to listen, so I changed direction and left for Java instead of Thailand. In Yogyakarta, I met a Frenchman who was willing to join me to go to the temple but then the voice came back to me and I realized something serious was about to happen, so I apologized to the friend and told him that I had to continue on my own. I knew this was important.

I climbed the stupa with a guidebook about the meaning of the statues and panels. Then I sat down somewhere on the lower levels of the Amitabha side and closed my eyes to meditate. I could feel that a group of people was approaching me, so after a while I opened my eyes and found myself looking directly into the eyes of the man standing in front of me. It was an intense moment. We smiled at each other. Usually when you meet somebody's eyes you look away after a while, so I closed them again and went back into meditation. That moment felt as if my body was made of glass. When I opened my eyes for the second time, the man was still looking at me. This time I couldn't take my eyes off him and I felt tears welling up. I could sense this was a holy being in front of me. This man was Lama Gangchen Rinpoche.

He had arrived there with his group that same morning to stay for a retreat that would last for three weeks; gradually I would start to join them.

After some days, I went to his room to talk to him for the first time. I told him that I was HIV positive. 'I don't think so', he said.

---

[16] Meditation method aimed at the development of clear insight into the nature of reality.

'You look healthy. Anyway, we will help you.' 'Who is we?' I thought. Then he looked at me and asked, 'But where did we meet?' I didn't understand his question not being used to his English. 'In Italy, in France, in Germany?' he continued. 'We met there,' I answered, pointing at the stupa. He said, 'Oh yes, I understand.' Then I left.

The next day I joined the group in the seminar room to listen to Lama Gangchen. Suddenly I felt tired as I had never felt before. It was something completely different, as if all the cells in my body were being shaken in some cosmic washing machine. I was exhausted. After twenty minutes it stopped and Rinpoche smiled at me, showing that he knew. 'You are very tired today,' he said later. I realized that I wouldn't be surprised at all if the test results would be different at my next annual medical check.

Nine months later I was back in France and in the hospital they couldn't diagnose me as HIV positive any longer. This was considered impossible, so the doctors declared me neither HIV positive nor HIV negative.

Back to that first time at Borobudur: In the morning at the start of the climb, Lama Gangchen gave us a flower and incense to offer to Borobudur as he always does. Several times he said to me, 'Bonjour! When you go to Paris you will meet Detchen.' Detchen? It could be a book, a person or a kind of cake; I didn't have a clue what it was but I would find out later.

In the meantime, like many of us, I started to have incredible dreams. It was so strong! I was asleep but sitting up in bed, I saw the five colors of the Dhyani Buddhas, indescribably clear and bright, moving around me. Later I realized it was a *blessing*[17] from this place. From that time, I started an incredible journey by means of the experiences that come with the visualizations and meditations of Vajrayana Buddhism. There are no words to describe that. Or maybe only Tibetan words can tell.

Back in France, I found out that Detchen was the Tibetan name of Dominique, a disciple who ran Rinpoche's center in Paris. She was already sick when I met her. We became friends but she passed away in 2012. We did *Guru Puja*[18] at her funeral with some friends."

---

17 The energy of gurus, holy beings and holy places that helps sentient beings on their spiritual paths and creates the conditions to transform body, speech, mind, activities and qualities.
18 An extensive practice with recitation, visualization and meditation.

Lama Gangchen and Ananda
at the unfinished Buddha statue

Following Buddha's footsteps

"In 2013 I went on a pilgrimage to follow the Buddha's footsteps in India. One day in New Delhi, I met up with an old boyfriend and from that moment something went on between us again. After a while, on a certain morning all of a sudden, I felt Dominique's presence all around me. I was walking through the streets, looking left and right as if I would see her. I knew this was unrealistic as, according to Buddhism, she would already have been incarnated again, 49 days after passing. It was one year later by now. But the feeling was inescapable.

Back home, I found out I was pregnant. I couldn't believe it; I had never ever wanted to have children. Besides, I was 43, and hardly menstruating any longer being in a pre-menopause phase. I phoned Rinpoche and told him I wanted to get rid of it. 'Dominique is coming,' he said. I didn't understand him. That day in Albagnano, some friends came to celebrate the Dominique's memory one year after her passing.

Next day I phoned again. And again he said, 'Dominique is coming.' Now I understood, and I realized I had to keep the baby. Things fell into place. Like the fact that before going to India, I had said to a friend that I didn't want children, but if I got a child I would call him or her Ananda as it means 'bliss' in Sanskrit. When I learnt that 'Detchen' means bliss in Tibetan, even this idea seemed to have a reason. So Ananda was born and Rinpoche gave him the Tibetan name Detchen Gyalpo, which means King of Bliss.

In 2015 we came to Borobudur with him. And on the exact spot where I met Rinpoche the first time, he gave Ananda refuge by cutting a piece of his hair and leaving it on the stupa while the group was singing the refuge prayer:

NAMO GURUBYE
NAMO BUDDHAYA
NAMO DHARMAYA
NAMO SANGHAYA
NAMO TRI RATNAYA"

From collection Museum Volkenkunde
Leiden, The Netherlands, ca. 1875

Chapter 2

The Garden of

Central Java

Working and living at Borobudur

March 1st, 2016, early in the morning. Lama Gangchen is sitting with a big group of monks and disciples at the foot of the stupa, reciting prayers and mantras. Suddenly Lama Gangchen interrupts the ceremony. He calls a passing Indonesian tourist guide, asks him to step up and share his story with the group. The man climbs the stairs, takes a seat next to Rinpoche, takes the microphone and happily starts speaking, "Lama Gangchen knows me very well. Fifteen years ago I started as a cleaner at the temple. Later I worked with security and was guarding the stupa at night. I never imagined being able to make it as a tourist guide one day, because I didn't speak English. But I have done it! Now I speak English and I tell tourists about the stupa. This is all thanks to Borobudur."

Many people who work on and around the stupa know Lama Gangchen from his yearly visits. In this chapter, some Javanese people who grew up near and with Borobudur tell their stories. Their love for the temple resounds through their words. They express their gratitude to those who created the building. The names of some villages in the area still refer to the time of the construction of Borobudur.

Gratitude to the builders

Borobudur is situated in the Kedu Plain, also known as the garden of Central Java. When you view the surroundings from the top of Borobudur, you understand why. There is so much green, so much beauty – it is a heavenly landscape. The fertile green valley is surrounded by mountains and volcanoes, which create a charmed atmosphere especially at dawn. The Menoreh mountains are visible in the South, the volcanoes Merbabu and Merapi in the East and in the Northwest are the volcanoes Sumbing and Sendoro. Active Merapi last rained its ashes in 2010, with great consequences for Borobudur and the whole area.

In his book *Borobudur, Buddhist Mystery in Stone*, the Dutch culture-historian A.J. Bernet Kempers describes Borobudur in the late 1960s beautifully and with love. He relates how the beauty of the surroundings influences those who find themselves in the holy atmosphere of the temple, "Initially it is even as if the plant world is continued in the rich decoration that spreads like a net of vegetation over the walls and balustrades of the galleries."

When you reach the top of the stupa the influence of the natural surroundings prevails and the serene stillness that it brings becomes part of the stupa, says the writer. In brief, the temple cannot be viewed separately from its surroundings. The lovely images of the animals and plants on the reliefs only enhance this picture. It also shows how the sculptors had an eye for nature, concludes Bernet Kempers.

In this way the historian honors the sculptors of Borobudur from the eighth century. Also let us not forget the stonecutters, the porters, the diggers, the ones that made the necessary tools, the people who took care of feeding them, *etc*. There must have been hundreds of people involved in the construction of this special Buddhist sanctuary. Some may have worked their whole life on the temple, which is now called the eighth wonder of the world.

It took fifty-five thousand cubic meters of andesite stone to build Borobudur. This volcanic stone was collected from surrounding riverbeds. The rocks were hewn into blocks that were fitted with dovetail joints or knob-and-socket joints. The size of the stones varies from between one hundred forty centimeters at the base of the stupa to thirty centimeters at the top. Besides that, numerous stones were needed for the life-size Buddha statues, the reliefs, the stone lions and the other mythical animals guarding the stairs.

Borobudur through the centuries

Year   Event

750   Construction

King Raja Indra of the Buddhist Sailendra dynasty on Java commissions the building of Borobudur. The Sailendras from Java are related to the kings of Sumatra. This large island is the center of the Buddhist empire Shri Vijaya (circa 680-1374). At its peak, the power of Shri Vijaya extends to parts of Cambodia. The island of Java is under Shri Vijaya for a while.

The Sailendra king initiates the construction around the year 750, with Gunadharma as the architect, so the story goes. It is estimated that the building takes seventy to one hundred years to complete, under the supervision of King Raja Indra, his son Samaratunga and his granddaughter, respectively. Afterwards, and for reasons unknown, the Sailendra kings suddenly disappear from Central Java.

850   Under a layer of ash and vegetation

With the disappearance of the Sailendras from Central Java not long after the completion of the building, Borobudur also vanishes from view. For centuries it remains quiet around the region of Central Java and the temple. It seems like the center of the Kedu Plain is completely abandoned because nowhere is there anything mentioned about it. There are no buildings from this era found in the region, nor any inscriptions in stone. Stone inscriptions are the only remaining sources of information from the past. Everything that was written on palm leaf pages has been lost in the humid climate.

Layers of volcanic ash, mud and vegetation cover the stupa until it is completely hidden in the jungle. In the meantime, from the year 850, the Hindu temple complex Prambanan – including some Buddhist temples – is built by a Hindu king in the nearby southern part of Central Java. A princess of the Sailendra dynasty is married to this Hindu king. Some centuries later, the Buddhist and Hindu principalities on Java gradually give way to Islam, which was introduced to the country in the thirteenth century.

1619   European colonizers take over

In the year 1619, the heavily armed Dutch merchant fleet, the *Verenigde Oost-Indische Compagnie* (VOC), take control over the port in Jakarta. The Dutch rename the city Batavia. This is the beginning of an era of Dutch colonial rule over Indonesia that will last for almost three hundred fifty years.

1814   The English governor hears about the temple

In the year 1814, during a short interlude of English predominance, the then English governor of British Java, Sir Thomas Stamford Raffles – best known for his founding of Singapore – hears about a mysterious temple in the jungle. At that moment he is in the coastal town of Semarang on Java and he sends out the Dutchman, Cornelius, to investigate. Following Raffles' orders, Cornelius starts the excavation, helped by two hundred men.

After some months the summit is accessible again, however it is in a deplorable state. In the century that follows, other parts are uncovered from time to time.

With the excavation of the stupa many things disappear, like complete Buddha statues or heads of Buddhas. Some pieces end up in various museums worldwide, such as the Rijksmuseum in Amsterdam, the Museum of Ethnology in Leiden, The Netherlands, the National Museum of Thailand in Bangkok and the British Museum in London.

1842   The mystery of the mother stupa

The Dutchman Hartman, a governor of the Kedu Plain finds a mysterious statue in the large stupa on the top. In this top stupa, which is also called the mother stupa, there are two voids: a round space with a square space above it. There are no entrances but there is a hole due to the decay. Hartman finds an unfinished Buddha statue in the lower space. Nowadays, this statue can be seen in the Karmavibanga Museum near Borobudur.

According to Lama Gangchen, it is inconceivable that this incomplete statue was meant to be placed in the top of the stupa. The mother stupa would have been reserved for the best of the best – perhaps a golden Buddha. Perhaps a golden statue was stolen and replaced by this unfinished Buddha statue.

Amongst the locals of the villages around Borobudur a story circulates to this day which also indicates the existence of a valuable statue: Amir, the Indonesian Borobudur-keeper at the time of Hartman witnessed someone taking a small object from the void in the top stupa and he saw the person wrapping it in a jacket. It was after that time that the unfinished statue was placed, according to the keeper. Amir gave his testimony in an official report. This story was told by one of Amir's successors to Mr Ariswara Sutomo[1] in his childhood. According to Mr Ariswara Sutomo, there was nothing particularly special about the unfinished statue that was found in the top; many similar ones were found around Borobudur.

1885   The hidden panels are discovered

The Dutchman IJzerman, chairman of the committee for archeology in Yogyakarta, discovers the hidden base of Borobudur. The hundred-sixty panels of the *Mahakarmavibanga* sutra, which depicts the law of *karma*[2] – the law of cause and effect – was hidden behind a massive stone wall. Due to this discovery Borobudur again receives a lot of attention. The hidden picture narrative at the foot of the temple forms one of the temple's mysteries. Some twelve thousand cubic meters of concealing stone had been placed at some point over the years that it took to build Borobudur, possibly because of the risk of subsidence.[3]

1900   A mega-umbrella on top of Borobudur?

In 1900, a committee for the conservation of Borobudur is established. The committee consists of three Dutchmen: The young first lieutenant Theodoor Van Erp (1874 -1958) who is posted in Magelang, superintendent Van de Kamer and chairman Dr Brandes. The rather extraordinary plan of Van de Kamer to protect Borobudur against sun and rain by placing a giant metal umbrella on forty pillars is rejected. Some years later, the committee approves the plan for restoration by Van Erp.

---

1 Read Mr. Sutomo's story further on in this chapter.
2 Literal meaning: 'activity'. Actions and their consequences. The process where actions of body, speech and mind with positive motivation bring positive results in the future. Actions that are performed with negative motivation lead to negative results. Actions done with neutral motivation lead to neutral results.
3 Refer to Chapter 8 for Lama Gangchen's explanation.

1907 Passionate restoration by Theodoor van Erp

Van Erp executes the first large-scale restoration of Borobudur. His main drive is to do justice to the original design. Hence, where original stones are missing, he prefers to leave an empty space rather than replacing them. The upper square platform, with the three round tiers above – including the 72 perforated stupas and the mother stupa – are completely dismantled and rebuilt under his supervision.

Originally in the eight century there would have been a pinnacle formed by three umbrellas and a crowning jewel on top of the mother stupa. Very little of that construction has remained; therefore Van Erp reconstructs the pinnacle with new stones. Now the stupa is no longer 35 but 42.5 meters high. However, afterwards the reconstructed pinnacle doesn't feel right to him. In his opinion there is too much 'new' to it. Hence the pinnacle is taken down again, after having been photographed first.

Van Erp decides to leave the subsiding walls of the four galleries and the base as they are, in order to do as much justice as possible to the character of the ancient monument. Necessarily, since he also lacks the means and technique to repair them. However, he addresses all kinds of parts of the stupa during the repair, like statues, alcoves, stairs, gates and arches. Van Erp finishes his work in 1911. Later, he will be involved extensively in and publish about the interpretation of Borobudur, its architecture and reliefs. Van Erp also left an extensive collection of pictures of Borobudur and all its construction details.

1973 UNESCO finances a large restoration

Sixty years later the state of Borobudur is worrisome. Rain is the main culprit. Despite the efforts by Van Erp to save the monument, rainwater has caused a lot of damage. The temple lacks a decent drainage system. The rainwater absorbs into the hill beneath the stupa and subsequently into the porous stone, which provides an environment conducive for lichens and algae and exacerbates the ongoing subsidence and cracking. The temple is at risk of collapse if no action is taken.

With financial support from UNESCO, Indonesia is able to thoroughly restore Borobudur during the 1970s. Over time, technical possibilities are developed which make it possible to completely dismantle and rebuild the whole stupa in order to conserve it for the future. Around the temple a large park is created and plans are made for the tourist promotion of Borobudur. The largest Buddhist temple complex in the world becomes a tourist attraction.

This mega-project takes around ten years. Six hundred people join in the work. The more than one million stones are taken down one-by-one and mapped accordingly. The temple is given a solid foundation and a good drainage system. By 1984, Borobudur is ready for the future.

1989   Lama Gangchen visits Borobudur for the first time.

1991   World Heritage

Borobudur is placed on the UNESCO World Heritage Site list. This brings along a certain guarantee of conservation and protection. The park around the stupa becomes an archeological site where discoveries are still made from time to time. For example, on a small hill west of Borobudur, the remains of an old monastery have been found.

The rescue

This latest restoration by UNESCO means Borobudur is rescued. However, the events have a strong impact on daily life of the local people. There are many changes and the new situation also brings along challenges concerning the conservation of the stupa. Up to the present day worries arise regarding the wear and tear of the stones due to the large numbers of tourists visiting. To avoid further damage some stairs have been fitted with protective wooden falsework.

In this chapter, some local people from around Borobudur share their stories. These include the hotel owner Mr. Ariswara Sutomo, Mr. Sucoro who wrote a book about Borobudur, and Jamal who drives tourists around in his vehicle. Each tells how their life is interwoven with the temple, how they have experienced the changes over time and what the sanctuary means to them.

Additionally, some disciples of Lama Gangchen retell their experiences with the inhabitants of the village where Borobudur is situated. Lidy Haarman visited an affected area shortly after a volcanic eruption. Laura Lau observed the pervasive spirituality in the area and how different religions live alongside each other in peace. Liana Casagrande was guest in the jungle with some artists and, lastly, Valter Berten describes his impressions of daily life around Borobudur.

Local ceremonies at Borobudur
Mr Sucoro (1952) Borobudur, Indonesia

We interview Mr Sucoro with help from his daughter who speaks some English. During the interview we watch a film of the ceremony, the Ruwat-Rawat, he organizes annually at Borobudur. We see an endless stream of people passing in colorful and festive clothes, carrying offerings of incense, flowers and food. We see dance shows, music, singing and speeches In brief, we see a huge event that radiates love and devotion towards Borobudur.

Creating balance

Sucoro was born and raised at Borobudur. Every year in June, he organizes a local ceremony at Borobudur. Hundreds of Muslims, Christians and people who follow local religions gather at the stupa. They come from the villages in the area and bring heaps of offerings like incense, flowers and food.

Sucoro says, "We are grateful to the ones who built Borobudur. We make offerings for peace and protection, for the prosperity of the people, the environment, Borobudur ... everything. The people believe that there are many bad spirits in the area. Borobudur helps us to expel these and to purify."

Borobudur is important for the livelihood of the inhabitants in the area. Each year, more than two and a half million tourists and pilgrims come to visit. This has a downside, says Sucoro. The economic value of Borobudur easily leads to greediness among the local people. This is detrimental to the awareness of the spiritual value of the stupa for the surroundings. This has to be pacified and that is why he started the yearly ceremonial ritual, which is called *Ratwan*. The ceremony aims to create balance between the tourist aspect and the spiritual aspect of Borobudur, and to protect the sanctuary. Ratwan is a local ritual; it is not Buddhist, even though it is reminiscent of it.

Moving out for restoration

Occasionally there is a special memorial ceremony held for the three villages that had to be moved to make way for the major restoration of Borobudur between 1973 and 1984. Indonesia received financial support from UNESCO and several countries for this huge operation. Some years later, in 1991, Borobudur was acknowledged by UNESCO as a World Heritage Site and since then the stupa has enjoyed the accessory protection.

Sucoro was in his early twenties when the restoration started. He lived on the premises of the temple in a house under a banyan tree, very close to Borobudur. As a child he played along the galleries of the temple, which was more and more corroded by water, vegetation and subsidence. When the restoration started he, his family and many others had to move out to make way for the work. At first, it was difficult to be forced to move away from the ground where he was born.

His daughter tells us, "Many people protested against this imposed relocation; it was overwhelming and sensitive. Also for my father; he loved Borobudur and was pushed away. The community was not really angry but they felt powerless. Eventually the people accepted it."

Inspired by Borobudur

"My father's connection with Borobudur was so strong that later he started to study the stories depicted on the bas-reliefs. One of these stories inspired him to create a Javanese dance. It is called: *A Love Story on Bhumi Sambara Hill*."

His daughter is proud of her father. In her opinion, her father has done something special by organizing the yearly ritual. Also he creates the most beautiful things for tourists. "First he was sent away from Borobudur; after that he made a study of it, created dances and now he is important for Borobudur as well as for tourists. We have many, many recordings and videos. He has established an art organization and everything he creates is related to Borobudur. Borobudur is his inspiration."

She presumes that her father believes in reincarnation even though he is a Muslim. "He studied the bas-reliefs of the temple and he also wants to understand their meaning. I think my father believes in the wheel of life. He believes in the message of Borobudur."

Resistance against desecration

Sucoro's mission at this moment in his life is to protect the sanctuary. That was why he initiated the yearly ritual. He also wrote a book about his life with the temple called '*Outside the Gates of Borobudur*'.

Riwanto Tirtosudarmo, Research Director of the Research Center for Society and Culture, LIPI in Indonesia, writes as follows on the back cover of Sucoro's book: "... but what needs serious attention is the role that Sucoro plays. I am convinced that many friends in and around Borobudur, aware or unknowing, silently offer resistance against the desecration of Borobudur."

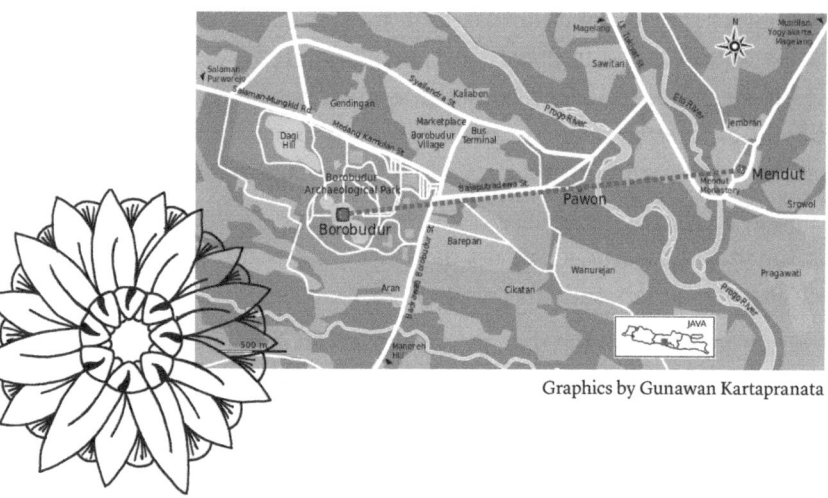

Graphics by Gunawan Kartapranata

A whole life with Borobudur
Ariswara Sutomo (1946) Ngaran II, Indonesia

Mr. Ariswara Sutomo is the owner of Rajasa, a family hotel right next to Borobudur. He elaborates on his life with the temple, which he also considers a mandala: a connection with the inner consciousness.

Playing, sleeping and dreaming

"I was born in a Muslim family, in Ngaran village, about five hundred meters from Borobudur. When I was a child, Borobudur was not yet fully restored and under the care of UNESCO – we could freely go and play there as kids. Often, high officials came to visit Borobudur, like Juliana, Queen of The Netherlands. Tito, Kennedy and Mao Tsetung also came. We children were standing along the road with flags to receive them. I would see the journalists taking notes to prepare their stories and I deeply wished to be one of them, not knowing that much later I would become a writer myself!

During our teens, my friend and I would sometimes go to see a performance of shadow puppets in another village and on the way back we would play on the ruin and fall asleep in the corner of a gallery. This happened more than once and every time I dreamt of huge dragon-like snakes – like nagas, and my friend dreamt of lions. Then we would wake up very frightened and hurry back home. I also had dreams about women, kings with crowns and people made of glass. I will never forget this.

My father told us that Borobudur was built by special people, not ordinary people, so we had to give high appreciation to it. We grew up with several legends and ideas about the temple. The local people believe that the different hand gestures on the four sides of Borobudur are connected to the meaning of the land in those directions.

In the East, we have the sunrise. The *bhumisparsa mudra* is the hand that touches the earth. It means the beginning of life. To the East side live many artists and craft workers who create things.

In the South we see the hand that gives; the *wara mudra*. The earth there is fertile and there are many rice fields and vegetable gardens.

In the West we find the hands folded as a sign of concentration and meditation; the *dhyana mudra*. The sun goes down in the West. It is where you become aware of the fact that life is ending and that it is important to meditate.

In the North is the raised hand that protects against danger; the *abaya mudra*. In this direction we find the markets and city life with their threats of riots, gambling, alcohol, prostitution and corruption."

Meditating in prison

"When I was 26 years old, I lived in Jakarta. It was the period when Suharto had just become president, and I had to go to prison for eighteen months because I was involved in the political activities for democracy. There was not much to do in prison; we had only one meal a day, so I became really stressed. Then I met a Chinese fellow prisoner who started to teach me yoga. Since then I took up meditation and yoga. After coming out of prison, I lived in Jakarta again. I met many artists and started to write short stories myself. Slowly, some newspapers started to publish my writing. Later I wrote several storybooks for schoolchildren, one of them about the way Borobudur was used as a settlement by Indonesians during the struggle for independence. The government bought all my books to be used in the schools. From this money, I bought some land near Borobudur and built a house there.

After eighteen years in Jakarta, I came back to where I was born. Since then, I have studied more and written about Borobudur. I am mainly interested in the legends and the philosophy, rather than the actual history or architecture."

Gold and yellow rice

"I learned that Borobudur is a mandala, not a temple. That means it is connected to the consciousness of the people. In my perception, Borobudur is not the name of the building, it is the place where it was built, it comes from the *Budur* hills. So the place is *Budur* and I believe the name of the place is *Gunadharma*, which means useful generosity. However, others say that *Gunadharma* is the name of the architect.

Then there are the names of the villages around it, they all remind us of the period the temple was built.

We have *Gopalan*, which in the ancient Javanese language means *guards*. This refers to the statues of gatekeepers, which in those days, were placed at the entrances to the temples. They have disappeared from Borobudur but the name of this village tells us that they must have been there before. They are still found at the Prambanan temples near Yogyakarta.

Bhumisambara, which means: how to reach step by step. This might have been a place where a monastery was situated.

Close to this place we have a village with the name: *Mendalan*, which obviously comes from *mandala*.

In the North we find *Bogowat, which* means: *place to eat*. Here the hundreds of workers were possibly provided with food.

Janan means *place for workers*. This was where the workers were accommodated.

Ngaran refers to the place where the stones were collected after having been taken from the river. It literally means *white empty spot*. Here the stones were selected and blessed with rituals before they were transported to *Bumisegoro* where, nearby the temple, they were processed.

The village at the *Pawon* temple, a small temple on the way to Borobudur, is called *Brojonalan*. This is derived from the ancient *Vajra Nala*, which means *pure heart*. At this place one purifies oneself on the way to Borobudur. During *Vesak*, pilgrims still respect this ritual.[4]

When Borobudur was restored, they found little pieces of gold, as small as rice grains, which they used to offer during all kinds of

---

[4] The Pawon temple is situated on a straight line between Borobudur and Mendut temple, at a distance of two kilometers from Borobudur and one from Mendut. During Vesak, both Mendut and Pawon are visited for worship and purification.

ceremonies. Nowadays, they use yellow rice for offering. So yellow rice represents gold.

The local legend about Borobudur is that there was a devil in the area that ruled over the hills. The ones fighting the devil sent him to Merapi and since then he resides inside the volcano. Sometimes, he gets angry and he shows himself by spitting fire, stones and ash. The people used these stones to build Borobudur, in order to protect the area from the devil. So in this way, they transformed something bad into something good and sacred."

Uniting with Borobudur's energy

"The people from around here may be Muslim but we are also still faithful to our local beliefs, which are called *Kejawen*. We mix it up somehow. *Kejawen* proclaims that God is energy, that there is no personification of God. It is like animism: everything has power and energy – even stones. So the local people do believe that Borobudur has power.

In my opinion, real Buddhism is not a religion. For me, Borobudur is energy. When I die, my energy will unite with this big energy. When I see Lama Gangchen, I can feel his power. He is an enlightened person.

After restoration, Borobudur became a money machine for the government. We regret it, because we can learn a lot from the wisdom of Borobudur. At the entrance of the stupa is a giant face that eats beings. So when you enter the mandala and you go to the top, it means you will be eaten. It reminds you that your life will surely end and you need to develop wisdom to cope with that. Borobudur is revealing that wisdom."

About betjaks and helping from the heart
Jamal (1970) Borobudur, Indonesia

Jamal provides transport for tourists around Borobudur on his three-wheeled motorcycle. When Lama Gangchen and his disciples are there, he always joins the group and offers his service to the pilgrims. He explains how he met Lama Gangchen and about an exciting encounter he once had with him.

Jamal and Champa Tsomo

The art of enjoying life

"I live in the village near Borobudur. Usually I take tourists in my vehicle to the area around Borobudur, because the temple is nice but the surroundings are also beautiful. In the countryside you can see what the real everyday life here is like. There is the tofu industry, pottery, rice fields... People are poorer than in Europe, but they possess the ability to enjoy life with little money. They are simply happy, being together with their family without knowing what tomorrow will bring.

The local people are mainly Muslim and some Catholic – not Buddhist. However, we all live in harmony with each other. When a Catholic dies, the Muslim cries and the other way around. People help each other build houses; that is what life here is like. We all like Borobudur very much. I cannot imagine what people here would be like if Borobudur wasn't there. When a volcano erupts, which happens every five years or so, even the farmers come to help clean the stupa, because it is catastrophic for the area if no tourists come.

The first time I met Lama Gangchen was three years before the millennium. Later, after the millennium, I started to help out during retreats. It began by driving one pilgrim, who asked me to take him to his hotel. Every morning I would pick him up and in the evening I took him back. He said, 'Jamal, you can join us at Borobudur with Lama Gangchen one time if you want.' So that is how I met Rinpoche and I could feel that he is a really great and special person. Also, the people who join him in the retreat are very nice. I think those who can make it to Borobudur with Lama Gangchen are very lucky because to me he is super mighty!"

Something cheeky

"That first time, I did something cheeky and a bit embarrassing. The group went out for dinner and they all rented cars. Some of my friends asked, 'Why don't they hire a *betjak*!',[5] because then more of the poorer local people would benefit, of course. Then, when I saw Lama Gangchen passing, I stopped the car and told him that the betjak drivers sometimes have to wait three hours or longer with no work. I feel a bit embarrassed that I did this. If I did something wrong, I am very sorry, please forgive me. But ever since, the group is hiring betjaks and horse carriages all the time.

I never have long conversations with Lama Gangchen but he always greets me with, 'Hello Jamal'. Every year I drive many people from the group. I also do odd jobs for Rinpoche like carrying his chair to the top of the stupa and every year I take pleasure in preparing the flower arrangements for the *gompa*.[6] I don't want any money for that; it is a present because I like to help in that way."

Helping people has nothing to do with religion

"In 2010, there was a fierce eruption and I remember that I went with a number of people from the group to help the locals who were in need. Some people couldn't stay in their houses; they needed blankets and a place to sleep. We collected money and used it to buy stuff for the children. Somebody did trauma work with the children who had experienced great danger and fear because of the floods

---

5 Bicycle taxi
6 Prayer hall

that came with the heavy rain after the eruption. Someone else came with seeds and planted flowers with the children. They liked these flowers that came all the way from England.

Helping people has nothing to do with religion; it comes from the heart, whether you are Muslim, Catholic or Buddhist."

The gate opened!

"In 2014, there was a very special moment. Because of an eruption the stupa was closed. But because all the people who work around Borobudur – like the ones from the hotel and also from security – love the lama, they opened the gate for him and his group. It gave me goose bumps. Fantastic! He has so much love that they opened the gate for him! All Muslims from here love him. Sometimes, the lama doesn't join the group walking, because he is tired from the night before. Then all the workers around Borobudur ask me, 'Jamal, where is the lama today?' And then when he comes to join the group later, they are all happy."

Stones as big as our living room
Lidy Haarman (1956) The Netherlands

Lidy Haarman visits an affected area after the eruption of the Merapi volcano, October 25th, 2010.

River of lava

"In 2011, the destructive consequences of the eruption of the Merapi volcano on October 25th of the previous year were still visible everywhere. Most of the levels of Borobudur had been cleaned and were accessible to visitors but the top was still covered by a thick layer of ash that had settled there. Much worse was what we saw in the surrounding countryside where I went to visit a refugee camp with some friends. We saw the river of lava that had swept through complete villages. Only the rooftops were visible. I still have a clear image in my mind of a piece of garment that I saw hanging on a roof.

Rocks as large as our living room had rolled through the streets, leaving a trail of damage behind. Bridges had collapsed, roads had disappeared, the river had changed its course. What struck me was the vigor of the people, how they helped each other without any self-interest. Or how they constructed alternative bridges themselves because the government didn't do it. How they organized a theatre and art festival for their children, so they could give vent to their emotions about this traumatic event.

I also noticed that different religions live together in harmony around Borobudur. One hears and knows about the conflict between Muslims and Christians, but here I experienced open-mindedness. For example, I know a Christian woman who is happily married to a Muslim man.

Moreover, one can tell that that there is great respect towards the Buddhist Borobudur among the population."

Many layers of religion
Laura Lau (1975) Singapore

Laura Lau, who speaks about her spiritual search in Chapter 1, is struck by the sense of spirituality in the surroundings of Borobudur. She recognizes a connection between the enchanting beauty of the garden of Central Java and the Pure Lands as described in Mahayana Buddhism.

Pure land

"Over the centuries and to this day, there are many layers of multiple faiths in the area around Borobudur. The stupa is surrounded by local mosques that resound over the area from dawn to dusk with the daily prayers. Every two years the Indonesian Buddhist Association organizes a Vesak festival at Borobudur, which includes every school of Buddhist traditions from all over Asia. There are even a few Catholic churches around the monument and more than one Indonesian bishops have come from the surrounding Magelang area. It is believed that there is a site sacred to the Virgin Mary nearby Borobudur. Recently, in 2011, crop circles appeared in the agricultural Magelang countryside. Alongside other Buddhist monuments of the era, there are also many Hindu temples in Java and the Prambanan temple complex located nearby is also a UNESCO World Heritage Site, which includes the ruins of another large Buddhist monument.

Geographically, Borobudur is located close to the confluence of two rivers, surrounded by four volcanoes. The most active is Mount Merapi: the volcano lies directly to the east of Borobudur and it is both giver and destroyer. Its volcanic eruptions might take away the lives and livelihood of the people. However, the spreading of volcanic lava and rains of ash create the highly fertile soil of the area that is covered in green and gives abundant harvests. In *Mahayana* Buddhism, the Buddhas reside in pure-land paradises. In Borobudur, the beauty of the environment and the extraordinary stupa bring the ordinary tourist visitor closer to experiencing pure-land paradise. For the devotees and especially for those following Lama Gangchen, Borobudur is the mandala of mandalas and a gateway to *enlightenment*."[7]

We come as spiritual tourists and receive something from the people who live here
Valter Berten - Jampa Chöpel (1957) Italy

Valter Berten feels a strong connection with the local people in Indonesia. He tells us how the country and its inhabitants made a profound impression on him.

A nicer place to live

"I come from a normal Italian Catholic family with father, mother and three sisters. We were Catholic on paper but we didn't practice. In school they told me to believe this and that, but at home it was not an issue. I am the oldest together with my twin sister. My youngest sister is no longer alive; she died of an overdose of heroin when she was 24. After my mother passed away, I went to Milan to visit His Holiness the Dalai Lama.

When I was there I met a Nepalese man, Pempa, who knew Lama Gangchen's center in Albagnano. He told me about the place, which seemed a nicer place to live than where I was at that time; there was no work and there was nothing to do except drink – every day, all

---

7 Complete liberation. A state of the mind in which a person is all-knowing and has developed infinite wisdom, compassion and power.

day. So the opportunity arose to come to Albagnano and stay a little while and do some work, but without my parakeet Gigio. At that time you couldn't come with pets or animals, but the following year Gigio arrived and we were united again. Gigio was pissed off initially; he was pretty upset because I had left him, but now he's fine again. We have been together for eight years."

Like meeting an old friend

"At the time I came to Albagnano, Rinpoche was in Tibet so I didn't meet him immediately. I was already aware, through stories of Rinpoche's friends and disciples, that perhaps Lama Gangchen was something very special. He had a different kind of energy going on. For me the image was of a high Eastern teacher coming, giving you a hug and then disappearing again. Finally when we met, I had the feeling that we had met many times before. Perhaps you hear something, then you meet somebody and you have a different experience from your expectation. But in this case it was absolutely familiar. Apart from the different clothes and appearance, it felt like meeting an old friend. I went to Borobudur one time, in 2013. I was so lucky because I was sponsored by Mr Jan. Mr Jan asked me to meet at breakfast in the center where he told me that he would like to offer me a ticket to Borobudur. I cried when he gave me the news. My only experience of Borobudur was other people mentioning it. To me it was a totally remote and distant thing where I knew there was a kind of connection. So to be suddenly presented with this offering and to be able to go was an overwhelming experience. I had already been in Albagnano for a while but the idea of being part of the spiritual group traveling in the company of Rinpoche on this pilgrimage was great. It was a moving idea."

The kindness of the local people

"The first thing on Java that really struck me was the attitude and behavior of the local people. I realized that we were coming there as spiritual tourists, and we were receiving something from them in the sense of their kindness and their way of life. At one point we went with some friends to visit the local village school that was kind of in the middle of nowhere. We brought them a whole bunch of books, pens and other school materials. I felt like a Martian arriving in the jungle; everything was beautiful and clean but completely without any kind of traffic, machinery and other Western technology. Another striking experience happened one day when we came out of Maya's bar and there were two local ladies, mother and daughter, who were visibly aged and conditioned by their hard life. They approached me gently with their hands out, asking for support. I turned around to pull my wallet out and when I turned back I found that they had dropped on their knees before me. Something like this had never happened before in my life."

A joyful and playful process

"The daily climbing of the stupa was like playing a game. Clearly all the other people had already been on Borobudur before, they were familiar with the procedures and gestures and so on. They knew what was coming. The process seemed one of joy and playing. I have never seen a spiritual activity with that energy and emotion before. The only point of reference, of comparison I had was my previous experience at home of processions, either at a funeral or the village festival for the local saint where only the local people were involved. Now, suddenly, I was in this other kind of spiritual event with people from all over the world, expressing a different energy. Visiting the market was also something special. I saw different kinds of clothes, there were dead animals for sale, and somebody killed a chicken to prepare it for the market. About sixty or seventy years ago, in Italy it might have been like that. Back then, there weren't any of the hygiene restrictions that exist now. Somebody would bring a chicken, break its neck and prepare it. Now the difference is that in Italy we have a huge hygiene industry. Everything here is sprayed with disinfectants, whereas in Indonesia things are just done in a natural way. Maybe in Italy, we pay too much attention to that aspect. I saw the toughness of the people. The women working in the rice fields, carrying heavy loads. I didn't see the whole spectrum of work done by the people but the heavy manual work that I saw was all being done by elder people and women. People who weren't even carrying anything were still bent over by having carried all that heavy stuff all their lives. I wouldn't be able to tell myself how the journey to Borobudur has changed my life; it is up to other people to judge that. But I heard them say that I became more integrated, loving, engaged, enthusiastic and socially appreciated."

Sleeping and dreaming in the jungle
Liana Casagrande – Champa Tsomo (1954) Italy

As a child Liana Casagrande dreams repeatedly about a mysterious temple in the jungle. Now she stays with people who live close to nature near Borobudur. There she meets a painter of dreams.

A buried temple

"Though my parents are both Italian, I mainly grew up in Zimbabwe, where I went to a British college for girls. Then I married a Scottish man whom I met in Zimbabwe and moved to New Zealand with him. After marriage, children, divorce, and several relationships, I came back to Italy to live in Intra near Albagnano and that's how I met Lama Gangchen.

Thinking about Borobudur, the first thing that comes to my mind is a dream that I used to have many, many times as a child. I often dreamed about a temple being buried in the jungle. The first time I saw Borobudur, I immediately felt a sense of recognition. But already – before arriving at the stupa – something strange had happened. On the way from Yogyakarta to Borobudur I saw my name on a billboard: Casa Grande Real Estate Agency Also my first name, Liana, is quite common in the area around Borobudur.

The first time I came to Borobudur was in 2010. It was the year before I became a nun. I stayed in a very nice room in the Rajasa hotel, with a view over the rice fields. It made me very happy. But after having enjoyed that nice guesthouse for a couple of days, my friend Ana Vogt came and said, 'My friend who lives in the forest really needs help because he has no money. Could you please go there and rent a room in that house? They are artists.' Of course I wanted to help them so I went to stay there. They gave me a room with just a mattress on the damp floor and that's where I had many adventures."

Painter of dreams

"The house was full of people that came and went. It was very strange and at the same time very nice also. It was so familiar; it felt like a déjà vu. It was as if I knew those people, as if we already were connected. The man who lived there was living a very simple life. He was a painter of dreams. He enters the world of dreams with his artwork in a very profound manner. You can discover many different things in his paintings. Lama Gangchen knows him also and calls him the fireman. He smoked a lot and I pleaded with him to stop and, after a long and respectful friendship between us, the last time I saw him in 2015, he made my heart sing when he promised he would do so.

I also met another artist there. This man had carved Lama Gangchen's face out of a tree-root. His girlfriend, a dancer, singer, and also a painter, took me to Borobudur every morning at five on her motorbike whilst we sang many beautiful songs together.

It was in the fireman's house that I woke up one morning and the room was a lake, the water had come in through the ceiling. However, despite these kinds of adventures it was a nice and simple stay. They were kind people and they gave me delicious local food. All the people I met in the house in the forest have this special healing quality and whenever we touched each other with a healing touch, we felt as if we were one."

Buddha's descendants

"For me it is clear that the local people have a connection with Borobudur. The people that live there have some unusual qualities. There is a gentleness and acceptance of each other's religions. One Muslim couple took me to the mosque, for example. A lot of young teenagers were there. I made them all break out in laughter when I prostrated in the wrong direction.

I am impressed by how they help each other, how they love each other and how they take responsibility for each other. They are really Buddha's descendants, Atisha's descendants. This I saw especially portrayed when I looked at a beautiful young mother with her amazingly relaxed baby, both dressed in the most beautiful rainbow colors. They shared a feeling of oneness that is rare to see."

Chapter 3

Indonesia &

The Netherlands

Collective karma

In the early years of the Albagnano Healing and Meditation Center in Italy, the 'Borobudur Temple' there was still under construction. However, there were already some impressive stone statues from Indonesia placed in the unfinished round building in the woods: the five Dhyani Buddhas. Because rain and wind could play freely through the open windows and doors, the temple easily turned dusty and dirty. From time to time, volunteers cleaned up the place. One day, we also picked up dusters and brooms with a group of Dutch guests to clear the temple from leaves and sand. During the cleaning work we sang purification mantras like the *Vajrasattva*[1] mantra. Someone in the group said, "It is right that it should be us doing this. As Dutchmen we have a lot to purify, we bear the collective karma of what happened in Indonesia."

The truth on the table

In October 2015, while we work on this chapter, the Dutch historian Professor Gert Oostindie from Leiden University publishes a revealing book about war crimes in Indonesia. Oostindie has researched fourteen hundred personal diaries, memoires and letters from Dutch soldiers who fought in Indonesia between 1945 and 1950. His conclusion is that there is so much excessive violence, execution and torture described in these hundred thousand pages of personal reports – over seven hundred incidents – that we have to acknowledge that Dutch soldiers systematically committed war

---

[1] A tantric Buddha who is connected to purification practices. One of the purification possibilities is to recite the one-hundred-syllable Vajrasattva mantra.

crimes on a large scale.² Hence, we can no longer maintain that these were excesses or exceptions. "Because when we extrapolate these figures to the whole army, it would concern tens of thousands rather than thousands of cases." According to Oostindie, one out of four soldiers in his research was actively or passively involved in these war crimes. The other 75 percent was unknowing or not involved.

This mentioned war is a dark chapter in Dutch history that we as a country have not easily dealt with to date. For example, it took until 2005 before a Dutch minister officially recognized the Indonesian independence date of 1945. In dribs and drabs, the victims of war crimes are given acknowledgement due to court cases through which they claim against the state of The Netherlands. The first time was in 2011, in the case of the widows from the Javanese village of Rawagede, where all 431 men were massacred by Dutch militaries. Two years later, in 2013, the Dutch government officially apologized for summary executions in Rawagede and many other places.

Gert van Oostindie doesn't plead so much for judicial prosecution of potential responsible living veterans from those days, "I find it much more important to get the truth on the table. That is justice in its own right."³

Three hundred fifty years of colonial rule[4]

The Dutch were active in the region since the beginning of the seventeenth century. Half of the Dutch merchant fleet – The United East-Indian Company (VOC) – consisted of soldiers. In 1619 the VOC conquered Jakarta on Java and called the city Batavia. From here, the Dutch conquered more and more parts of the archipelago, which would later be called the Dutch East Indies. Over three centuries later, during the Second World War, Japan occupied the country. Dutch and East-Indians with mixed blood were put into camps for forced labor. The defeat of Japan due to the atomic bombings at Hiroshima and Nagasaki resulted in a power vacuum in Indonesia during which the politician Ahmed Soekarno declared independence for the Republic of Indonesia – in Jakarta on August 17th 1945.

---

2 Oostindie, G. (2015), Soldaat in Indonesië 1945-1950 - Getuigenissen van een Oorlog aan de Verkeerde Kant van de Geschiedenis, Prometheus

3 *Zwarte bladzijden* October 27th 2015, Report on Dutch TV about research by Gert Oostindie in: Brandpunt

4 www.isgeschiedenis.nl/archiefstukken/politionele-acties-bevrijding-werd-oorlog/

Holland did not accept this and went to battle in an attempt to regain a foothold in the country that had bolstered the Dutch coffers for centuries. The mainly young Dutch soldiers who responded to the call of the Dutch government had the idea that they would free 'East-Indies' by 'police-action.' However, they ended up in a bloody guerilla-like war. There were victims on both sides; Indonesia lost one hundred fifty thousand people; on the Dutch side six thousand out of the two hundred twenty thousand military force died. In 1949 Holland sounded the retreat, due to international pressure. Twenty years later, in 1969, reports about the horrifying cruelties of this war in the *kampongs*[5] came out for the first time on a large scale in the Dutch media. After research, the government dismissed these crimes as incidental excesses.

Recognition and acknowledgement

Together as Dutch, we bear the collective karma of what Holland has done in Indonesia. Gert Oostindie pleads for openness about what has happened there. Also from a Buddhist point of view, it is important that we openly recognize and acknowledge our negative actions and that we purify them. Only when things come to light can healing take place; for the people of Indonesia, and also for those concerned in The Netherlands, and their families. On both sides, people have been traumatized.

Tibetan Buddhism has various methods to purify negative actions; in all cases the four opponent powers[6] are essential:

1. Generate an opposite attitude, like an attitude of love and compassion.

2. Acknowledge what has been done and sincerely regret it.

3. Be determined not to repeat it.

4. Do something positive. This can be anything, like cleaning the gompa, reciting a mantra or doing the Self-Healing practice.

The following stories relate the connection between Indonesia and The Netherlands. Toet de Best grew up during the time of the battle for Indonesia. She tells what she sensed as a kid in this

---

5 Settlements, villages
6 Lama Michel, February 13th 2016, Teaching: *Lojong, Seven-point Mind Training,* part 2, AHMC, Albagnano, Italy

respect. Thresia Flora Bernet is a child of East-Indian parents who had to flee to The Netherlands after the war. With her story about a lecture she gave at Borobudur, Kitlyn Tjin A Djie stresses the importance of healing the pain in the relationship between Indonesia and The Netherlands.

Toet de Best

Paragon of love and compassion
Toet de Best (1942) The Netherlands

When she is about five years old, Toet de Best's uncle goes to Indonesia to serve as a soldier. Only much later in her life does she get an idea of what has happened there.

A name from Indonesia

"My uncle Frits had served as a military in Indonesia. I must have been six or seven years old when he came back. 'You are my sweet little Toetie,' he used to say to me. *Toetie* is Indonesian for sweetheart or honey. I was so delighted by this that I changed my name. Riekie became Toet.

What exactly happened in Indonesia we didn't know. Nobody spoke about it. I remember our neighbor coming back from the front. That was a huge celebration. The front door and the street were decorated with flags. He arrived in uniform and was received as a hero. That makes sense in a way; he had come back from a war and he was unharmed.

It was when I was a bit older that I first heard about the cruelties. A colleague of mine who had fought in Indonesia told me that they sometimes wanted to get rid of somebody. They let this person free in a part of no-man's-land and then he got shot in the back. This made a deep impression on me. Later he told me another story – the intense silence of the dark tropical nights with only the sound of crickets was the worst thing for him. It was mentally killing, he said, because the Javanese could sneak up on you from behind, barefoot, and cut your throat with their *klewangs*[7] just like that. These were the kind of traumatic experiences he had had.

What Indonesians endured during this war and the traumas it must have left, recently became literally visible in late 2015 when a large private collection of photos and slides with images of the cruelties committed by the Dutch was made public."

Fluent in Dutch

"When I came to Borobudur for the first time with Lama Gangchen in 1991, we once had dinner in the Sarasvati restaurant. Ms. Sri Ayati, the owner, was very kind and happy but I was almost in shock because by then I had some idea of what had happened during the war. I couldn't believe that somebody was so friendly after all the things we Dutch had done to Indonesia. She spoke with me in fluent Dutch. She was a very special woman, a paragon of love and compassion. She had been the one to accompany our queen Juliana during her visit to Borobudur. In 1993, at the request of Lama Gangchen Rinpoche, Ms. Sri Ayati gave a lecture for his disciples and friends in the Manohara hotel. She spoke lovingly and proudly about 'their' Borobudur. She also indicated how the people who used to live literally at the foot of the temple had to relocate during the big restoration between 1973 and 1984. Currently, the Borobudur Archeological Park is located on the exact spot where they lived. This all struck me deeply."

---

7 Traditional sword

Following in the footsteps of my father
Thresia Flora Bernet (1952) The Netherlands

Thresia was born in The Hague to Dutch-Indien parents; descendants from the colonial past. 'Indien' nowadays means having Indonesian as well as Dutch or other European blood running through your veins. Late in the 1940s, after the war, her father and mother were coerced to leave Indonesia. Thresia's story is about her father who escaped from a Japanese Prisoner of War camp to pay a visit to Borobudur. Years later she followed in his footsteps.

Breaking out to the temple

"I didn't go to Borobudur because of my affinity with Buddhism, though I am somehow interested in Taoism and Buddhist wisdom. Tai Chi works quite well for me as a form of meditation. I went there mainly because I wanted to learn about Indonesia as it has become now; not to have an "Indien" experience in the way I know the Dutch Indies from the stories of my parents and grandparents. My mother grew up in West-Java and my father in East-Java, but they met in Holland, after the war. They both left because they couldn't stay.

I wanted to go to Borobudur because my father had been there, in the period before he came to Holland. During the Japanese occupation he was imprisoned. He was very lucky to be taken to a civilian camp and not a military camp. There he met several people who felt a need to do something with their intellect, besides the technical aspects of the education they had received. My father studied Social Economics & Sociology and later, Indien law. In the period before his imprisonment, my father was taught by various professors about Javanese culture and mysticism. He had a short intense period of education under difficult circumstances.

This brought him a wide socio-cultural and theological-mystical interest that he always retained. Here the seed was sown for his interest in comparative religions, which occupied him until he passed away. During his time in the camp in West-Java, my father stayed in the same building as some fellow students from Leiden University and the University of Batavia, the current Jakarta. My father told me that among his fellow prisoners there were some students who realized that life could possibly become very tough. They thought, 'Let us be occupied with interesting stuff because you don't know how long you will live.' They knew about the existence of a Dutch professor, Bernet Kempers, an archeologist who had conducted research on the excavation and restoration possibilities for Borobudur and they managed to contact him. Together with him they plotted this 'study tour' to Borobudur and they temporarily escaped from their imprisonment, with help from the guards in the camp.

Before my father died, he told me: 'Because we were busy with this group of people, with the mythology and culture-philosophy of Java and related things, we weren't thinking all day about food and how hungry we were. It was very fortunate.' He mentioned the visit to Borobudur in the context of how they had mentally survived this period in the camp, which lasted three years. That is why I also wanted to go there."

Lost in time

"It was in 1994, right before our wedding. It was more or less our honeymoon. I thought, 'It is now or never'. Our idea was to get to know certain regions of Java and Sumatra. A visit to Borobudur was essential for me. We left Yogyakarta very early in the morning, with a small group in a mini-van. We wanted to avoid the troupes of tourists we had heard about. After arriving at Borobudur, everyone went their own way. After we had entered together, Dirck and I also decided to climb the stupa separately, each at our own pace.

Next I was walking around very relaxed. I took my time, mainly looking around me and taking in the environment, the nature and looking at some restored parts. At a certain moment I thought, 'Well, I have been on my way for quite some time now I guess.' I didn't have a watch and there were no cellphones. I didn't have a clue about the time, so I slowly started to descend the stupa. Then I saw a museum, where I wanted to take a look as well.

At some point I realized I didn't see any of my group members around anymore, so I decided to check where they had gone. It appeared that they all had been waiting for me in the bus for a long time! I must have been gone for three hours. Apparently I had had a kind of blackout whilst circling the galleries on that Borobudur. Later I heard a story that exists in the monks' world of a certain gallery.

If you walk that gallery a specific number of times, you go into a trance, a higher state of consciousness. I thought, 'My god, is that what happened to me?' In my experience I was only walking and looking, drinking in the scenery, thinking about my father who had walked there as well. Bernet Kempers was an archeologist, but my father was really interested in Javanese mysticism and that was why he had been there.

I thought about that. I admired the beauty of the temple and the surroundings – as he may have done. I enjoyed simply sitting there, a unique experience, as it was so pleasant and calm that early morning."

The visit to Borobudur was his rescue

"After Japan had surrendered and my father had been free for a while, he lived with his parents in Surabaya. Afterwards, Surabaya was set on fire by Indonesian freedom fighters, which again caused a lot of misery. The freedom fighters were fed up with Dutch people or Indien mixed people – Indonesians simply hated everything that was European because of the three hundred years of colonial attitude and rule. Men and women were taken to separate camps. After some months, the English and Indiens freed my father just in time. But that is another story...

In Holland, government officers had advised people like my grandparents and great grandparents to remain in Indonesia because there was not much to do for them in The Netherlands. 'You are too old to re-integrate.' Around the year 1949, my father came to Holland anyway. He has always cherished his memories of this group of friends and the visit to Borobudur. The network and the trip were part of his rescue.

Until his death, his attitude was to only be concerned with things that matter. He always retained his interest in mysticism and culture. I went to Borobudur to see what he might have experienced there. The trip was so essential for me because my father had walked there under special circumstances, before he got married. He wasn't there anymore when I went – he passed away in 1994 – but the fact that I walked there shortly before I got married somehow brought us together for a moment one more time."

Kitlyn Tjin A Djie

The power of purification
Kitlyn Tjin A Djie (1953) Suriname

Kitlyn was born in Suriname – like Indonesia, a former colony of The Netherlands. She has worked in the Netherlands as a family therapist for many years.

The children of Sulawesi

"In 2015, during the retreat at Borobudur, I gave a lecture about the power of purification in families. It was about the importance of families in relation to Lama Gangchen's words, 'Your family is the first circle where you can intend to listen to each other with kindness, speak to each other with kindness and to generally use your senses in a peaceful way.'

When families argue or fight, or if the continuity of the family is at stake, it is important that the family uses its power of purification. Every family has this power. Not only families: any system, any religion possesses such wisdom, and this was what we were talking about. But often we have forgotten, we have no access to it or we don't think about it, especially in Western families where we have abandoned many rituals and traditions. In this way, the idea came to my mind to give the example of the context where we work in The Netherlands. Holland has had difficulties making use of its power of purification, to dare face the darker chapters of Dutch history, like its colonial past, slavery and the East-Indian history. It was a joyful fact that, precisely during the week we were on Java, the children of Sulawesi were proven right by the court in the Hague: The Netherlands state was held responsible for the damage caused to the children and widows of the more than three thousand men executed by Dutch militaries in South Sulawesi in 1946 after they had rebelled against Dutch rule.

The bereaved were proven right almost seventy years later and were enabled to claim compensation. Hence the claim was acknowledged and approved.

This is the start of purification – and since then, an increasing number of cases about Dutch actions in Indonesia has become apparent and revealed."

Healing the relationship

"While speaking about these children of Sulawesi and the decision of the judge during this lecture, I became very emotional. Tears streamed from my eyes; I felt them trickle down my face. It was as if there, at Borobudur, I could feel in the deepest parts of my heart and soul what the meaning of purification is, and the impact it can have. Because we were in Indonesia and obviously it plays a role as well in my history, in my mother country Suriname. I realized the purification that can take place if Holland dares to face the slavery and its whole colonial history. And I was aware of the fact that there are possible opportunities in the relationship with the Caribbean and Suriname. So in one way or another, at that exact moment I could feel in my whole body what it means to purify, what the power of purification is. That is what happened.

Purification means to face it, to look it in the eyes, to be able to bow, to have the courage to admit you were wrong, to be able to apologize or to make it right with the other. For example by talking about what needs to be done to make up for it, what needs to be done to heal the relationship. You can purify with rituals; there are many forms. But I find it most important that you can bow your head and that you can admit that mistakes are made and that you show courage by being open about it.

After a traumatic event in a family, but also in a country, the consequences are not always known, though usually they are sensed consciously or unconsciously. Children and grandchildren have changed DNA after suffering trauma. The impact is transferred from generation to generation. This holds for descendants of slavery and also for Indonesia. According to Shamanistic as well as some Christian traditions, it takes seven generations to solve a trauma. The suffering needs time to heal. Using the power of purification is helpful for that."

Chapter 4

The Stupa

Deciphered

About a wedding ring and female Buddhas

During a stay in The Netherlands, Lama Gangchen visited the library of the Kern Institute[1] of Leiden University. The librarian had placed some open books about Borobudur especially for him to look at. When Lama Gangchen entered the room, he said, seemingly casually, "The Buddha was married, you know." Then he walked towards an open book with pictures of Borobudur reliefs and indicated, "Look! the ring." On the photo was the image of a Buddha with – unmistakably – a wedding ring.[2]

Buddha gives a ring to Gopa

---

1 The Kern Institute is the national center of expertise for Southern Asia and the Himalayan region in The Netherlands.
2 The relief on the first gallery from the Lalitavistara, about the life of the king's son Siddharta Gautama, shows how he offers his own ring to Gopa. She becomes his wife.

These words of Lama Gangchen, spoken in Leiden, possibly refer to the hidden meaning of Borobudur. He possesses the knowledge of Vajrayana Buddhism, of how the stupa-mandala is suitable for all four kinds of tantric practice, including the highest yoga tantra where the sexual union – *Yab Yum*[3] – symbolizes perfect harmony between male and female energy; compassion and wisdom. "But there are no Buddhas in sexual union found on Borobudur," is the argument that scholars bring against this position, "There are no female Buddhas at all." But with his remark about Buddha's wedding ring, Lama Gangchen implicitly states that the feminine aspect is indeed present on Borobudur.

However, the story continues.

While Lama Gangchen visited an exhibition about Indonesia in the Museum of Ethnology, also in Leiden, his way of indicating pictures and making remarks aroused the interest of the curator about the level of knowledge the lama might have. They started a conversation and eventually this led to an invitation for a congress at Borobudur at the beginning of July 2008.[4] Because of the festivities around his birthday on July 7th, Lama Gangchen could not go himself. Instead, he sent Lama Caroline who has conducted a lot of research on Borobudur together with him. She would participate on his behalf. Around fifty scholars were present at the congress, coming from all over the world. Lama Caroline was one of the youngest participants and she was the last person to speak.

While showing slides to illustrate her talk, she spoke of Lama Gangchen's many discoveries, which indicate that Borobudur must be a Vajrayana mandala. For example, the presence of *vajras*[5] or *dorjes*[6] at the foot of the staircases on each of the four sides of the stupa; the curved *makaras* – mythological water beings – that form the actual spokes of a vajra. When viewed from above, together the stairs on the mandala form a crossed vajra, called in Tibetan a double dorje; a well-known symbol in Vajrayana Buddhism.

---

3 Literal meaning: father-mother.
4 International Seminar, *Uncovering the Meaning of the Hidden Base of Borobudur*, July 1st - 5th 2008, Organized by the National Research and Development Centre of Archaeology – Indonesia
5 Literal meaning: 'diamond'. An indestructible scepter. This ritual object – held in the right hand and used together with the bell in practice – symbolizes method: the masculine aspect. The bell in the left hand symbolizes wisdom: the feminine aspect. Combined they symbolize the union of bliss and emptiness.
6 Tibetan for Vajra.

Also various images of vajras are depicted on the reliefs at the stupa. Besides that, an actual metal vajra was found in the area nearby Borobudur. The latter indicates actual practice of Vajrayana Buddhism.

The most significant eye-opener presented by Lama Caroline to the scholars present is the fact that there is a female Buddha[7] next to each male Dhyani Buddha.[8]

Great Mother Mamaki on the left side next to Dhyani Buddha Akshobya

After her speech, Lama Caroline's presentation and statements were acclaimed by one person in particular: the great scholar Professor Lokesh Chandra (1927), from India. He speaks over 24 languages and has written more than three hundred sixty scholarly books and articles, many of which are about Buddhism. He claims that the Tibetan Lama Gangchen apparently knows best how we should interpret Borobudur. According to him, if we want to understand Borobudur we should listen to the Tibetan lamas because they are the ones still practicing the original Indian Buddhism. The

---

7 These are the *five Great Mothers*; the female Buddhas connected to the five elements. See Chapter 10.
8 Seeds for Peace IV – *Homage to Borobudur: Ocean of Mandalas* (2011), contributions Lama Gangchen: '*Discovering the Meaning of Candi Borobudur*', p. 351, and Lama Caroline: '*A Short Explanation of T.Y.S. Lama Gangchen's Theories about the Meaning of the Sacred Geometry and Mandala Symbolism of Candi Borobudur in the Light of Academic Scholarship on the Subject*', p. 359, Lama Gangchen Peace Publications.

encounter between Lama Caroline and Professor Lokesh Chandra at the congress of Borobudur marked the beginning of an intense friendship between Lama Gangchen and the Indian professor.

The scholars in the conference room were surprised. They could hardly believe that they had never noticed the presence of any female Buddhas on Borobudur themselves; they had not recognized the images as such. The accepted position had always been that Borobudur is not a tantric mandala because there are no female Buddhas present. After the presentation, Lama Caroline invited the participants to join her at the stupa where she showed them the female Buddhas: beside each of the alcoves of the 432 Dhyani Buddhas on the four sides is a square frame in which a female Buddha is seated.

It seemed odd that not a single scholar realized the fact that these figures were female Buddhas. Lama Caroline explains this was a possible blind spot. She herself had not noticed this either during her first visits to Borobudur, "We often only see what we expect to see. This is a common phenomenon in science. It is a Buddhist fact." The Western scholars saw Borobudur since the beginning of its 'discovery' as a Mahayana temple, which was probably understandable – knowing that in the nineteenth and twentieth centuries, many translations of Mahayana sutras were published in German and English. However, Vajrayana tantras were unknown.

"They were hardly translated; it didn't match the Protestant culture of that time," said Lama Caroline.[9] Besides, people often have a single focus on their own area of expertise. In that case it is hard to see the complete picture.

Meanwhile, various academics have started to see Borobudur as a yoga-tantra mandala – thanks to the insight that there are male and female Buddhas sitting next to each other on the stupa. However, there is no physical evidence present on or around Borobudur that helps academics further prove the meaning of Borobudur as a mandala for the highest yoga tantra, which is usually demonstrated by the image of male and female Buddhas in intimate embrace.

---

9 Lama Gangchen and Lama Caroline, LGIGPF-workshop *Make Peace with the Environment – Regenerate the Female Energy – The Female Buddhas in Relation to Borobudur*, November 29th 2014, Diessen, The Netherlands.

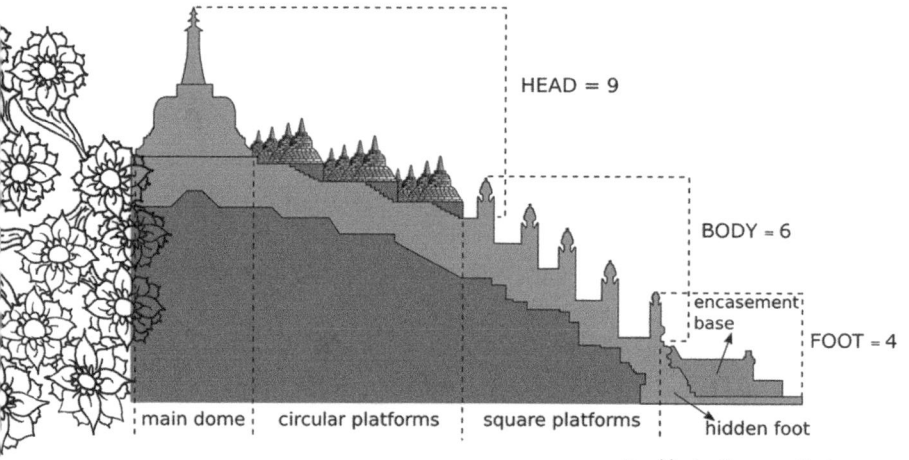

Graphics by Gunawan Kartapranata

Mandala for all traditions

Since the first time Lama Gangchen visited Borobudur, he sees the stupa as a multi-mandala, suitable for the practice of all three main traditions of Buddhism: *Hinayana, Mahayana* and *Vajrayana*, including all four stages of tantra.[10]

The three 'Yanas' or vehicles sometimes go together or form part of one another. Hinayana resembles the Theravada path that – as opposed to Hinayana – is still practiced on a large scale. We will now explain Borobudur in relation to Theravada, Mahayana and Vajrayana following Lama Gangchen's interpretation.

Theravada

Theravada is the path of liberation of the individual. Meditation and helping others are important practices as well as developing the ten perfections: generosity, morality, renunciation, wisdom, energy, patience, truthfulness, determination, loving kindness and equanimity.

When we view Borobudur according to the Theravada path, we can give the following explanation.

---

10 Lama Caroline, *How to Understand and Use Borobudur Now and in the Future*, p. 24, syllabus Lama Gangchen World Peace Foundation, International Conference Borobudur, March 1st -3rd 2013

Borobudur is constructed from three parts:

1 The base

2 The five stacked terraces

3 The top with the three round levels and the mother stupa.

These three parts represent the world of desire, the form world and the formless world, respectively.

Graphics by Gunawan Kartapranata

1. At the base the *Mahakarmavibanga* is depicted, although hidden behind a thick wall. The reliefs show in detail how the law of cause and effect works, how positive, negative and neutral actions lead to positive, negative and neutral results in the future. Here one finds oneself in the 'Kamadhatu', the world that is ruled by desire and attachment.

2. On the galleries of the five terraces the pilgrim passes by numerous bas-reliefs with stories about and teachings of the Buddha. This is the form world, 'Rupadhatu'. In particular the *Jatakas, Avadanas*[11]

---

[11] Jatakas are stories of the earlier lives of Buddha Shakyamuni, sometimes as a human, sometimes as an animal. In each of these tales, he develops a specific quality.
Avadanas are similar stories in which the good deeds of the main character are related to events in subsequent lives.

and the *Lalitavistara*[12] show on the Theravada level how the world of desire leads to the path of enlightenment.

3. On the three highest levels the shapes become round and there is space and light. Here the pilgrim reaches *nirvana*. Narrative bas-reliefs on the walls are lacking here. This is the formless world, 'Arupadhatu'.

Mahayana [the great vehicle]

Those who follow the Mahayana path strive for enlightenment for the benefit of all sentient beings. The path of the *Bodhisattva*[13] of the *Gandavuyha* is depicted on the reliefs that are found on the walls of the galleries on the second, third and fourth levels. These tell the story of the merchant's son Sudhana who encounters more than fifty teachers on his way to becoming a Bodhisattva.

Lama Gangchen gives, amongst other teachings, the following three Mahayana interpretations of the stupa:

1. The base plus the five square storeys represent the six perfections: generosity, morality, patience, joyful effort, concentration and wisdom.

2. The five square levels represent the five-paths of preparation, accumulation, seeing, meditation and no more learning.

3. The base, the five terraces and the three round levels plus the mother stupa together form the ten *bhumis*,[14] or the ten stages of the Mahayana path. In this case the great mother stupa on the top represents the ultimate objective: enlightenment.

Vajrayana [the fast vehicle]

In Vajrayana, the fast vehicle, special meditation techniques are applied to achieve quick results. In the past, these techniques were usually top secret, but nowadays there is more openness. It is important to always follow the instructions of a qualified teacher,

---

12 Description of the life of Buddha Shakyamuni.
13 A person who has the unchangeable, spontaneous mind of *bodhichitta* and is still in the process of perfecting his or her body, speech, mind, quality and actions.
14 Literal meaning: 'ground' or 'stage'. The ten bhumis refer to the development stages a bodhisattva goes through on his or her way to enlightenment.

when practicing according to this fast vehicle.

The Vajrayana aspect is visible in the mandala structure of Borobudur, where its five Dhyani Buddhas are seated in the 432 alcoves on the four sides of the stupa, each accompanied by a female Buddha. On the three round highest levels are the 72 perforated stupas. Here no images are found of female Buddhas, however according to Lama Gangchen the female energy is surely present.

The Buddhas in these stupas touch their ring fingers together. According to Lama Gangchen this mudra symbolizes the union of masculine and feminine. Lama Gangchen is the only one who gives this explanation of this mudra. Scholars interpret this gesture as the dharma-chakra mudra, symbol for turning the dharma wheel.[15] However, in the dharma-chakra mudra one does not usually see the tips of the ring fingers touching each other as they do in the mudra of the 72 Buddhas in the top stupas.

Hence, the sexual union aspect of the highest yoga tantra is represented here in an encrypted form, through the mudra of the connecting ring fingers, or the 'mudra of union'.[16]

Buddha with mudra of union in bell stupa

Photo by Gunawan Kartapranata

---

15 *Borobudur, Majestic Mysterious Magnificent* (2010) contribution by Noerhadi Magetsari *Buddhism in Tenth Century Java*, p. 85, Taman Wisata Candi Borobudur, Prambanan & Ratu Boko.
16 Lama Michel, May 5th-8th 2016, Teaching *NgalSo Tantric Self-Healing*, Diessen, The Netherlands.

This encoded tantric articulation serves to make all people and Buddhists of all traditions feel at ease. In this way, Borobudur is a true multi-mandala.

This symbolic gesture represents the perfect balance between method, the masculine aspect, and wisdom, the feminine aspect. Lama Michel explains that the ring finger is connected to the energy of great bliss, and therefore we sometimes block the basis of this ring finger with our thumb while doing certain mantras, to remind us not to be attached to bliss and in order to realize that our objective is to work for the benefit of all sentient beings. He believes that wearing the wedding ring on that finger has a similar meaning.[17]

About Tibet and Indonesia

Professor Lokesh Chandra says that in the present time, it is the Tibetan lamas who can read the mandala of Borobudur. How is it possible for a Tibetan lama to know how to unlock the wisdom that is hidden in this temple on Java?

Lama Gangchen recognizes Borobudur as an early manifestation of his own Tibetan Vajrayana tradition. Tibetan Buddhism was given new impetus around the year 1040 – after its first introduction to Tibet by Padmasambhava – thanks to the great Indian master Atisha (980 - 1052). Atisha practiced Hinayana, Mahayana and Vajrayana and brought numerous texts and transmissions from India to Tibet. Lama Gangchen's Gelugpa tradition leads directly back from teacher to teacher to Atisha. Over the course of time, Vajrayana Buddhism in India and Indonesia have given way to Hinduism and Islam. However, in Tibet it has remained a living tradition all those years. Therefore Lama Gangchen is capable of understanding and reading the stupa-mandala.

Atisha visited Borobudur

Atisha was connected to the Buddhist monastic universities of Nalanda in Northern India, but he also had a connection with Indonesia. In the year 1011, long before he went to Tibet, he went on a long dangerous journey by sea, accompanied by 125 monks, to study with the great Buddhist scholar Serlingpa on the Golden

---

17 Lama Michel, March 17th 2015, Teaching on Borobudur stupa-mandala, Indonesia

Island, the current Sumatra. His aim was to develop *bodhichitta*[18] for the benefit of all sentient beings. Bodhichitta is the motivation to help others, which is a central theme in Mahayana Buddhism. Developing empathy, love and compassion is vital, and goes together with developing wisdom.

Atisha promised not to leave the island before he had realized this. Atisha had more than one hundred fifty *gurus*,[19] but Serlingpa became his most important teacher; the story goes that Atisha's eyes filled with tears of emotion, whenever he heard Serlingpa's name.

According to Lama Gangchen, Atisha made pilgrimages to Borobudur during his stay on Sumatra. He also spent time in the monasteries at Mendut temple near Borobudur. It is very likely that he introduced the building style of Borobudur to Tibet. Today in Tibet there are still some stupas – 'kumbums' – from Atisha's time that strongly remind us of the way Borobudur is constructed. They are buildings with circumambulatory passages and square and round terraces. Recently, relics of Atisha have been brought to the monastery at the Mendut temple. This temple is connected to Borobudur as a kind of gateway for arriving pilgrims.[20]

Noerhadi Magetsari from Indonesia is one of the few scholars who carefully shares his assumption that higher yoga practice was performed in the early years of Borobudur. He recognizes the similarity between the position of the five Dhyani Buddhas and the highest yoga tantra mandala of *Guhyasamaja*. He describes that he can imagine how Atisha received the secret transmissions of these practices from Serlingpa near the Buddhist study center at Borobudur. According to him there must have been many more temples and monasteries in the past.[21]

---

18 Mind of enlightenment; the deep wish to reach enlightenment with the objective to help all sentient beings.
19 A guru is a spiritual teacher who conveys to his or her students the correct methods for going beyond suffering
20 LINKS V, '*Borobudur 2013*' *World Congress - An Education for the Third Millennium*, lecture by Lama Caroline, p. 79, Lama Gangchen Peace Publications
21 *Borobudur, Majestic Mysterious Magnificent* (2010), contribution by Magetsari, Noerhadi, '*Buddhism in the Tenth Century Java*', p. 102, Taman Wisata Candi Borobudur, Prambanan & Ratu Boko.

Numerology and connection with the cosmos

At Borobudur, nothing is by chance. Everything in this multi-mandala has a meaning or function. It is a temple in the sense that it is a place for meditation and contemplation. It is a mandala that connects with the inner world and the outer world – the cosmos. But it is also an observatory of the surrounding environment and the stars and planets in the sky.

The numbers 108 and 1008

❊The number 108 is a sacred number in several Eastern religions. On each side of Borobudur there are 108 Dhyani Buddhas.

On each side of the lower square terraces, there are 92 meditation Buddhas:

In the East is the Dhyani Buddha Akshobhya.

In the South is the Dhyani Buddha Ratnasambhava.

In the West is the Dhyani Buddha Amithaba.

In the North is the Dhyani Buddha Amoghasiddhi.

On the walls of each side of the highest square level are 16 statues of the Dhyani Buddha Vairochana.

That makes a total of 92 + 16 = 108 on each side.

Then 4 sides times the 108 Buddhas makes a total of 432 Buddhas.

On the three round top levels, there are another 72 Buddha statues in the perforated stupas, which are sometimes called the sixth Dhyani Buddhas. According to Lama Gangchen, these Buddhas represent Vajrasattva.

Cumulatively, 72 + 432 = 504 statues.

When we calculate that each Buddha has a female counterpart and therefore duplicate this number, we come again to a sacred number: 1008 Buddhas.

❊In 1993 Geshe Yeshe Wangchuk from Tibet visited Borobudur together with Lama Gangchen. With a group of monks and Lama Caroline, they started working with a piece of rope, chalk and a pin. They measured and checked the dimensions of Borobudur. The way they worked used the same method employed to draw Tibetan sand mandalas. What they suspected appeared to be true. The stupa-mandala has exactly the same proportions as a traditional two-dimensional mandala. The most important characteristic they found is that certain lines consistently measured 108 units. For mandala-drawing, body parts are usually used as the unit of measurement and in this case the measure was based on the size of somebody's foot.

🌀According to Professor Lokesh Chandra, there must once have been 108 small stupas around Borobudur. He had seen the remains of these with his own eyes, before the renovation by UNESCO.

Observatory

🌀A morning in April. The sun rises from directly behind the volcano Mount Merapi. The first beams bathe the top of Borobudur in a golden glow. It is a magical sight that can only be witnessed twice a year. It is even more special when you know that there were exactly 108 days between the two sunrises from Merapi in the early years of Borobudur. It is not without reason that Borobudur was built on a natural hill that has been slightly moved and raised by 25 meters in height with eighty thousand cubic meters of earth. Why did all this extra work need to be done? Because the location was measured very precisely.[22]

Borobudur is connected to stars and planets and is exactly aligned with the temples, mountains and volcanoes in its surroundings. Borobudur was built as a kind of observatory, says Lama Caroline, from which the stars can be read:

🌀The stupa is aligned exactly in the four cardinal directions. A deviation of 1.5 degrees from North can be explained from the position of the polestar, which at the time of construction of Borobudur deviated by 1.5 degrees in comparison to its current position.

🌀Merapi volcano is situated in the East. Those days the Ashvini star – in Indian astronomy, Ashvini is an indicator for a new era – appeared in the sky in an exact straight line above the volcano.

🌀As we saw earlier, at the time of construction of Borobudur, exactly 54 days before the summer solstice the sunrise aligned exactly from Merapi and exactly 54 days afterwards, the same alignment occurred again. It is possible to count a corresponding reference to this with

---

22 UNESCO (2005) *The Restoration of Borobudur*, p. 241 - 250

the 54 Buddhas on each side of the staircases.

❀When connecting lines are drawn between the king's town Yogyakarta – which literally means city of Yogis, Borobudur and Merapi, the result is an equilateral triangle, the Buddhist symbol of the fire element. This refers to the fact that Borobudur was built on this precise spot to protect ancient Yogyakarta from the fire of the volcano.

❀The 72 stupas on the top possibly refer to the three hundred sixty degree rotation every twenty-five thousand years of the starry sky above us. It takes three hundred sixty times 72 years before the cycle is completed.

❀The triangles on the rims of the gallery walls form a tool for measuring the positions of planets and stars from Borobudur, which functioned as an observatory.

❀The slight differences in the number of steps on either side of the stupa (each around 365) can be explained by the difference in the number of days of the solar and lunar years.

In this chapter, four of Lama Gangchen's earliest Western disciples share their experiences with us about their first visits with their guru to Borobudur. We start with the story of Toet de Best who has already recounted about her childhood and Indonesia in the previous chapter. She seems to have an old connection with Serlingpa, Atisha's teacher in Indonesia. She was also present during Lama Gangchen's visits to the Museum of Ethnology and the University of Leiden in The Netherlands. Claudio Cipullo heard about the sanctuary from other lamas even before he became Lama Gangchen's translator; and Dominique Nayir Detchen relates the first visit with Lama Gangchen to Borobudur. Finally, thanka painter Leonardo Ceglie remembers the search for indications of Vajrayana Buddhism on the stupa.

Silver coins for a lama
Toet de Best (1942) The Netherlands

When Dagpo Rinpoche came to visit The Netherlands, Toet de Best offered him a collection of Indonesian coins without knowing why. Later she discovered the connection.

Reincarnation

"In the year 1987 I was introduced to Tibetan Buddhism, and that same year I met Dagpo Rinpoche in Holland. It was shortly before I met Lama Gangchen, I think. In those days I collected coins and I had a complete collection of silver coins from the Dutch East-Indies, the former colony nowadays called Indonesia. And without knowing about Dagpo Rinpoche's connection to Indonesia, I brought him this collection as an offering. I arranged the coins nicely in a pretty little box and offered this to him with a *khata*[23] and an envelope.

It was only later that I learned that Dagpo Rinpoche is the reincarnation of Serlingpa, an important teacher from the eleventh century in Indonesia. Serlingpa lived on Sumatra and he was visited by people from India who came to study Buddhism. Atisha, who is of great importance for Tibetan Buddhism, also travelled to Sumatra. Atisha studied with Serlingpa for twelve years. According to Lama Gangchen, he must have visited Borobudur during his stay in Indonesia."

The letter to the queen

"Lama Gangchen visited both the Museum of Ethnology and the University of Leiden in Holland a couple of times. On both occasions I was present. During the last visit there was a photo exhibition about Borobudur. That day, the curator received Lama Gangchen in person. He asked her to explain the different panels that were exhibited and to give some specific background information on Borobudur. During this conversation he learned about a specialized Borobudur congress for scholars, professors and other Borobudur experts to be held in the Manohara hotel at the foot of the stupa-mandala in July 2008. When the conservator learned that Lama

---

23 A traditional silk scarf with interwoven Tibetan Buddhist symbols, offered at various religious and social occasions.

Gangchen had visited Borobudur annually since 1989, that he thoroughly studied the mandala and the panels and that he came to interesting conclusions, she immediately invited him to attend and to speak at the congress.

In the museum itself, very little of what they possess from Borobudur is exhibited. Most of the pieces and Dhyani Buddha statues are stored in depots. It is possible that this has to do with an uneasy feeling that, in the past, original pieces were stolen from the place where they belong. We have tried to get access to the stores of the museum three times, but we have never succeeded. Rinpoche would have liked to perform Self-Healing at the Dhyani Buddhas there. Later, he wrote a letter to Queen Beatrix requesting her to give the Borobudur pieces a better place than the vaults of the museum where they are now.

This was after Rinpoche saw the Corpus Museum in Oegstgeest, Holland from the car. We told him that Corpus is an interactive museum and congress center. Immediately Lama Gangchen responded, 'In this way we can also create an interactive and educative Borobudur museum and congress center here in Holland. The Dutch are connected to Borobudur and Indonesia forever.'

The letter to the queen was eventually never posted because a scholar from Leiden University told us that the queen did not have such influence. However, it does show how much Lama Gangchen is concerned that Borobudur relics are displayed rather than stored, in order that they can radiate their blessings.

We were permitted access to the archives in the library of the Kern Institute, where Lama Gangchen pointed out the Buddha with the wedding ring. In the archives, there appeared a marvelous collection of Borobudur pictures, all taken around 1900 before the restoration by van Erp. At these archives, Lama Gangchen and his retinue were able very briefly to perform Self-Healing."

Borobudur is everything for me

"I have participated in seventeen Borobudur retreats. To be able to describe seventeen Borobudur retreats and a multitude of extraordinary experiences, one must probably be a poet, which I am not; I am a down-to-earth Dutch woman.

Borobudur is everything for me: *Kalachakra*[24] - the Wheel of Time, and all-inclusive. If I could have the chance to make one more journey with Lama Gangchen and I could choose one place, it would be Borobudur. During my very first visit in 1991, Rinpoche and I walked around the stupa hand in hand. He was looking around, did his prayers and said: 'Here a meditation center.' 'Yes, and I will come and live here,' I replied. But that wasn't meant to be. Later I said to Lama Gangchen once that it would be okay for me to die at that place. For me, Borobudur is the most esoteric place on earth; light, space, timelessness all at the same time in one experience."

The map to Shambala
Claudio Cipullo (1948) Italy

Since the 1980s, Claudio Cipullo has travelled with Lama Gangchen and translated for him. He tells about other Tibetan lamas who visited Borobudur and he gives us an interesting story about one of Lama Gangchen's previous lives.

Lama Zopa's bag

"The first time I heard about Borobudur was sometime in the 1970s. At that time, Trijang Rinpoche was still alive so it must have been before 1981. Anyway, I was already a monk so it was most likely around 1977. I was the assistant of Lama Zopa, and I was travelling together with him and Lama Yeshe. We were relaxing and having tea in a cafeteria in Bangalore airport, Southern India while waiting for our next plane. I had never heard about Borobudur before.

So we were just sitting there when, all of a sudden, the secretary of His Holiness the Dalai Lama entered the cafeteria. His name is Dooboom Rinpoche. Of course the lamas invited him to sit with us. He is a very nice, quiet and tall man. I knew him quite well because in those days I was pretty close to the Dalai Lama and occasionally I went to see his secretary to make an appointment for me with His Holiness.

---

24 A highest yoga tantra in which the microcosmos is related to the macrocosmos, this world is connected to Shambala and the possibility is offered to reach enlightenment in one lifetime.

Anyway, he sat down and at the same time Lama Zopa stood up to make him move closer to Lama Yeshe. While Lama Zopa was standing up, Dooboom Rinpoche saw his bag lying on the chair. 'Borobudur!' he said, while pointing at it. The name was printed on Lama Zopa's bag.

I was immediately aroused by this name. 'Wow, Borobudur!', I thought. It was the first time I heard about Borobudur. 'What is Borobudur, Rinpoche?', I asked the secretary. 'Borobudur is the map to go to *Shambala*,' he replied very kindly. Within myself I thought that this was the chance of my life, so I asked him, 'Rinpoche, where can I find that map?' We were quite close, so I could ask him that. The lamas were exchanging glances, looking at me smiling and at the same time being serious. 'That you must ask your guru,' Rinpoche said. So I asked Lama Yeshe, 'Where is it possible to get that map?' Lama Zopa started laughing; they joked that I was the King of Shambala myself and everyone ended up in a big laugh altogether. Apparently they had been visiting Borobudur, and this was the first time I heard about it.

So, many lamas had already been visiting the sanctuary for a long time, but only Lama Gangchen Rinpoche has the key to Borobudur."

Very first visit to Borobudur with Rinpoche

"I met Lama Gangchen because I was asked to translate for him in Italy, so I went to see him in Nepal and followed him from there. We were invited by Mr. Kok to come to Malaysia every year and Rinpoche gave many initiations there. One evening, Rinpoche asked Mr. Kok if he knew about Borobudur and if it was possible to go there. So Mr. Kok found out the travel arrangements and soon afterwards we went there for the first time. I was excited because, after all, I had heard it was the map to Shambala.

It was a small group; Franco from Italy, Mariette from Canada, Claudia from Brazil, Detchen-la from France, Mr Kok and me. The Manohara hotel at the foot of the stupa had not yet opened – it was still being built. So we had to travel to and fro between Yogyakarta and Borobudur, which is about an hour's drive.

The first time we arrived at Borobudur was quite late at night, so we couldn't enter the stupa because they closed at six. However,

Rinpoche was standing in front of the stupa and doing some very strong prayers. Over the following days we went around the galleries. But that first visit, Rinpoche didn't really show us much about the meaning of the mandala.

Rinpoche had yet to devise the NgalSo Self-Healing. That practice was revealed much later in 1992, some ten years after the first time we were there. However, after that first trip, every year when we were in Malaysia we would visit Borobudur."

The jewel of inner peace

"I have now visited Borobudur 27 times - and as long as my body and my mind allow it, I will go. It is very difficult to explain about the experience of Borobudur because there are no words to express the greatness of that jewel that Rinpoche tries to show to the whole world. It is the jewel of inner peace.

Rinpoche is a healer, which is special because there are many lamas, but few of them are healing lamas. I was translating in many places for many years and Rinpoche always pointed out his healing capacities. He has this special quality and is the holder of this special lineage, NgalSo. He has already been healing in all his lives."

Indrabuti and Laksminkara

"In an earlier life, Lama Gangchen was Laksminkara, the sister of Indrabuti, who was king of Oddiyana in Buddha Shakyamuni's time. In those days, kings were highly developed beings; they were not just rulers but also researchers – and Buddhism was not just a religion; it was also a research method, like science.

Indrabuti heard about Buddha's incredible teachings and he was determined to see this so he went himself. He was very much impressed but because he had a kingdom and was responsible for many people, he couldn't be away for long. He was not in the position to become a monk or renounce the mundane life in any way due to his duties as king, so he asked the Buddha for a method to integrate his teachings in his worldly life. He was a very intelligent man. But Buddha, who was of course even more clever, did not respond immediately. He pretended to think about it and told the king to go back home. 'I will come to your place', Buddha said.

We think Buddha was a human being, and Siddhartha was, but then he became a Buddha, and a Buddha can take on any aspect he likes in order to benefit others; he can be a god, a man, a woman... anything really, to help sentient beings. So what Buddha did was to manifest as a king like Indrabuti himself and he came to Oddiyana to teach tantra as a means to integrate the dharma into the life of the five sensory pleasures. He actually taught Guhyasamaja there, many kings listened, as well as the sister of Indrabuti, Laksminkara, who was also there to receive Buddha's teachings.

Indrabuti practiced as much as possible; however, he didn't have much time, given his regal workload. But his sister, Laksminkara, who had no husband to take care of, no children to attend, and many servants who took care of her, had all the time on her hands. She was a princess after all. So she practiced and practiced until she reached enlightenment."[25]

Back in Oddiyana

"One day, on one of our many travels, I was in Oddiyana with Rinpoche and he took me to the actual spot where the Buddha had taught the kings the Guhyasamaja tantra. This place is now in Pakistan. The Muslims destroyed many things like stupas and statues, but some relics were still there. Rinpoche took me to the exact place where the Buddha had been. We went on the slope of a mountain, then came to a small valley, and later came to a large valley. There the place was very clear and in the middle was something that looked like a throne. This was the place where all the kings had gathered for Buddha's teachings and where he first taught Guhyasamaja. I have never seen Rinpoche happier. 'Oddiyana, Oddiyana, Oddiyaaanaaaaaaaa!!!!,' he shouted out loud. He remembered; he could feel the blessings of the Buddha there.

So in my opinion the first person to reach enlightenment following tantra was a woman and it was Rinpoche. And that's how he became the lineage holder of NgalSo."

---

25 See also Lama Caroline's lecture about the life of Mahasiddha Laksminkara on p. 53 in *LINKS VII, Borobudur 2015 World Congress – An Education for the Third Millennium*, Lama Gangchen Peace Publications.

The boy with the precious key
Dominique Detchen Bock Nayir (1945 - 2012) France

Dominique Detchen joined the three first pilgrimages to Borobudur. In 2012 she passed away. She wrote these words just weeks before her death.[26]

A special proposal

"It was during a damp and rainy Western winter that Lama Gangchen proposed to a few friends to visit the magnificent stupa of Borobudur in Java. Franco, Francesco - who was a monk, Mariette, who was the secretary of Rinpoche and who was a nun, Claudio and I had the good fortune to be part of the first trip to the land which, so long ago in the eighth century, was Buddhist. Following a safe flight to the Soekarno airport of Jakarta, we hastily took a domestic flight with Garuda Indonesia, with rather old planes!

After about half an hour into the flight, we all got our tissues out to mop up the water coming out of the air conditioning vents everywhere. And moreover, before arriving at our destination, no longer water, but smoke was escaping from the same orifices. When we finally landed on the tarmac, I was relieved to leave this dilapidated and potentially dangerous aircraft. Anyway, being with Lama Gangchen, my fears were rather relative!"

Immediately to the stupa

"At that time there were only one or two major hotels in Yogyakarta, about forty kilometers from the stupa of Borobudur, without any of the guest-houses that can be found around now. It was late when we arrived but Lama Gangchen still wanted to go immediately to the stupa to pay homage and make a few short practices. At the hotel they confirmed that the stupa would be locked - it closed at six o'clock in the winter - and that we would not be able to enter.

Listening only to his own faith, the lama ordered two taxis in which we rode cheerfully. Sure enough, when we arrived everything was dark and shut up. Then, suddenly a boy came up to us and said

---

[26] This story was published previously in LINKS VI and has been shortened and lightly edited. Read more about Dominique in the story of Annabel Nguyen Tat in Chapter 1.

he knew the person who held the precious key. Lama Gangchen was delighted, 'Not possible, possible!', he said laughing. Then he asked the boy to guide us. Indeed, we were able to enter the stupa. Not to do the entire circumambulation; that would have taken too long. But to make prostrations, chant mantras and do some practices for half an hour. Then the taxis waiting for us outside took us back to the hotel in Yogyakarta, about forty kilometers away.

The next morning, we returned to the stupa and this time we went to the third level with beautiful offerings that we had brought with us. Over the centuries, people no longer had the habit of these Buddhist practices to honor Buddha with offerings of incense, light, food *etc.*, but they allowed us to carry on. During those few days spent in Indonesia, we met two young Englishmen who studied there. They were delighted to meet Lama Gangchen on the stupa who provided them with many explanations, especially about the different levels and the five Dhyani Buddhas.

Usually, when we made practices on a mandala, we had to imagine everything during the meditation. Here on the other hand, we were directly on the mandala and it was wonderful to meditate whilst climbing the successive levels of the mandala itself. The bas-reliefs stones mingling with the surrounding dark grey lava-stone, told the story of the significant periods of the Buddha's life and we were transported back to ancient times, to the time of Buddha Shakyamuni."

Leonardo Ceglie at panel with Vajrapani holding a vajra

The vajra in the hand of Vajrapani
Leonardo Ceglie (1954) Italy

Being a thanka[27] painter, Leonardo Ceglie always observes the stupa with an artist's eye. He tells us about the search for physical evidence of the Vajrayana mandala in Borobudur.

Looking for proof

"It was around the year 1995-96. By that time, we were already sure that the Borobudur stupa was a Vajrayana mandala but now we wanted to find the proof. So we had to look for symbols that are connected to Vajrayana Buddhism. Usually during a retreat, we went to climb the stupa long before sunrise. After finishing the practice around ten or eleven o'clock, we would come down to the hotel, have some breakfast together and then retreat in the room, take a shower and have some rest. We were usually very tired at that point.

But one day, Rinpoche called me and said, 'You go back to the stupa and look for a dorje.' 'Yes, sure,' I said, 'I'll go back.' And I went around the galleries once again, checking for this significant vajra symbol. We had already discovered many dorjes, but they were

---

27 Tibetan Buddhist scroll painting. The images of Buddhas and symbols are depicted following specific procedures and are used in meditations and ceremonies.

never complete, in the sense that they were part of a bas-relief, a statue or an ornament.

The most important evidence that we had found up to this point was at the bottom of the stairs of the temple. Years before, when Rinpoche saw this for the first time, he already knew. On the banisters on both sides, there are two big animal heads, like water monsters. If you look at them from above, you see the shape of a part of a dorje. This is exactly how the symbol is used in a specific Vajrayana mandala.

Now Rinpoche sent me on a mission to find a full dorje. So there I was again, climbing the Borobudur, by myself, walking through the galleries, checking all the levels. It took me four or five hours. Then, finally I discovered one! A very big, complete dorje! I have never seen one like that in my life! I found it on the west side of Buddha Amithaba, on the third level, in the hand of Buddha *Vajrapani*;[28] not the wrathful Vajrapani that we usually see, but the peaceful one.

I remember well where it is because, on the ground on this side, there is a huge lion that I like very much. Usually the lions at the entrances are all the same size, but there is one at the Amithaba entrance that is much bigger.

When I came back to tell Rinpoche about my discovery, I was full of emotion and very happy for many reasons. It was not simply a dorje that I had found but I found it with Vajrapani, which was a very auspicious and wonderful sign to me.

From that time until now, we have discovered many, many things that confirm the ultimate Vajrayana mandala. And still, every year on Borobudur, we find new things and we continue to understand more about its meaning. Since then we have convinced many important scholars about our findings. For example, nobody considered the existence of images of female Buddhas on the stupa. But we have proven that it is full of female Buddhas! Then, there was supposed to be no sign of the tantric sexual union, which represents the union of feminine and masculine energy. But we proved that there was. You can even find the hugging mudra depicted in the lava-stone. These are all elements that are part of the highest tantra practice, which is Vajrayana Buddhism."

---

28 Buddha of spiritual power.

The images help us to visualize the inner mandala

"As a thanka-painter myself, Borobudur is an example of true art. Our guru Lama Gangchen is always together with Borobudur, you cannot separate them. Though he is not an artist, he teaches me everything about thanka painting. What is unique about Tibetan thankas is that they are the only religious paintings used in that way. Maybe other types of Buddhism, Hinduism or even Christian religions use their art for devotion and meditation. But none use the images in the same way that Vajrayana Buddhists do. We may receive permission from the guru to visualize ourselves like a divinity. Then we put the painting in front of us and we visualize ourselves as being the divinity. In this way, over time, we wish to develop the same qualities as this *deity*. This is exactly what Borobudur does for us.

Rinpoche says that all the images and pictures in stone are there to help our mind to visualize an inner mandala. By doing our Self-Healing practice on the stupa, Borobudur helps us to realize an inner movement in our minds. With a pure mind, a pure motivation and a pure action, we can go inside our inner mandala and enjoy being a part of that."

Art in a traditional way

"Being an artist myself, I am much impressed by the style of Borobudur. It is not just Indonesian style; you also find Indian influences. When the architect and the king at that time in the eighth century decided to do the job, they must have called for the best artists and for sure some of them came from India. Imagine how it was not a job for one person. There must have been over a hundred people. The result is unique! On all my travels around the world with Rinpoche, I have never ever seen anything like this. Thinking over the fact that more than a hundred artists must have worked on it over several generations, it is incredible to see that the style is exactly the same all over the monument. All the panels, statues, ornaments, decorations are as if made by the same hand. From my experience, this is a sign that this job was being done in a real traditional way.

When you visit a Tibetan monastery, you may find five, ten, even sixteen monks making a perfect mandala together. They have this special ability to work in perfect harmony with each other. They don't have a meeting beforehand or afterwards. They all work as if they are one artist. They can, because they work in *samadhi*: they have realized perfect single-pointed concentration. For me, being on this side of the world, this is something magical.

When the Borobudur was built, the artists must have realized samadhi due to many different causes and conditions. Maybe in that time and place it was easier.

I feel there is a big difference with the way we create things in our Western world nowadays. For example, the airport in Madrid is incredibly big. So much money is being spent on space for the car park, metro, travellers, *etc*. When I look around there, I imagine it could have been a big temple and I wonder why humanity changed its mind so much over the centuries. In the time of Borobudur, so much money and time was spent to create a beautiful temple where ceremonies could be held, where life could be celebrated! During that time, the artists had the ability to realize something very deep inside while they worked together on this immense project."

Perfect single-pointed concentration

"Tibetan monks destroy their mandalas after making them. We Western artists write our names on every little thing we create and make sure people know it is *me* who did the job. Art is an expression of the values of the society. Different times and places show different meanings of art. Sometimes it simply has an aesthetic purpose, meant only for decoration. In other cases, art is holy and full of meaning. It can be an expression of someone who feels a deep connection to the universe. The Borobudur is exactly that. Numerous different people over several generations worked in deep, single-pointed concentration on the same project. The outcome is a miracle.

We have discovered a lot about the symbolism of Borobudur. What is next is to discover the deep connection that it brings us about the universe around us. Borobudur is a way to show us how to feel the truth. The temple is a teaching – a big, wonderful, incredible teaching."

Chapter 5

Magical Experiences

Around the Sanctuary

Energy field

The first man on the moon, Neil Armstrong, looked from his extraterrestrial position to the Earth and saw a light shining. When it was investigated where the light came from, it appeared to be Central Java; exactly the spot where Borobudur is situated.

Sometimes special light effects or light balls appear on the pictures that are taken during retreats with Lama Gangchen. Moreover, people have witnessed actual light shining up from Borobudur.

We see Borobudur as a stone mandala but within it, on an energetic level, is an actual wisdom mandala that enables extraordinary occurrences and appearances to happen.

Lama Caroline says, "When we are at the stupa with Lama Gangchen, he brings Borobudur to life. He knows how to open this energy field. And when he leaves, he closes it down again and everything turns back to normal. At Borobudur many amazing things happen. When we did Self-Healing in 1993, we saw white nectar coming from the stupa. It squirted up from the stone. We could sense a special energy. In another moment, after a Kalachakra-initiation by Lama Gangchen, a rainbow appeared on one of Borobudur's corners. The rainbow went straight up, like a light beam in a science fiction movie."

NgalSo Self-Healing is the key to Borobudur

According to the Indian scholar professor Lokesh Chandra, Lama Gangchen brings Borobudur to life with NgalSo Self-Healing, the Tibetan Buddhist practice that Rinpoche has introduced as a meditation method that is suitable for modern people.

However, though the practice is very suitable for contemporary society, it doesn't mean that on a certain day Lama Gangchen just created a simplified and compact meditation method.

In the early 1990s, after Lama Gangchen had visions on Borobudur, he developed Self-Healing. Lama Gangchen said, "In the winter of 1992, during my fourth visit to the Borobudur stupa-mandala of Indonesia, I experienced a kind of revelation that was accompanied by many visions of Buddhas, holy beings and my gurus. At this time something opened in my mind and I began to regain the wisdom lineage of one of my previous Tibetan incarnations who was called Jampa Pel or Truphul Lotsawa ...

These ancient memories from the twelfth century are called mind *termas* or mind treasures. They are true healing methods that come from my subconscious mind in new and modern forms that are more suitable to heal the people of this polluted modern time." [1]

The fact that ancient wisdom is revealed in a later era is a well-known phenomenon in Tibetan Buddhism. The rediscovered wisdom is called terma: a hidden treasure. In this case, Lama Gangchen is the treasure finder, or the *terton*. A terton is a person who possesses the quality to reveal ancient precious texts that have been hidden in water, earth, fire, or the space of the subtle consciousness.

Authentic practice

Lama Michel explains that everything about NgalSo Self-Healing is completely coherent with the original teachings of the Buddha. The knowledge and insights of Lama Gangchen can be traced back from teacher to teacher to the founder of our Gelugpa tradition, Lama Tsongkhapa (1357 -1419), Atisha (980 - 1052), who reintroduced Buddhism to Tibet, and eventually to the original Buddha Shakyamuni (±560 B.C.)

Lama Michel speaks about Lama Gangchen's visions, "These visions are not just a creation of one's own mind; they are in fact the ability to come into contact with existence itself, an existence that is there on a more subtle level. It is what we call holy existence. So, when Rinpoche came to Borobudur, he had a vision, which basically

---

1 Lama Gangchen, T.Y.S, (2009) *Zhing Kham Yong So - Making Peace with the Environment*, p. 8-19, Lama Gangchen Peace Publications

brought us the practice of Self-Healing. The stupa talked to him, so to speak, and showed him the practice of Self-Healing. This is why it is so precious, because the practice of Self-Healing was not based on a theoretical aspect – it came through the pure connection that Rinpoche has with his own gurus and with the Buddhas. He actually had this precious experience, this precious vision, which was like the stupa talking to him, like the stupa showing him the practice itself." [2]

A poetic miracle

Professor Lokesh Chandra was the first scientist to confirm Lama Gangchen's insights that Borobudur is a mandala and, thanks to him, the conservation of Borobudur as a World Heritage Site became a reality due to his strong lobbying at UNESCO. Professor Lokesh Chandra attended a retreat with Lama Gangchen and his disciples in 2013. During a lecture, he described how the silhouette of the architect Gunadharma might be described in the contours of the surrounding mountains, and he continued his story with these moving words,

"... I asked: 'Gunadharma, when will you come down to the Buddha-land? Borobudur has been restored.' I came many times, but Gunadharma did not descend from the mountain. Suddenly his incarnation Gangchen Rinpoche appears. I am happy that prayers to Gunadharma have not been in vain. His incarnation is with us. We sit beside his incarnation, who is going to create other Borobudurs ... Lama Gangchen has done a poetic miracle in giving new life to the Borobudur ...

I have the deepest respect for His Holiness Gangchen Rinpoche because he has done what I thought could never be done. I thought Borobudur would remain a monument of silence." [3]

The six perfections

During his stay at the retreat, Professor Lokesh Chandra himself experienced the magical impact of the wisdom mandala that manifests at Borobudur in the presence of Lama Gangchen and

---

[2] LINKS VI 'Borobudur 2014', Proceedings - An Education for the Third Millennium, speech by Lama Michel, p. 10, Lama Gangchen Peace Publications
[3] LINKS V 'Borobudur 2013' World Congress - An Education for the Third Millennium, speech by Prof. Lokesh Chandra, p. 45-46, Lama Gangchen Peace Publications

Silhouette of Gunadharma

with Self-Healing as the key for entering it. In the early morning of February 28, 2013 the professor sat hand in hand with Lama Gangchen on the lowest steps of the stairway on the East side. Around him he saw the sculptures and statues of animals, like the lions. During the renovation by UNESCO, 38 years before, the workers had asked him about it – Where should the lions be positioned? What have they to do with Buddhism? Professor Lokesh Chandra found, "I had no answer for 38 years. Suddenly the vibration from the hands of Gangchen Rinpoche flashed across my mind the solutions to several questions. I suddenly realized that the lions, dolphins, elephant tusks *etc.*, designed on the eastern entrance were symbols of the six paramitas." [4]

Next he explained how the five animals and a dwarf that adorn Buddha Shakyamuni's throne are related to the six perfections, referring to certain works of Buddhist literature:

---

4 LINKS V 'Borobudur 2013' World Congress – An Education for the Third Millennium, contribution by Prof. Lokesh Chandra, 'Ploughing the Fields of the Mind', p 66-68, Lama Gangchen Peace Publications

The garuda (a mythological bird) represents generosity.

The naga (a mythological snake) represents morality.

The makara (a crocodile-like creature) represents patience.

The dwarf represents enthusiastic perseverance.

The elephant represents meditation or concentration.

The lion represents wisdom.

In his speech, Lokesh Chandra continued describing several insights that came to him while at the stupa with Lama Gangchen. He realized that the statues and reliefs must have been plastered over and colored, and the spires of the stupas with the Buddhas inside must have been gilded during the era of the Sailendra rule on the Golden Islands.

Symbols of six perfections

The real miracle is transformation of the mind

In the following stories, several miraculous events are featured. These are very interesting and appealing indeed. However we shouldn't lose sight of what the spiritual path is really about. Lama Gangchen once said: "The real miracle is to change the mind."[5] We can have many magical experiences, but if we don't get to work with our inner processes, they are completely useless.

---

5   Lama Gangchen, Initiation of the 84 Mahasiddhas, November 1st 2014, AHMC Albagnano, Italy

First, Alen Kok shares with us how he witnessed several magical events around Borobudur. Lola Hernandez had an impressive vision while she was on the stupa. She saw Borobudur in the way it must have been during its early days: colorful and lively. Following these, Gabrielle Lo Re speaks about the origin of Self-Healing and a meaningful dream she had in this respect. Ulrich Hüschelrath took a miraculous picture of the stupa. Irene Zwaan's story is about how her prayers on the stupa were answered. Finally, Laura Oliveira had a special experience when Lama Gangchen advised her to climb the stupa by herself early in the morning.

The mind that can make things happen
Alen Kok (1967) Malaysia

Alen Kok shares some miraculous and magical experiences he witnessed at Borobudur. For example, he met a very special woman on the stupa who helped him to solve a personal problem.

Many lives

"It was almost thirty years ago in Malaysia that I met Lama Gangchen. The first time I saw him, I cried. This was so surprising to me because I didn't know that it was possible for me to cry! At that time I spoke only Chinese and Rinpoche spoke no English either. So we communicated with two translators. I felt very close to him. He said that it was because some of us have been together already over many lives. That was when I decided to learn English, to be able to communicate with Rinpoche. He also started to learn English from that time and nowadays we speak English to each other. We also have a group and a small center in Malaysia now."

Tara in the sky

"While we are at Borobudur with Rinpoche many magical phenomena may happen. For example, the first time I was there I did some prayers at night outside, while everybody else was fast asleep. Then I saw a cloud with some light inside, not so far away. While I was doing my prayers it moved steady to the top of the stupa and after a while it moved away again. Then, when I continued my chanting, it moved to the stupa again. This happened three times!

Another experience was when we arrived at night and did the *kora*[6] with prayers around the stupa straight away. Suddenly Rinpoche looked at the sky, so I also looked and I saw something there, but we were moving fast and I couldn't focus. Sometime later he looked again and when I followed his glance, I saw *Tara*[7] in the sky! Then I started to see more symbols like a double dorje, a lotus, a dharma wheel, garudas ... all aspects from the Self-Healing practice. It was as if I was looking at images in a book or on TV. I couldn't believe it myself. But the next morning Rinpoche asked in the gompa who had seen phenomena appear in the sky the night before and other people confirmed they had seen Tara and the other things, exactly as I had. It must have been a dedication to us by the holy beings because they were happy that we are there, praying and practicing."

The oracle woman

"One time, before I came to Borobudur, I had some serious financial problems at home related to investments in the stock market. I was deeply worried and dedicated many prayers during my stay at Borobudur to the solution of this problem. One morning, I met a Chinese lady from Surabaya. She was having a tea in front of her hotel room while we passed by, returning from our daily kora at the stupa. She saw Rinpoche and said, 'That man came to my house. He was standing at my door last week and told me to come to Borobudur, so now I am here!' I told this to Rinpoche, who then asked me to invite her to come with us to the stupa the next day. I passed on the message; she came and on the way I translated the practice for her into Chinese. After we had finished, she said that she knew I had a problem. She instructed me to go to a specific Buddha on the Amitabha side and to wish there deeply for the solution, so I followed her advice. This was the only time I have seen the woman; after two days she was gone again. When I came back home, my problem was solved in a miraculous way. Later, I asked Rinpoche about the woman and he told me she was an oracle."

---

6 Ritual or ceremonial circumambulation around a holy place or temple.
7 Female Buddha, occurring in different forms. The green and white Taras are best known.

Making rain

"There are many examples. For instance, that time when we were lighting the ten thousand candles on the stupa, while the sky was filled with dark heavy clouds about to burst into rain and thunderstorm. Rinpoche looked up at the sky and then I saw a hole appear in the middle of the cloud formation. Around the stupa it started raining. On the stupa it was dry until we finished the candle offering.

Even more astonishing was the time when everything was covered by ash from a volcanic eruption. As a Malaysian, I also understand the Indonesian language. On my arrival, the people from the hotel asked me to ask our guru to help make it rain because it had been dry for weeks and the air remained filled with dust. I told Rinpoche about their wish and then he said, 'Okay, our first job here is to make it rain.' We had all just arrived so everybody took a shower first and afterwards we gathered in the conference room. Rinpoche said, 'We ask the bodhisattvas now to make it rain for the benefit of the community here because they are suffering, and we need to chant with a compassionate motivation. You will all do the guru mantra now, I will do the rest.' So we did that for at least half an hour, while Rinpoche was performing prayers with a dorje and a bell. Suddenly there was a big explosion of thunder and lightning. BAM!!! Then the rain came. It went on for at least twelve hours. It was heavy rain that gave a strong wash to the stupa. When the sun came out, everything was bathed in golden light. I saw it with my own eyes – it was so powerful! Rinpoche explained that this was possible because the inner elements are linked to the outer elements. They are of the same nature and they can communicate. I have no doubts about that.

These things happen and the holy beings are there to increase our faith. This faith helps our minds to overcome our disbelief in the power of mantra. It helps to develop the mind that can make things happen.

I come to Borobudur with Rinpoche every year. It is a place for purification. In *samsara*[8] there is a lot of stress, but in Borobudur everything gets better."

---

[8] The infinite cycle of death and rebirth in which lives are determined by karma and mental defilements. The only way out of samsara is the path to enlightenment.

Mendut temple

A myriad of colors
Lola Hernandez (1978) Spain

The dreams started while she was on her way to Borobudur, in Jakarta. Upon arrival at the stupa-mandala, many visions began to occur. In this way, Lola Hernandez got the opportunity to check out the past.

Borobudur didn't appeal

"Since I was a child, I have been interested in psychology and art, and I studied art history and art restoration. I met Lama Gangchen in spring 2008 at the Madrid Tibetan Medicine Congress and, while I wasn't too sure about what it meant, I decided to follow him in all aspects of my life. From the moment I met Lama Gangchen, I have heard him say that Borobudur should be visited at least once in a lifetime. However, it wasn't particularly appealing to me and I didn't have the money to go anyway. But when I was offered sponsorship in 2014, of course I was happy to go and visit the famous stupa.

Lots of people told me about their experiences there, how it feels, the magic that engulfs the place... But to be honest, I didn't expect to feel or see anything like this. I must say that I didn't know anything about the stupa by then. I wasn't particularly interested,

I didn't really care and I didn't even know the Self-Healing practice very well. I was simply happy to go and have a good time. The day we travelled, we heard that a volcano in the area had erupted and that planes couldn't reach their destination. I was still determined to go anyway. A call from Rinpoche gave us confirmation and we headed to Jakarta. However, as we arrived there, we were informed that there weren't any connecting flights to Yogyakarta, so the whole group had to stay in a hotel. I shared a room with my partner. We were very happy to be on the other side of the world, so we went to sleep early looking forward to arriving at Borobudur. That's where my experience started."

Feeling of nostalgia

"In my first dream, a beautiful path opened up in front of me; a wide street full of people talking and arguing, most of them dressed in white, carrying texts. There were temples on both sides of the road. Later I realized that the Mendut Temple near Borobudur is similar to those I saw in my dream. Down the road was Borobudur. There were people walking around it, others went up and down its stairs. But it was different from now; it wasn't black but colorful, a myriad of colors. White, gold, green, blue, red... I also recall a spire that crowned the mother stupa – golden, dazzling under the sun.

The next day we could fly to our destination. I remember entering the street where you can see the stupa far away... I was thrilled to see it; it was incredible to be there. But I really expected to see more temples around it, so when we got nearer to the stupa I felt a bit disappointed. During the retreat I felt a strong need to be alone. I didn't want to practice but simply to sit down looking at the stupa, and that's exactly what I did. Anyway, the stupa was closed due to the volcanic eruption, so we couldn't climb it. Then one day we got permission to enter briefly. I stayed slightly behind the group because there were a lot of people. At one point I almost fell from the steep stairs so, spontaneously, I grabbed a bas-relief to keep my balance. And that's when I had a vision that deeply, deeply touched my soul as it has never been touched before.

A tanned and slender man, wearing nothing more than a kind of white skirt, barefooted, with deep black wavy hair was carving an elephant in a dark volcanic rock. It was hot, I was sweating ...

I felt an outburst in my chest and started to cry... I looked where I had put my hand and there it was: the same image that I had seen the man carving. It was there, behind my hand, and the most intense feeling of nostalgia I had ever experienced in my life came over me. I couldn't stop crying while a voice inside me told me over and over again that I was back home. I was home... Suddenly everything around me changed.

I wasn't me, I wasn't Lola, I didn't recognize myself. We kept on walking around the galleries and climbing the stairs to higher levels. The feeling of familiarity didn't leave me. I looked around and felt incredibly happy and bewildered at the same time. Everything around me felt so familiar but it was also different."

Glimpses of a past life

"Days passed by and I felt like being at home. I loved everything about it and was happy. I didn't want to go back to Spain; I wished to stay there forever. Dreams kept coming, everyday scenes of Borobudur, landscapes from the past... There is one dream that I remember particularly, where I could see the whole complex from above. I was looking at it from the highest point of a temple very similar to Mendut. I looked down and there were people on the stairs. I remember the whispering conversations and far away seeing Borobudur in its former glory, fully colored, with its golden spire.

Back in Spain the dreams didn't stop, they were all very similar. I will never forget these dreams, feelings and experiences because they were so vivid that I had no other choice but to share them with Rinpoche. First I talked to Lama Caroline, since she has great knowledge about Borobudur and I told her about my dreams and experiences. She told me that it is only recently known that Borobudur must have been colored at some point. In those days there was a whole complex of temples around it. She also told me that I should tell Rinpoche about my experiences, so I did.

His answer left me speechless. Indeed, he confirmed that Borobudur and its surroundings back then were exactly as I saw them in my dreams. He also told me that the dreams and visions were glimpses of a past life in which I worked on the construction of the stupa. Probably the stone I touched was carved by me in that life, and that's why that memory came back to me. He also added that he had great plans for me, and that we would build another Borobudur together.

I always wondered why I was following Lama Gangchen, and how I could be useful ... Now I understand the connection. I understand many things and I am immensely thankful for being where I am, together with my master again, being useful for him in this life and collaborating in his projects."

Each time I reach a point where my mind is still and happy
Gabriella Lo Re (1971) Italy

Gabriella Lo Re saw more than twelve rainbows when she traveled with Lama Gangchen to the place in Brazil where a new Borobudur temple is being built. This phenomenon is familiar around Lama Gangchen. In Holland and Italy, she saw the same.

Permission of the Holy Beings

"I have been to Borobudur twenty times and there are many stories, auspicious signs and experiences to tell, but what I want to share now is this special dream I had in 1996.

I was alone in the desert and next to me there was a pot filled with blood. The sun was hot and I was naked. In my understanding, the meaning of this in the East as well as in the West is that you are free of mental concepts. From far away, there came a gigantic Garuda – a mythical bird – flying towards me. The bird alighted next to me and started to drink the blood. I woke up with a very special feeling; I was not in the least anxious or shocked.

When I told Lama Gangchen my dream he reacted differently from normal. Usually he is very restrained if we come to him with our special dreams, so we can keep both feet on the ground. But this time he said, 'The dream tells us that our lineage is uninterrupted. It means that I have permission from the holy beings. This is very auspicious'."

Vision

"The term terma is known in Tibetan Buddhism. Termas are sacred objects and teachings that are hidden on the land, in water or space. The termas are waiting there until the time is ripe to be revealed. In 1993 at Borobudur, Lama Gangchen received the termas of the Self-Healing in a number of visions.

His mind is vast; we don't know how it works, but after the visions he knew how he could transmit tantra to Westerners of this time. We live in a Kaliyuga era, a degenerate time, which also means that we have no time and that our minds cannot easily deal with long texts. Lama Gangchen's Self-Healing is perfectly suited to this kind of mind.

The practice is mainly focusing on visualizations. You can compare it to Twitter. In a few words it goes straight to the essence. It is also a very balanced and safe system that protects people who have had insufficient preparation, to avoid inner harm. This has to do with the inner winds and how these flow through our channels. People who meditate in a wrong way and without good guidance might sometimes completely lose it.

So, my dream was a small confirmation of the fact that Self-Healing refers straight to the teachings of the Buddha and that it is not 'just another idea' of Lama Gangchen. The Borobudur stupa is a mandala for many practices; it started with Self-Healing but, year by year, Rinpoche opens another door to this Ocean of Mandalas."

Rainbows

"Lama Gangchen has the wish to bring the energy of Borobudur to the world. Thinking about what I should relate, I realized that I have been to all three other places with Rinpoche where this was intended: the temple in Albagnano, Italy; the Borobudur under construction in Minas, Brazil and the replica on exhibition at *Floriade*[9] in the Netherlands.

Many people know that a lot of auspicious signs appear in Albagnano, like the rainbow that came when the central channel in the temple was filled with thousands of crystals. But I was also there when we flew in a private jet with the Brazilian businessman Marcus to a large piece of land where he wanted to build a Borobudur temple a quarter of the size of the one in Indonesia. The number of rainbows that appeared during the trip was bizarre. In total we saw twelve rainbows within two hours! The last one we saw was on the gigantic plot that is used for grazing cows. We were near a small farm building and Marcus was somehow worried in what direction we should look. 'No worry', Rinpoche said. Immediately the rainbow rose from a spot on the land... Rinpoche had no doubt where this Borobudur should be built. He says that we may see rainbows but that he sees holy beings. This is thanks to his vajra eyes, his great realizations.

We went to the spot that was indicated by the rainbow and we

---

9 Floriade: World horticulture exhibition, held once every ten years in alternating locations in Holland.

also checked the surroundings. There happened to be two rivers and there was a water source, exactly as in Indonesia and in Italy. These are specifically auspicious conditions for a holy place. At this moment, the creation of a duplicate of the Borobudur at this spot is underway.

In The Netherlands we visited the Indonesian stand at the Floriade exhibition near Venlo. We wanted to check if the replica of the Borobudur stupa built there was suitable for an activity with our group. At the moment we arrived, a beautiful rainbow showed up in the sky. Lama Gangchen truly carries Borobudur's energy with him; I have seen it many times. If Rinpoche and Borobudur come together, the wisdom beings are present for sure!"

Inner peace

"But the most important thing for me is the inner peace that Borobudur gives me. Borobudur is almost always on my mind. Sometimes I use the word Borobudur as a mantra. I have been there twenty times with Lama Gangchen and every time I pray that I can go again – because it feels like coming home. Each time I am there, I reach a point where my mind is calm and happy. This gives me the confidence that meditation does work. It is truly possible to achieve this state of mind.

Lama Gangchen said lately, 'I offered this stupa-mandala to you as a place of refuge.' This is so true for me because, at Borobudur, you feel uplifted to another level of consciousness: the mind is clearer. You peek through a crack in the door and get a glimpse of the bright light out there. This energy of peace, harmony and joy is what you can touch within yourself. In daily life, in good times and in difficult times, just by thinking of Borobudur, I am reconnected to this blissful energy.

This helps me to continue my meditation consistently. Please note that it is an experience, not a realization (because then you would have this sensation all the time). It begins with a few minutes, later you can feel it for half an hour, maybe for a few days, and so on until you reach full enlightenment."

Loosening karmic knots

"Because I work for Rinpoche, in recent years I have been much busier with the organization of the retreat than before. In the early years we came with ten people; by 2014 the number had gone up to two hundred fifty! So in the past I had much more time to do the real retreat, but it makes me very happy now that I can do something to make it possible for other people to have similar experiences. I realize that I am in a very fortunate situation, having been able to go so often.

It makes me happy if others can make it to Borobudur as well. I have seen big changes in people's lives. Inner changes, but – with people who suffered from karmic knots that perturbed their life situation – I saw also changes in their economic or social situation. Once, a man with a tumor came – the doctors had given him one month to live. I believe he is still alive. I know someone who had no money, no job and no house. His last thousand euros – the only thing he possessed – he spent on a trip to Borobudur. After that, things in his life changed for the better. At Borobudur, you are offered the chance to change yourself and your life!"

The impossible is possible
Ulrich Hüschelrath (1969) Germany

Sometimes people don't sense that much at Borobudur. Yet, even in that case, all of a sudden something miraculous might occur. This is what happened to Ulrich Hüschelrath.

What is wrong with me?
"Borobudur is the most important place for me to go to. I have been there almost every year since the first time in 2010. For me it is not something I feel, but rather something I know – because whenever I am there, I have a theme of something that bothers me in my life. And when I go back home, the year after that journey the situation changes for the better. The whole year is improved. It is simply always like that.

For example, we had a lot of conflicts, quarrels and discussion on the board of Dharma-Chakra, the German organization for Lama Gangchen's NgalSo practices. After every board member apart from me had changed, this conflict remained, so I concluded that it must be me who caused the negative vibe. I was the problem. So one year during the Borobudur retreat I went to Rinpoche and asked him, 'What is wrong with me! What is my problem? Because I want to change this.' Rinpoche replied, 'Nothing is wrong with you.' Then he coughed a bit, looked in another direction and after a while he said, 'I will give you an answer later.'

A little confused, I went outside and sat by the fountain in front of the conference hall – our gompa to contemplate what had happened. Then something popped into my mind. It was crystal clear. 'You are not the problem', I thought. 'However, you are the one responsible to take care of this issue.' So there was the answer; I was responsible, and it worked! I took care of it. After that retreat, I started to take more responsibility for my actions and the decisions that needed to be taken. Since then things became much better and smoother in my life."

The miracle picture

"On March 13th 2012, something happened during the initiation of the Bodhisattva Vows. We were sitting outside at the foot of Borobudur. I had put my camera next to me on a small hill in the grass. The year before, I had already taken some night shots of the stupa and so I knew the settings of my camera very well.

In general, such a night picture takes a long exposure; the lens stays open for a long time after triggering the mirror. In this way, more light is captured by the sensor and the shot is bright. Everyone can imagine the effect of underexposed shots, which are too dark, or overexposed images like a car at night, where a long red strip is pulled from the rear light through the picture. This has to do exactly with this mechanism.

That evening, sitting with the masters and the group on the field in front of Borobudur, I pressed the shutter of my camera and heard the mirror close again immediately after pressing. Click-clack. Normally I would have heard a click and then after about ten to thirty seconds the clack. So I was disappointed because I assumed that it was impossible that the picture would come out well.

The next day when I looked at the images of the day before on my laptop I was very surprised! The photo showed a brilliant stupa

Photo by Ulrich Hüschelrath

as if light shone from the inside out. It was not at all like the other pictures I had taken before, where the stupa was clearly illuminated from the spotlights around.

I showed the photo to Lama Caroline and told her how the image had come about. I said to her, 'This is like a miracle.' Lama Caroline replied: 'No, it is not like a miracle, it is a miracle.'

Usually I analyze everything. However, this experience I had at Borobudur with the miracle picture made me realize that the impossible is possible. Maybe I don't feel it. But I know it."

My mother's dream
Irene Zwaan (1968) The Netherlands

While Irene Zwaan intensely dedicated her prayers for her mother's health, her mother had a special dream at home.

Extremely healthy

"Before I joined a Borobudur retreat myself, I had heard many stories from others. Family members, friends, people who are close to me had already been there a couple of times. What struck me about their stories was that nobody really attempted to explain the real meaning of the pilgrimage. There are simply no words to describe it because it is so huge, special, intense and magical. This I only realized when I was there myself for the first time, in February 2013. In daily life, since a burnout, I have always lived with fatigue, hypersensitivity to sounds and light, headaches, a buzz in my head and a bad memory. To be able to do my work, I lived an isolated life and I needed a lot of rest. In Indonesia, much to my surprise, I was extremely healthy from day one! For example, the continuous noise of traffic near the hotel didn't bother me at all. Three times a day I enjoyed meals, accompanied by the lively chatter of fellow pilgrims.

Every morning, without hesitation, I woke up at four o'clock to attend the meditations at the stupa that lasted for hours and hours. In the afternoons, I didn't skip a single meeting in the conference room. And in between, I joined in social activities. In short: For two weeks I lived the life that I had not been able to live for the previous four years in Holland. To me, this was a magical experience, a miracle. But the real miracle was of a wholly different nature. A week before the start of the retreat, my mother became very ill, so I went to stay with my parents, to help and to be there for them day and night. I strongly considered canceling the journey to Borobudur. But my sister came back from her holidays to be with my parents and she insisted that I should go, so in the end I decided to head off to Indonesia. My sister had been to Borobudur a couple of times before, so she knew where I was going and she wished for me to have this experience."

Another crisis

"For me, it was difficult to leave my mother behind in her vulnerable state. Previously, she had always been very strong. I decided I would take her with me in all my prayers. During the retreat, I contacted home regularly and I felt very sad when I heard she had had another crisis.

During the daily climb of the stupa early in the morning, I usually stayed a bit behind the group, because it was more relaxed. The group consisted of around two hundred people, who made their way to the top, walking through the narrow galleries at a slow pace under the guidance of Lama Gangchen. Once the highest level is reached, everybody stands in a circle around the mother stupa, touching their foreheads to the black lava stone, reciting the dedication prayers, usually followed by a long, deep silence. But there is not enough space around the top stupa to perform this ritual with two hundred people at the same time. Only the ones walking ahead get the chance to undergo this experience together with Lama Gangchen."

Close to Rinpoche

"Now, on the day before the last day of the retreat, my mother was in such a bad state that I decided to try my best to walk in front so I could do my concluding prayers in the presence of Lama Gangchen and the other teachers. It took me some effort and I somehow elbowed my way through the crowd, but I managed and eventually I had a good spot close to Rinpoche on the highest level of the temple. There, I prayed very, very deeply and intensely for my mother's health and for her to feel a little bit better."

Sitting at the guru's feet

"That same day I asked Rinpoche, who already had given some advice to my mother, if he could recommend her a specific mantra. He said 'Tara', and looked at me with a smile. So I sent her this message and the next day I received an email from my sister: 'Could I contact her quickly through Skype', she asked. She wanted to tell me something special about our mother. The fact is that my mother has always been pleased that my sister and I are connected to Rinpoche. She even met him once in The Netherlands. Our father is Protestant and our mother has always been interested in spirituality but she never committed herself to any movement or religious group. I managed to establish a connection though Skype and my sister told me that our mother had had a very special dream. In the dream she saw me sitting with Lama Gangchen. She was present, together with my father. She saw a beam of light or energy; whatever you may call it, flowing from Rinpoche's heart to mine. In the dream she thought, 'If my daughter can have this connection, then I can too.' Immediately, balls of light came from Rinpoche's heart to hers. She experienced the deep love and compassion that Lama Gangchen sent to her and she felt completely calm and relaxed. Then, the lama reclined in a relaxed way and at that moment my mother realized she was there, sitting with my father at his feet in the same way as Jesus' disciples sat at his feet. This thought was comforting for her and also my father was calm and accepting of the situation."

A cloud of love and compassion

"Next, she woke up in a cloud of love and compassion. This feeling stayed with her for a long time and she felt supported by Rinpoche. Over the following days, her health improved a great deal. Her energy level increased and the many discomforts bothering her reduced substantially. To me, my mother's experience was a confirmation of the powerful and undoubted significance of Borobudur. The fact that my mother got the chance to meet Rinpoche in her dream while I did my prayers and asked Rinpoche to help her, is a grand miracle. I am forever grateful to Rinpoche: for his support, that I met him and that he offered me the chance to come to Borobudur in his company."

The sun and moon in line with the stupa
Laura Oliveira (1961) Brazil

While being alone on the stupa, Laura Oliveira experienced how Borobudur is connected to the stars and planets.

A very special gift

"One morning I woke up very early at Borobudur. I left my room and at the same time, Lama Gangchen came out of his room. He said: 'Go to the stupa now, there is something there for you.' 'Shall I first call my sister?' I asked him. 'No no, you go,' he said. So I did and I climbed all the way up. When I arrived at the top of the stupa, I looked up at the sky and what I saw was stunning. The sky was

Panel with the moon, the seven planets and the sun

clear and the sun and the moon were extremely bright – positioned perfectly in line with each other and with the stupa. It was exactly the same as the image on a thanka. At the same time, I was overwhelmed by an incredible strong energy. It seemed to last for a long time, and it felt as if I was taken back to somewhere that I cannot describe. I am very sensitive and this was simply too much; I needed to talk to somebody, so I ran down back to the hotel, where I met Rinpoche. He smiled at me: 'Did you like your gift?' he said. And that's what it was: a gift, especially for me, that is why he wanted me to go alone, with no one else.

There were other times when magic things happened. Rinpoche used to make water manifest from the stupa. He touched the stone at the top with his head, and then water came out exactly where he had put his head… I have seen rainbows, round ones, in a full blue sky… I have seen a big scorpion coming out of the stone floor after Rinpoche's blessings…

What does it mean, the gift I received? I don't really know. It may have been a big purification. Even when you ask Rinpoche about these things, he doesn't always give you an answer, because you are not really ready for it. For me Rinpoche is a living Buddha: wherever he touches, light comes out. He can remove obstacles. He can do anything if you allow him. He is pure crystal."

I feel young again

"The energy of Borobudur is so powerful; it takes you back to the time when it was built and how it was built. The first time I came – I was much younger and slimmer – I saw all those semi-naked images sculpted at the stupa and immediately I felt part of it, I felt I was home again. And every time I go there I feel young again.

The energy there is so different. I need little sleep and I don't feel tiredness. It is like a spaceship. If you let yourself go, things happen. I don't sit much to meditate. I do other forms of mediation, like *karma yoga*[10] *etc*. But there it is much easier to practice. It is where I belong."

---

10   Those practicing karma yoga follow the path of unselfish actions and servitude. Karma yoga offers the possibility to turn all kinds of daily activities into meaningful practice.

Chapter 6

The Feeling of Borobudur

Golden light

"On the last night of my first retreat at Borobudur, in 2009, we recited the same long mantra endlessly. It went on and on. During this recitation something happened to me. I knew I was in the gompa, but at the same time I was at the top of the stupa. I saw a golden light, magic and radiant – it was beautiful. I only felt peace, happiness, calmness and softness. Inexpressible. I was beyond the fears, discomforts and discontent that one usually carries all the time as a human being. It was as if I was allowed a glimpse of how 'It Is', how it can be. Infinite peacefulness. I was one with the stupa; there was no more distinction between us. I have never had such a feeling again. It is wonderful that I had this experience because now I know that that state of being is possible." Karin Zwaan (1964) The Netherlands.

The feeling of Borobudur is not easy to capture in words. It is something personal, and different for everyone. However, it is the most important aspect that we want to highlight in this book.

Lama Gangchen is the King of Feeling

When we started with this book, Lama Gangchen said, "It is not about history or architecture. It is about the love for Borobudur; a love that is greater and deeper than the love for one's husband or one's wife, for one's child or one's parents."

The love for Borobudur is a feeling that grows as we visit again and again, as we learn more, as we know more and as we meditate more. There are no words to describe the feeling. At the same time, it is a feeling that connects people from all parts of the world who come with Lama Gangchen.

Lama Gangchen and Ruedi Schneider

Lama Gangchen often explains how the senses are connected to one's experience, one's feelings. He often speaks of the 'taste' of things: you have to taste it. This tasting is also applicable to Borobudur: it is an experience, a sensation. Also, Lama Gangchen teaches us that everything is made out of energy and that everything has its own sound or vibration.

The artistic, cultural and historical aspects are all very interesting; hundreds of books have been written. But the most important thing is to experience the feeling of Borobudur. The Swiss family doctor Ruedi Schneider explained during his speech at Borobudur in March 2015, "Borobudur is a feeling school and Lama Gangchen is the King of Feeling."

Lama Gangchen knows what bothers you

In 2013, Professor Nirmala Sharma joined Professor Lokesh Chandra on his visit to Borobudur. She is an Indian scholar in Buddhist studies and art history. It was the first time she had met Lama Gangchen and after some days she expressed her feelings publicly during her speech. She said she was delighted to have been invited and very much impressed by Lama Gangchen, "... You are just silent there and he knows it, right? He knows what the pain in you is before you have spoken to him ... He does so many things in this meeting ... It is not just that you come here, you chant, make friends and go away, but that there is so much happening inside."

Over the previous three years, she had professionally studied mandalas and she was happy that now she had the chance to experience the meditation aspect of it. "Going around Borobudur and chanting ... has done wonders for me ... Everybody should come and have this feeling inside ... I thank Lama Gangchen for all he is doing; it is just great. There are no words ... I wish Lama Gangchen a very long life."[11]

A lotus on a lake?

Borobudur arouses feelings, not only with Buddhists but also with people who, over the years, have worked on the conservation of Borobudur or who have researched the temple. In books and texts about Borobudur, we repeatedly find descriptions that exude love and admiration for the sanctuary.

Borobudur and its situation in the surrounding landscape led the famous Dutch artist W.O.J. Nieuwenkamp (1874-1950) to the appealing idea that, once upon a time, the temple must have been in the center of a lake or inland sea. Nieuwenkamp had studied Hindu and Buddhist culture and architecture. He spent many years on Bali. Borobudur on Java appealed to him strongly and he often went to visit the temple.

Nieuwenkamp saw the stupa as a white plastered lotus throne rising up out of the water, forming the seat for the future Buddha. His idea that Borobudur had once been completely white derived from the fact that small pieces of white plaster were found on some of the stones. He depicted his ideas in paintings.

Years later, geological research regarding the presence of water has proven that Nieuwenkamp's ideas cannot have been true. There might possibly have been a prehistoric lake, but it would have been long before the construction period. Also the presumptions of others that Borobudur must have been situated on a riverbank appear to be mistaken.[2]

However, according to Lama Gangchen, there must have been a water source near the stupa in the past.

---

1 *LINKS V 'Borobudur 2013', World Congress - An Education for the Third Millennium*, Remarks by Professor Nirmala Sharma, p. 51, Lama Gangchen Peace Publications
2 UNESCO (2005), *The Restoration of Borobudur*, p. 247

All in all, this special construction seduces the imagination of many with fantastical ideas about what was and what will be.

The following interviews relate to the feeling of Borobudur in various ways. Daniel Calmanowitz, Lama Michel's father, describes what Borobudur does to us and what the effect of a retreat is. Mieke Marchand speaks of impressions that go beyond reason. Peter Webb tells how he experiences the energy of the stupa in relation to the elements – earth, fire, water, wind and space. And his partner, Bel Cesar, Lama Michel's mother, has dreams where the Buddha statues talk to her.

A power plant that radiates cosmic energy
Daniel Calmanowitz (1953) Brazil

Daniel Calmanowitz uses beautiful words to express the meaning of a visit to Borobudur. On one hand it is a huge positive experience with many blessings. On the other hand it is nothing special, he says. "We simply feel quiet, cool, happy and smooth, as if everything is okay as it is."

A happy time

"The first time I came to Borobudur was in 1992 and since then I have joined the retreat almost every year. For the first few years, the retreat was very strong for me because it was a mirror of my own defilements. Whatever my negative mind was projecting, it would immediately come back, like ping-pong. That is the difficult part of Borobudur, but in fact we go there for that. In that way I learned a lot about myself, because it was shown to me like a reflection in the mirror – and it also purified many things.

Ever since that first visit, I have wanted to come back every year. If you don't go, you have the feeling you are missing something, but in fact you are connected forever.

After that first visit to Borobudur, we were to remain in Asia because I would accompany Lama Michel to Sera Monastery in India. I was going to stay there with him for two years. Those were happy times: being his father, supporting him there. Being Lama Michel's father has always made sense, not in an intellectual way,

Lama Caroline, Lama Michel, Lama Gangchen and Daniel Calmanowitz

but it was natural. It was very comfortable; I never had any doubt about what I was doing. I was happy and I did what had to be done. There were difficulties, but I knew that we would overcome any interference; nothing was a real threat. In many aspects of my life and in my samsaric mind things weren't that clear, but regarding Lama Michel there was never a single moment of doubt. This was of course thanks to Rinpoche's blessings. But that feeling has nothing to do with Borobudur.

In 1999, around New Year, we spent one month in Borobudur. Can you imagine? – a whole month with Rinpoche! We held parties with people from all over the world; everyone was preparing their own songs in their own language, drawing on their own customs. My daughter Fernanda performed a traditional Indian dance. We did the samba. We did so many things because we had the time. Besides that, we went to the stupa daily, we did our practice and we received teachings and initiations. It was amazing."

More important than Tibet

"Rinpoche always says, 'If there is one place you should go to, it is to Borobudur, even if you are very old or in a wheelchair.' Visiting

Borobudur is even more important than going to Tibet because all of the paths, the very essence of Vajrayana practices, is there. In Borobudur we purify a lot, we gain lots of merit and we receive so much positive energy. We get completely revitalized. We get a glimpse of how it is in the pure lands. And at the same time, it is nothing special. We simply feel quiet, cool, happy, and smooth, like everything is okay as it is. These are strong blessings, difficult to put into words. Of course, we all have our own experiences and miracles, but it is not those particular personal 'highlights' that makes Borobudur special. The amazing feeling Borobudur gives is a constant, stable positive sensation that is there when we are present with Rinpoche.

Actually when we get home, each one of us struggles to keep this energy stable, though we lose it again very easily. Once again, we become trapped in daily life. We become anxious, nervous or sad and we start following our negative mind and patterns. But once we are back in Borobudur, it doesn't take any effort to return to the peaceful, quiet energy. That is because of Rinpoche's blessings and the connection that we have with Rinpoche. We simply tune in through our connection."

Embodiment of Self-Healing

"Borobudur is an energy power plant that spreads cosmic energy everywhere. Of all the holy places I know, Borobudur is the strongest. I guess that is because it is the embodiment of NgalSo Self-Healing, which in itself is the essence of all tantric practices as taught by Buddha Shakyamuni. So Borobudur is the essence of all tantric teachings. Another thing is that each time you visit Borobudur you are able to acquire more knowledge. Not just intellectual knowledge but deep knowledge, a deep understanding of how things are. As if you have the basis to understand things better.

We don't know how lucky we are because normally we have no access to the dimensions that can show us that. Borobudur was built over a period of a hundred years around the year 800. Not long after, it was covered by lava and ashes and it stayed hidden under a layer of earth for centuries. This was probably fortunate, because we don't know what would have happened to it when Muslims invaded Indonesia around the year 1200. Only now, in our time, has it been excavated and protected. At the same time, we are with Rinpoche, who happens to have chosen this time to unveil the sacred and invaluable secret meaning. We are not able to see what happens to us there. We feel something, but we are like small children. We haven't got a clue about the impact our visit to Borobudur has on our path to enlightenment.

To be happy is simple; that is the message we get from Borobudur. We don't have to look here or there, everything is present inside us. That is what Rinpoche calls, 'The good thoughts supermarket'. Each time you visit Borobudur or any other holy place, it becomes easier to tune in to this feeling. You accumulate the positive experiences.

It is all there, but you have to develop the eyes to see it. That comes with practice. The deep meaning and experience of tantra is confirmed at Borobudur. It is not just a heap of stones. With Rinpoche's presence as an enlightened being, it shows itself as a pure land. It is playing – showing how phenomena manifest.

In 2011 I was ordained as a monk in Borobudur, together with Liana[3] and Peter.[4] The wish to be ordained was always there, but that year Rinpoche suggested the time was ripe. I consider myself very lucky to have received my vows in Borobudur, because we know how sacred the place is. Rinpoche was so happy!"

Lama Michel with his father Daniel Calmanowitz

---

3 Read Liana Casagrande's story in Chapter 2.
4 Read Petrus Linnemann's story in Chapter 9.

Mieke Marchand on the round higher levels

Father and mother at the same time
Mieke Marchand (1944) The Netherlands

In 2009 Mieke Marchand traveled without her husband Peer to Borobudur. Their farewell was special. Only later did she realize how this goodbye had prepared her for his death.

A special farewell

"Halfway through the 1990s I went to Nepal and Tibet for seven weeks with my husband Peer. It was a beautiful journey and a good experience. After the trip, Peer said to me several times, 'Why don't you go to Borobudur?' 'Only if you join me,' was my invariable answer, because I wanted to make these kinds of big journeys together, and also financially I found it a bit difficult. But he didn't want to come along and so I accepted the situation. But somehow a desire to make the trip remained in the back of my mind.

However, in 2008 Peer came to me with the announcement, 'I will go to Borobudur!' 'Then I will join you,' was my obvious response. We planned to go in 2009, but eventually I went alone, because in the end Peer decided he preferred to make a trip to the Arctic.

He took me to the airport, we had a coffee, talked a bit and then said goodbye. Usually he walks off without looking back. But this time it was different, because while I was heading towards customs I saw him standing still, looking at me. At that moment I was overwhelmed with a feeling of loneliness and sadness – as if I had said goodbye to him forever. What I didn't know then was that he was already ill and would die that same year."

The white elephant

"During the first part of the flight I was pretty much occupied by the sensation of this goodbye, but slowly, slowly the feeling faded away and I started chatting with my fellow pilgrims. I told them about a special dream I had had. In the dream, there was a white elephant, and I also felt the presence of Lama Gangchen and Peer, though I am not sure if they were there. The day, after we arrived at Borobudur, we stopped to feed the elephants that we pass during our early walk around the temple on the tarmac road. For me the Borobudur retreat was already a success, so you can imagine how surprised I was when Rinpoche picked me, out of all hundred fifty pilgrims present, to give a coconut to an elephant.

In the summer of 2009 Peer fell ill, and in the autumn of that year it became clear that he was going to die. I took care of him at home. Now I can see that the farewell in the airport was a preparation for both of us.

On one of the last days I was afraid to leave him alone in the house, so I asked a friend to stay with him while I went to the supermarket. In the store I met a friend and I asked her how she was doing. But in that moment when she took a breath before answering, I realized I didn't have time to chat, so in a flash I tapped her on the shoulder and said, 'Tara is Light.' Then I rushed home.

On the way home something special happened. I had almost reached our street when I suddenly heard a short, loud hissing sound. Pfffhhht... I looked up and saw a huge green Tara in front of me – with all her details, colors and characteristics. This experience has helped me a great deal in all aspects of the farewell process with Peer.

A couple of months after his passing, I joined the trip to Borobudur again. We were on the foot of the stupa, reciting preliminary prayers.

The group was pretty big so I couldn't see Lama Gangchen. And once again I hear that same sound. Pfffhhht... Before me, in the sky, I saw huge-sized Lama Gangchen. His image wasn't static – his hands moved. Someone else might think that I am crazy but I had seen Tara before and I knew it was alright. During the whole circumambulation that morning, I was floating. I felt intensely happy.

Afterwards people said to me, 'You were so focussed!' I was indeed; maybe Rinpoche helped me with that. I did manage this time to do the inner meditations with deep concentration, which had been a wish that I had expressed earlier. I had seen it with others and that was what I wanted to achieve myself."

As soon as you start thinking, it disappears

"At Borobudur I had very intense experiences a couple of times. These things are not easily explained in a rational way. Things that occur in a flow of energy. As soon as you start thinking, it disappears.

In this way, one morning after meditation, I saw someone from the *sangha*[5] at my guesthouse coming outside as a gorgeous, stunning young man. I saw this person was so radiant and lively! At the same time it struck my weak spot: attachment. When I gave him a good look again later, I didn't see what I saw before. How odd! Apparently I had seen the most inner beauty that he contained, the fullest potential that he can develop.

Another occasion was in the conference hall, where the monks were preparing a *Rabne Chenmo* – a purification ritual. Rinpoche sat with the monks, while the group did meditations on the stupa with Lama Michel. I felt ill that day and decided to stay in the gompa as well. Suddenly – no thoughts: in a flow of softness, I stood up, walked to Lama Gangchen and sat next to him behind the conference table between all those realized people. Lama Gangchen laid his hand on my chest, on my belly and then on my knee, very natural... Then my nose started running. I didn't want the moment to cease so I muffled a tissue in my nose and stayed there beside him, still without thoughts.

The first thought that came up was when should I go? – I could simply allow myself to be there."

---

5   The spiritual company, ranging from the highest realized beings to the ones who are at the beginning of the bodhisattva path.

May I never forget the dharma

"A recurrent fear is that I might forget the dharma. Last time at Borobudur this deep fear came up strongly. 'May I never forget the dharma, may there always be someone to remind me,' I prayed in silence. A little later I saw Duccio[6] the thanka painter sit at a table. I asked him if I could give him a hand. He said nothing, but did the mudras of the Self-Healing in a very brief and subtle way. There was my answer; there was someone to remind me ...

At another moment Rinpoche embraced me very intensely during the circumambulations around the galleries, exactly on the spot where the hugging mudra is depicted on a bas-relief. At this panel he always asks the couples that have gotten married in Borobudur to hug each other. While Rinpoche embraced me I thought, 'I am always yours in dharma.' It brought me an experience of deep happiness and bliss. Rinpoche is always there for me. He is my father and mother at the same time, from the beginning."

Borobudur softens our rational mind
Peter Webb (1954) Australia

Permaculturist Peter Webb visited Borobudur for the first time in 2014. He gives his own distinctive interpretation of how the elements of earth, fire, water and wind interact there at the stupa-mandala.

Cleansing and peeling

"I met Lama Gangchen and Lama Michel through my partner Bel,[7] which was wonderful for me. They gave a new meaning to my life. In 2014, I went to Borobudur for the first time and it was amazing. I am a very down-to-earth type. For me, it was important to feel Borobudur, the way it was made; that language touched me every time I was at the stupa. Borobudur is such a special place because it is a place where there are active volcanoes. Just before the retreat, there was an eruption at the nearby Mount Kelud volcano. The ashes that showered down are now fertilizing the whole country. But the

---

6 Read Leonardo (Duccio) Ceglie's story in Chapter 4.
7 Read Bel Cesar's story further on in this chapter.

ash was not only fertilizing; it was also cleansing, and peeling the environment. Borobudur still exists only because it was covered with ashes for a long period of time."

Peter Webb

Here is how the earth was born

"We can see Borobudur is like a volcano, just as primitive tribes would symbolize natural forms. It is a difficult energy because it is situated on a small island in the middle of an ocean, where the earth is filled with fire that is cooking the water on the stove. In Albagnano, the fire comes from the sky in the form of lightning, but here in Borobudur it comes from the mountains and the earth! What a strong energy! And there we are, all praying together, some also physically getting a fever. That's why we come with the lama. He is our friend, he takes care of us, and he perceives the subtle energy.

Here is how the earth was born, here is new energy coming out all the time. Borobudur itself is even made out of lava stone. One day it will become soil again; it will be recycled and then everything will end up in the sea. The whole planet has gone through these cycles many times. Everything manifests and dies, manifests and dies. This is what you see on the images in the bas-reliefs. This is the *impermanence*[8] of Borobudur.

We think that the elements water and fire are opposite but in tantra they go together. Before humans arrived, nature was looking for balance, not competition. The elements are communicating amongst themselves to create a happy environment.

Around Borobudur, it is warm and gentle. There is lightness in the stones. The people are so soft there. Borobudur has the ability to work on our imagination. It softens the rational mind and the concepts that we have. It helps us to have dreams, images, and to see things in a different way, which is wonderful."

An image of waves

"Thinking about the relationship between the practice and the processes of the elements: in my opinion, transformation always comes from the marriage between two or more elements. One element can always choose between two consorts. And the moment that they meet is important. Plants connect to light. In my understanding, plants are actually at the symbol stage – before we become a Buddha. And so we are surrounded by symbols all the time. The lama has prepared us so that we can see that.

Every day on Borobudur, I had an image of waves. At first I thought it was water, but when I started to draw them, I realized they were more like the waves that I had seen in the clouds. I connected the waves to the space element of Vairochana that manifested in this way to me on the stupa. Then I saw the similarity with the waves in the structure of plants. Fire, water, earth, wind – it feels stable on the stones, but there is movement ... I am sitting on fixed stone, but I experience waves - Borobudur is a happy environment."

---

8 The constant transformation of phenomena.

Lama Michel and his mother Bel Cesar

Borobudur brought me love
Bel Cesar (1957) Brazil

The first time Bel Cesar visited Borobudur she saw nectar coming from the stupa. She managed to put some drops in a bottle that she has kept. Later she had dreams where the statues spoke to her.

Deities and nectar

"Thinking about precious experiences, the first image that occurs to me is a memory of my first Borobudur retreat, in 1991. There were only twelve of us, sitting on the stupa. The air was fresh though hot; we did some prayers, then meditated in silence. Rinpoche gave us coconuts. We recited OM AH HUM three times, and then Rinpoche said we could drink the coconut milk. So we drank in silence, looking around at the stupa. It felt special. 'Don't look at the stupa,' Rinpoche said. 'Look at the *deities*.[9] They are working for you as if they are working in an emergency room in the hospital.'

---

9   A deity is a being considered holy, divine or sacred. Deities occur in various religions. In Buddhism, deities usually represent manifestations of Buddhas

For me, this was so incredible. We learned in this way that there are things beyond what we see. All these dakinis flying in the stone images, gentle and smiling; they are working for us. I realized we come to Borobudur to be healed, to recover, to be attended to in the presence of our guru.

A couple of years later we were on top of the stupa when some liquid dripped out of the stone. 'This is real nectar,' Rinpoche said. I happened to have a bottle of cognac with me, where I normally keep the flower essences that I sometimes give to my patients. So this bottle was there, just waiting for that precious water! Rinpoche collected some drops for me in the most gentle, caring way. The way in which he gave value to this was beautiful. Rinpoche knows that I still have the bottle and sometimes he asks me for a drop.

The importance of this example is that, once again, it shows that there is subtle energy, and that we can be in touch with it. Subtle energy has much more power than the gross and it is never exhausted, as it is always there. However, we tend to forget. Being at Borobudur with Rinpoche gives you the opportunity to connect to this subtle energy container, because it allows you to see beyond the gross level."

Panel with deity

Bodhichitta mind

"Back in 1991, I had a dream. Somebody wanted to kill Rinpoche. I jumped in front of him and said, 'If you want to kill him, you will have to kill me first!' Then there was an earthquake and everything fell apart. When I told Rinpoche about the dream, he said, 'This is your bodhichitta mind. When you activate your bodhichitta mind, the whole universe comes to help you.' It still moves me to tears when I remember this.

At that first retreat, I was very sad and lonely because I was just divorced. Rinpoche told me that I could make a request to the stupa, so I did. I asked to learn about the dharma through relationships: to learn about concentration, patience, satisfaction, generosity, enthusiasm, and compassion with somebody. Shortly after that I got married again, and that marriage lasted for nine years."

Looking for Rachel

"Twelve years ago, Peter[10] came in my life in a miraculous way. I had bought some land to establish a spiritual center. By then, Rinpoche had this idea to bring Buddha statues made out of lava stone from Indonesia to important sites all over the world, to empower the places in the same way that acupuncture enlivens the nervous system. So we brought seventeen tons of stone statues to the land I bought. It might look easy but it is a big garden and once you have put them somewhere you are never able to move them again. So I had to really make a plan about where to put the statues and I asked somebody to give me advice. That man said I needed somebody who knew about permaculture. I did not have a clue what that was but I was convinced it was important. I learned that it had to do with balance and friendship between different plants, but I could not find anyone and the statues were about to arrive! One week before the statues came, I had a dream. In my dream the statues spoke to me, 'When we arrive, things will be open.'

So they arrived in Sao Paolo and some days later – before they were delivered to my premises – they spoke to me again. One statue said, 'When you are looking for permaculture, you have to look for Rachel.' When I woke up I was thinking, 'Who is Rachel? My aunt is

---

10 Read Peter Webb's story earlier on in this chapter.

called Rachel!' And indeed, I found that a permaculture specialist, Peter Webb, was working on my aunt Rachel's land. Consequently, he helped me with organizing the land, planning and preparing the site for the arrival of the statues. So it happened that we fell in love and we are still together. I had asked the Buddha statues to teach me about dharma through love and it was the statues that answered me and brought me love."

Chapter 7

A Place of Healing

Comprehend the cause

"After two years of headaches I started to worry if maybe there was something serious going on. Therefore I asked Lama Gangchen for help. He felt my pulse, looked in my eyes and comforted me. Nothing serious, but he also told me to go back to the time I was 49. Recollecting what had happened that year, I immediately knew what it was. I had a serious accident and it took two years to recover. I even had to use a wheelchair for some time. 'This must be it,' I thought. But the headache didn't go away. I didn't pay attention to it anymore because Lama Gangchen had said it was nothing serious.

Around six months later I suddenly had a hunch. During that period of rehabilitation my ex-husband had offered me treatment for my leg muscles, which was very effective. Due to that contact I went back to live with him and – actually under pressure and against my will – stayed with him for ten more years.

As soon as I had this insight, I was sure this was the event Lama Gangchen had indicated. And at the same time I realized this was a rather unhealthy pattern in my life, the fact that sometimes I was doing things that I did not really want to and that were not good for me. Now that I saw this, the headaches vanished for good and never came back." Jampa Drolma (1942) The Netherlands

Invited by the King of Sikkim

From an early age Lama Gangchen has been involved in healing activities. In the 1970s, he visited a Tibetan family in Sikkim, a small kingdom in the Himalayas. During his stay there, he started helping people. The King of Sikkim heard about the special healing lama and invited Lama Gangchen to help his mother, who was almost blind.

Lama Gangchen gave the King's mother the *Chenrezig Open Eye*[1] initiation and a special medicine. The queen was cured – she could see again. Out of gratitude they offered Lama Gangchen a house in the capital of Sikkim and the King opened the borders for Tibetans by making the visa requirements more flexible.

Later Lama Gangchen cured many more people with eye problems in Sikkim, and they started calling him 'Open Eye Lama'.[2] This is only one of the many special stories about Lama Gangchen. He has possessed extraordinary qualities since he was young. When he was nineteen, he was imprisoned because of his healing activities.

Some years later he fled to India, like many Tibetans. He stayed with the great Tibetan teacher Zong Rinpoche for seven years. Once Zong Rinpoche said about Lama Gangchen, "Gangchen Tulku is different from my other students. All his actions are beneficial to others. Even his breath can heal diseases, and even if he does the ritual wrong or says the wrong mantra, it still really works and heals others."[3]

What is healing?

With the energy of Lama Gangchen present, Borobudur becomes a place of healing. The Self-Healing practice is energetically connected to Borobudur. But what do we mean when speaking of healing? Tibetan medicine is completely interwoven with Buddhism. In Tibetan Buddhism, body and mind go together and are considered as a whole.

However there is a difference between physical and mental suffering. According to Lama Michel, people in the West mainly suffer mentally, from fear, depression, anger, jealousy, dissatisfaction... Even if people have an illness they usually suffer most from the fear of the pain or other consequences of that disease. Meanwhile in other poorer countries, people mostly suffer physically due to diseases, poor healthcare or lack of food, water and shelter.[4]

---

1 Chenrezig is the Buddha of Compassion.
2 Gammon C. & Back C. (2013), *Gangchen - A Spiritual Heritage*, p. 60, Lama Gangchen World Peace Foundation, CH
3 Gammon, C. & Back, C. (2013), *Gangchen, a Spiritual Heritage*, p. 43, Lama Gangchen World Peace Foundation, CH
4 Lama Michel Rinpoche (2015), *Compassion in (Mental) Health Care,* lecture transcript, p.7, Lama Gangchen Peace Publications

Buddhism is based upon the assumption that things occur when some causes and conditions come together. Lama Gangchen says that any physical disease also has an underlying mental cause. Under certain circumstances, the disease – from which the mental cause may already have been present for a long time, manifests. Sometimes the disease is at such an advanced stage that a cure is no longer possible. But the underlying mental cause can still be healed by recognizing and purifying it, as recounted by Jampa Drolma in the example about her headaches earlier in this chapter.

From the moment Lama Gangchen came to the West, an increasing number of sick people came to see him for healing. In his early years in the West, he gave them Tibetan herbal pills and the mantra of Buddha Shakyamuni: *Om Muni Muni Maha Muni Shakyamuniye Soha*.

In the early 1990s, after having worked as a Lama Healer in the West for ten years, he said that he was convinced that all the illnesses of his patients were triggered by a stressful emotional event, "This event, like a divorce, a break in the family, a fight or a dramatic change in living conditions, created strong negative emotions and energies in their body and mind. These damaging and disturbing energies are the true cause of their disease."

Then, he compared this energy to the information held on the hard disc of a computer,

"This energy can stay dormant in the subtle body and mind of a person for a long time: on his inner hard disc. At the moment a specific combination of conditions occurs the 'illness program' becomes activated."

Hence, it is not sufficient just to take medicines against illness according to Lama Gangchen, "Taking medicines is good, but not enough to completely regain the strength of our body and mind. To achieve that, we also have to delete the 'illness program' from our hard disc by practicing the Self-Healing methods of sutra and tantra."[5]

So diseases arise from a combination of various negative conditions, like poor diet, pollution, toxins *etc.*, together with the

---

[5] Lama Caroline, November 1st 2015, workshop: *Seven Point Mind Training (Lojong)*, Diessen, The Netherlands. Lama Caroline cites from a non-published text by Lama Gangchen.

deeper underlying energetic pollution and disturbances. Lama Gangchen often gives the example of smokers: not all people who smoke get lung cancer. "If smoking cigarettes was the only cause of lung cancer, then everybody who smokes would die of that disease. We know this is not true."[6]

Energy in motion

The Self-Healing practice helps work on transforming and purifying the physical and mental disturbances in one's body and mind. During the course of life there are many events, experiences and actions, positive and negative, which lead to certain emotions. Emotion – which literally means 'energy in motion'[7] – can be sensed in the body, but it also lodges in the subtle body in the form of imprints. As we saw in the previous section, Lama Gangchen often compares it to the information stored on the hard disc on a computer. By transforming the imprints of anger, jealousy, envy, sadness and so on, one heals oneself on a subtle level.

Many of the damaging imprints that are stored in our subtle body and mind are not easy to recognize by ourselves. Lama Gangchen helps us – for example through the Self-Healing method – to identify the blockages, to become aware of them and to heal ourselves. Lama Caroline explains that this is usually a subtle process. We might have special dreams that help us feel something has changed energetically. Sometimes we become aware of a certain problem in our life, or we have an emotional release that helps us let go of negative imprints.[8]

Positive use of the senses

Borobudur is sometimes called the World Peace Stupa. Lama Gangchen states that developing inner peace is the best foundation for world peace. By using all our senses and our body, speech and mind in a friendly and peaceful way, the world around us will also

---

6 Lama Caroline, November 1st 2015, workshop: *Seven Point Mind Training (Lojong)*, Diessen, The Netherlands. Lama Caroline cites from a non-published text by Lama Gangchen.
7 Lama Gangchen, T.Y.S. (1994), *NgalSo Tantric Self-Healing III*, p. 178, Lama Gangchen Peace Publications
8 Lama Caroline, November 1st 2015, workshop: *Seven Point Mind Training (Lojong)*, Diessen, The Netherlands.

become more beautiful. We create greater and greater peace inside us and around us by looking, speaking, listening, working, playing, studying, sporting, driving, *etc.*, with softness and friendliness.

By training ourselves to use our senses and functions in a positive way, we gradually develop an 'antidote', which transforms our negative emotions. Lama Gangchen says, "Emotions arise as an immediate reaction to what we see, hear and feel. The minds of ordinary people are very small and sensitive and the normal reaction to their sense consciousness is to allow negative emotions like anger, jealousy, pride and attachment to arise. There are many different methods to deal with this negative moving energy ... It is better to use positive mental antidotes to transform the poison into medicine."[9]

Where there is love, compassion and inner peace, anger cannot exist. In the book *Choose Peace*, Lama Gangchen gives an answer to the question, "Why should I give up my anger?" He says, "Anger is very destructive. If we keep anger in our mind, we have no peace; instead we experience many painful mental and physical sensations."

There are several ways to bring more softness and friendliness into our life on different levels, for example in the way we speak and the words we choose. Lama Gangchen advises us to call the daily obstacles in our life *small difficulties* rather than *problems*, "This will give us a greater capacity to deal with and peacefully accept our real sufferings and genuine problems like living with chronic disease or facing death."[10]

The following stories illustrate the effects of Lama Gangchen's healing principles in practice. Professor Paola Muti tells how, after a long search, she found a missing link for medical science in Buddhist philosophy. The stories of Janne Zevenberg, Moreno Sartori and José Mutsaerts show how the impossible can become possible. May Heerkens and Rob Assmann share their special healing experiences at Borobudur. Carlotta Segre was able to rid herself of depression

---

[9] Lama Gangchen, T.Y.S. (1994), *NgalSo Tantric Self-Healing III*, p. 178, Lama Gangchen Peace Publications

[10] Lama Gangchen, T.Y.S (2013), *Choose Peace, A Gift of Wisdom for a Less Expensive Life*, p. 98-99, Lama Gangchen Peace Publications

due to her deep faith in Lama Gangchen. Claudia Rapisarda received help from Lama Gangchen after she saw him at Borobudur in a vision. Finally Renata Zincone speaks about her dog's surgery and recovery during her stay at Borobudur.

Buddhist philosophy provides a missing link in science
Paola Muti (1956) Italy

Professor Paola Muti is a medical scientist and a leading figure worldwide in the field of cancer epidemiology and cancer prevention. She felt that there is a missing link in the approach to this disease; there must be more to it than only environmental factors. She resides in Canada but found answers to her questions in her motherland of Italy.

I couldn't stand it anymore

"For me, Borobudur came as the final step on a long path and at the same time it was the first step on a subsequent path.

I had been working for a large part of my life on scientific knowledge related to cancer causes. I was looking at population risks, the relationship with environmental factors, with lifestyle factors such as diet, physical activity, metabolic factors, glucose ... and I realized that the connection between environmental factors and the body did not explain everything. When you look for example at the relationship between smokers and lung cancer, not all smokers get cancer; although out of hundred patients, ninety have been smoking. I felt that there was something else that we should be taking into consideration.

On a personal level, I have always been searching on the spiritual path. Science requires a constantly attentive and devoted mind. However, I found that this was not enough for me. I really needed something that would allow me to help people with more than just providing them with assistance, care, advice and indications. In cancer care, the constant relationship with death is something that makes you wonder about life and the life of others. You talk with a person and you know that in a few months he will not be here anymore... How could I use this awareness in a positive way for the person and for myself too? I couldn't stand it anymore.

First, I looked at the so-called monotheistic religions, but the fact I had to trust something without question didn't suit my mind. After all, I was always looking for cause and effect. Then I started to consider myself to be an atheist. But deep inside me, there was still something questioning. Even since I was a child, I have always been upset about the events of life, needing answers.

So I needed to continue my search and I looked at all kinds of philosophy traditions, like the Greek philosophers, to see if there was any solution for these questions."

I feel part of the universe

"Finally I found this Italian-speaking Buddhist teacher, Lama Michel, on the Internet! He even had a Genova accent, because native Portuguese speakers who speak Italian sound exactly like the people from my home region. So I started to listen to his teachings and, not much later, I was so much enthralled that I couldn't wait to get home after work to start listening again. While I was listening, I was structuring the different ideas and explanations. It was like putting my puzzle together. Buddhist philosophy provided the missing link with science.

So two years ago, in 2014, I went to Albagnano for the first time. And in 2016, I joined the trip to Borobudur. Now that I have been there, I realized that it was the end of my scientific search for spirituality. Being on the stupa on the first day, first of all I was fascinated by the structure of the building, the statues, the surroundings... Up to that time I had only been to China. I was so charmed by the environment.

The second day, when I sat and did my meditation it was like being in a whirlpool. And the third time I really felt something was different – like a presence, a vibration. The colors were different – purple. It was like I was in an energetic environment. And the energies did not leave me while I was walking around the stupa. When we arrived at the top I felt completely exhausted, but not in a physical way. No more thoughts... it was very magical.

For the first time in my life I let go of everything. I could sleep well after five years of restless nights. Finally, all my anxiety was gone. So Borobudur was a medicine for me, I felt much better when I was there. It was a tough and strong experience, but the more time that passed there, the more I felt connected.

Before traveling to Borobudur, I was already so happy to have found Lama Michel on the Internet. He was my main driving force. It was a kind of rational happiness, due to being able to put the missing pieces in the puzzle. But now I feel connected on a much deeper level, to both of them, Lama Michel and also Lama Gangchen. The composition of the puzzle of my life is happening right now, since Borobudur. When I do my daily meditation, I am moved to tears by the depth of all this. I feel part of the universe, no longer isolated. It is not with arrogance that I say this: I know that anything may happen to me and I might suffer, but I am happy now."

At Borobudur I could accept myself as I was
May Heerkens (1947) The Netherlands

The retreat at Borobudur helped May Heerkens in her recovery after a severe accident. While on the stupa, she had an impressive healing experience.

My securities were no longer there

"In 1998 I got seriously injured in an accident. I was riding my bicycle, carefree, when suddenly somebody opened a car door right in front of me. The smack caused me severe brain damage. From the hospital, I remember that I was floating out of my body quite often. I saw myself from above, lying in that bed. For a while, I was on the verge of death.

As I recovered little by little, I realized that things were not okay with me at all. I wasn't able to communicate as before; when somebody asked me what I had been doing, I started at the beginning of the day and step by step I went through all the activities of that day, while looking for words – somehow I didn't manage. Also my behavior changed then. I could suddenly react quite sharply when somebody said something to me and I was scared without knowing why. One can feel unsafe in a house, but I felt unsafe in my head and my body. My securities had vanished; they were no longer there."

Singing mantras

"Because I had changed so much, my husband didn't want to move on with me any longer. We divorced in 2007, after having been together for 35 years. Indeed, I was angry with him quite often in the years after the accident. Strangely enough, after we separated the anger was gone, as if he took it with him. Later, my daughter told me that from that moment she felt that she had her old loving mum back.

By coincidence, two years after the divorce, I met Mieke Marchand[11] at a presentation of various religions in a synagogue, where she sang mantras. And wow! The way she performed and what she transmitted there struck me deep inside. People sang with her and so did I. I had known her for quite some time, but I had never had any interest in her Buddhist path.

From that moment on things happened pretty fast. I joined her a couple of times going to the center in Italy, I started to practice the Self-Healing and in February 2011 I traveled with Mieke to Borobudur! She offered me the trip. I could hardly believe it!

To my own astonishment it felt like coming home; until then I had always believed I was more of an Africa and South America person. Getting up early and walking in peace to the stupa was also very pleasant to me. I managed simply to go with the flow there, without worrying about mantras and meditations. I really felt that there was no urgency to know everything by heart. Beforehand, I had been too eager to learn and understand everything, but now I was in peace and I could let myself go."

All heaviness vanished

"On the ninth day of climbing the stupa, something special happened to me. The upper levels were still closed due to cleaning activities after the volcano eruption at the end of 2010, so we didn't perform our usual closing ritual on the top, but we finished on the highest of the square levels. We all held each other's hands and stood in a big circle facing the inner wall of the gallery. All together, we laid our heads against the stupa. At that moment, something happened within me in my head. Somewhere deep in the back something burst. I have the image of a kind of pea from which something was

---

11 Read Mieke Marchand's story in Chapter 6.

launched to somewhere high above me, and then there was just air, light... All heaviness had vanished from my head. For an instant, I didn't know who I was or what had happened. It was a very intense and pleasurable experience.

When I looked up again, I asked the woman next to me if she would hold me. She did, without words, even though I didn't know who she was. There was nothing to explain and also this was a beautiful and positive experience.

This experience helped me to move on a lot. All of a sudden I knew: I can go my own way. It was as if something had literally been set free. I can allow myself to be who I am – this was a liberating insight to me.

I rely upon myself much more now. I realize that I am the only person who can change me. Nowadays, I am also more able to take responsibility for my defilements. I don't look around me pointing the blame at others so much any longer. It may happen that I am suddenly sharp, but much less than before, and if it happens, I notice it immediately. I learnt that through the Self-Healing. Looking back, I can also see that I didn't accept the fact that my ex-husband couldn't accept me.

In fact, the accident has woken me up in a strange way. People say I became more open. In the beginning, I had been searching for resolutions and for years I was busy dealing with myself. But it was not until Borobudur that I could accept myself as I was.

When I told my experience on the stupa to Lama Gangchen, he held his thumbs up, 'Wonderful!' he said a couple of times. That gave me the feeling that it's okay. Nowadays, I just have to remember that experience, that light feeling in my head and the energy balls floating upwards, and I am back in that moment. Exactly on that spot; I can even point it out. So beautiful! From the bottom of my heart I can say, 'Thank you Lama Gangchen'."

More physical and mental stability
Moreno Sartori (1975) Italy

As a dog trainer, Moreno Sartori helps people and their animals. After his first visit to Borobudur he noticed big changes in his life and work.

He did not mention climbing Borobudur

"Three months after I took refuge with Lama Michel in Milan, I met Lama Gangchen. It was 2011, and from that moment I started to practice Self-Healing with many positive results. When I found out that Self-Healing had been conceived in Borobudur, I felt a strong attraction to the place. I wished to go there and asked Rinpoche if that would be feasible for me. Since I was born, I have had spasms and moving and walking is difficult for me. It is a problem to carry my own luggage, for example. Rinpoche answered, 'Only if somebody accompanies you.' He said nothing about climbing Borobudur. A fellow traveler was soon found and that is how I came to Borobudur in 2014. My first experience was strong. I had received four Reiki initiations previously, so I knew something about energy, but this surpassed everything. When I was confronted with Borobudur, an extremely powerful energy came towards me from the stupa. At night, I sensed an energy flowing up and down my spine all the time. So the only problem I faced was actually how to get enough sleep..."

Anchored in the earth

"There were some instant positive effects while I was at Borobudur, but most of the positive results came later, when I was back at home. The first things I experienced were internal. For example, my practice became more stable and the meditations during my practice got much better. The second positive effect was that I gained physical stability. I didn't lose my balance as easily as before at work, and I felt anchored to the earth while being busy.

Physically my job as a dog behaviorist is not so tough, but mentally it requires a lot. Talking to people while I closely observe their dogs takes a lot of effort and you can lose your attention in an instant. Thanks to Self-Healing and daily practice, I am more capable of regulating my energy to work in a better and more efficient way."

Helping people

"There were several large and small positive effects, some of them appearing only months later.

It was important for me that I had asked Borobudur for an increase in my capacity to help others. In my job I have to deal a lot with people also. It is all about harmonizing the relationships between dogs and humans. After I had expressed my wish, more people came to me for help, especially with spiritual problems. That was so beautiful because I had the tools to apply a new way of working that had nothing to do with the conventional methods that I had learnt years ago. Nowadays, I mix these with the things I learn from Rinpoche and Lama Michel. I also apply Reiki and meditation at work.

Being aware that I can always return to Borobudur is a very comforting thought, the fact that it is possible for me! According to Rinpoche, the only obstacle was the journey. However, the stupa itself was another story. I did indeed manage to climb and descend; my spastic movements had actually diminished somehow while being at Borobudur. But I certainly needed the help of others to support me while climbing the steep stairs. That first time there were not as much people spontaneously helping as the second time in 2015. In 2014, I had to approach people and ask them for help. In 2015 that was not necessary; they were simply there when I needed them."

Rejoice in the happiness of others

"Borobudur means a lot to me. Besides the fact that it is a magical place, it is also true that whatever happens in Borobudur happens in no other place that I know of. When Rinpoche arrived, I was already there and it intrigued me that, somehow, tranquility arrived with him. However, the greatest blessing is that I have learnt to rejoice in the happiness and realizations of others; that was something that I was never very good at before."

A turbo experience that gave me a boost
Rob Assmann (1964) The Netherlands

While at Borobudur, Rob Assmann got almost desperate from the pain caused by an injured shoulder in combination with severe sunburn and internally he asked for Lama Gangchen's help. Then extraordinary things started to happen to him.

Relaxed in collision

"One afternoon in October 2012, I was driving on the highway. It was very busy. Before me, I saw brake lights. I let go of the accelerator, hit the brake... There were thirty meters of space ahead of me, but I hit the car, not too hard, on its back. No problem. In a split second, in the rear mirror, I saw two headlights approaching me from behind at high speed. I turned on the hazard lights, placed my right hand in the left on my lap and sat relaxed in meditation posture. Then the car behind me crashed with great force into the back of my car. A little shaky I got out, nothing broken. Only my shoulder was injured.

Later, I heard about someone who had braced himself in a similar accident. This person had suffered several fractures and had a long period of recuperation. It was thanks to my long term experience in the practice of Self-Healing that I was able to sit calm and still in this frightening moment."

Dreadful pains

"Some months later, February 2013, I traveled to Borobudur, fourteen years after my first visit. After a couple of days, we went swimming with some Dutch friends at a hotel: a beautiful old colonial-style building. A glass of juice there was four times the price of juice in Holland. It was a luxurious treat to go there, which I allowed myself to enjoy. Actually, that was my theme that journey; to appreciate myself and allow myself to enjoy things. I had recently sold my self-refurbished sports car, that was how I could afford the trip.

I never used to swim and hadn't even planned to go sunbathing. My skin is extremely pale and we got the idea to apply some sunblock only after thirty minutes. Hence I got completely sunburned. Over the following days I was suffering from such dreadful pain, it made me vomit. My left shoulder was still hurting from the accident, and I couldn't lie on my side nor could I lie face down. The only thing possible was to lie very still on my back. Every slightest use of a muscle hurt, the itching drove me mad, I couldn't carry my backpack. In moments of clarity, I laughed about the situation. I realized it would pass. Also, I thought it would be daft to bother Lama Gangchen with my mishap. However, one night, I did explicitly ask for help inside myself."

Light being

"Early the next morning, when I wanted to walk to the stupa, there was a motorbike parked next to the house that I rented. I had not seen that before, as the house was quite remote. I was glad and asked the driver how much the ride would cost, to avoid problems afterwards. 'I help Lama Gangchen, there is no need for you to pay me,' the driver said to my astonishment, and he took me to the stupa.

That night in the congress room, I chose to sit in a quiet place, with my painful shoulders against the wall, so no one could suddenly touch me or lean against me. But what happened? The woman, who sat next to me, cheerfully hit me on the shoulders, while saying something. I shouted out loud from pain. Immediately I had the clarity of mind to comfort her, because I had scared her with my reaction. Then, I decided to lay down on a mattress in the back of the room.

I was exhausted and fell asleep. After some fifteen minutes I opened my eyes. A woman dressed in white sat at my feet. She blew over my body and all pain disappeared; I felt an intense calmness wash over me, and I felt happiness and clarity. When she had gone a moment later, I wanted to go back to sleep. But I realized I was fit and awake. I stood up and wanted to thank her. I asked someone sitting near me where this woman dressed in white had gone. She must have passed by there. But she hadn't ... the woman didn't exist.

For me, this experience is a strong confirmation of the power of Lama Gangchen and of Self-Healing. I have performed this practice since 1998 and I know it works, but deep down I do not always have strong faith. This was a kind of turbo experience that gave me a huge boost."

A question for the guru

"Once in the beginning of the retreat, I was looking for Lama Gangchen to ask him a specific question about the relationship with the guru. He approached me on the path and I asked him, 'Do you have time for me or are you busy?' His answer was, 'I am busy.' Obviously that was a lesson for me to better consider the way I formulate my questions.

At the end of the retreat, I wanted to say goodbye to Lama Gangchen and I walked with a khata to his room. Again, we met on the path and he came towards me. I offered the khata. It was a short encounter, almost while passing, but he was really there for me. I realized that he noticed me one hundred percent. I said, 'Thank you for all you have done for me.' For me, it was evident that he had sent the motorbike and the female light-being, or that it was he, himself. Also, I had received answers to all my questions, in conversations and interactions with other pilgrims. He laid the khata over my head and said, 'I will see you in Italy.' Back home in The Netherlands, my shoulder appeared to be cured. The physiotherapist thought it was thanks to the tropical heat, but I knew better."

Working with blessed oil and healing nectar
Janne Zevenberg (1959) The Netherlands

At Borobudur Janne Zevenberg wished for more work in her Shiatsu practice. When back at home, she started working in a different way and soon more and more clients came to see her for help.

Yellow horses

"In 2014 I went to Borobudur for the first time and, even at the beginning of the retreat, I had an intense experience. We were on the stupa and during the meditations, yellow horses were running from my arms! I really saw them going. For me, it was something incredible and very huge. Later, I found out that in NgalSo Self-Healing this image symbolizes that the negativities that are connected to the navel chakra are leaving the body.

In those days we were living in financially difficult times. I was helped by friends to be able to go to Borobudur, which was already something very special. My husband could hardly believe that there were people simply depositing money into your account for this reason."

More work

"After this intense experience, being at Borobudur and in connection with Lama Gangchen I wished to get more work. I run a practice as a Shiatsu therapist and at Borobudur I had an inspiration that I should start working in a different manner. I had no idea what this meant.

But when I was back at home, an increasing number of clients with physical and mental problems came round. Since then, I have asked people to choose the oil they want me to use, which I then briefly put at a special place near a picture of Lama Gangchen and Lama Michel. Following that, I help my clients to relax with the blessed oil, while internally I do mantras and prayers from the Self-Healing. When their body has calmed, I start with the acupressure points. While applying pressure, I visualize that healing nectar flows in and that all pains, negativities and problems come out.

The people whom I treat don't know all this process, but it has worked really well. They feel lighter and happier – as if they have let go of something. And my wish has been fulfilled. Since I started applying this method more and more people have come to my practice. From now on I plan on going to Borobudur every year to get revitalized. That first journey has changed my life. I feel truly supported and helped."

Panel from Lalitavistara: The Bodhisattva receives monk's robes

Rinpoche saved my life
Carlotta Segre (1971) Italy

Carlotta Segre suffered from depression and panic attacks and couldn't imagine she would make it to Borobudur one day.

Not feeling happy

"I belong to a very Catholic family; my mother and I both were practitioners. I loved to go to church, but at the same time I was missing something there. I didn't like to pray to a cross, even though I realized it was a kind of symbol. I preferred to pray to Holy Mary. I knew there must be something else...

Internally I was not feeling happy, it was a difficult time for me. In my family and social context, the next logical step was to go see a psychologist and so I did. From the moment I started the sessions with the psychologist, I began to feel really depressed and I developed panic attacks. My doctor gave me antidepressants and anti-panic medication."

Lorenzo

"One day I was at the hairdresser reading a newspaper. There was an article on a Buddhist monastery in Scotland. It touched me because I had felt an urge to meet Buddhist monks for some time. Just outside the hair salon, I met an old high school classmate, Lorenzo. 'How are you! Let's have a drink!' I suggested. So we chatted about our lives, and I don't know why but I told him about the article I had just read.

'Oh,' he said, 'I went to Tibet last summer, following a tulku,' and he told me about Lama Gangchen Rinpoche. Lorenzo promised to let me know when Lama Gangchen would be teaching in Milan again. In this way I was introduced to Rinpoche in 1995."

Something changed inside

"While I was already with Rinpoche, I was still seeing this psychologist and taking medication. This was not going well; I was depressed, sad and had a heavy mind even with the medicines. I was not myself anymore.

Someone asked me if I was going to join the trip to Borobudur. I knew Rinpoche was traveling all over the world to spread his peace message. But I was not even able to take a train without getting panic attacks. It was not the fear of the journey itself; it was fear of not to be able to stop when I needed to. If I was with my own car, I had no fear at all because I was more or less in control.

My friend Giusy insisted, 'At least you should ask Rinpoche.' When we called Rinpoche, he said, 'Yes! You come. Good!' In that moment, I felt something change inside myself. 'If Rinpoche says I can make it, I can.' Even though I had only been with Rinpoche for a few years, my faith was strong. That must be something from a previous life; otherwise I cannot explain it.

In the end, I found myself with a ticket and a few weeks later I was on the flight to Borobudur.

I felt safe with my dharma friends. Giusy helped me all the way and shared a room with me. The panic didn't come back on this journey. I was convinced I was on the right path, doing the right thing. In fact everything went well."

Experience of growth

"After coming back from this trip, I realized that the moment to stop the medication had arrived. Rinpoche supported me and advised me to take some herbal vitamins. It was also an experience of growth. Rinpoche helped me to find my own way out.

Some days after I had returned from Borobudur I had an insight – I remember it very clearly. Thinking about this still makes me emotional, because it was realizing something so important and so deep. I was walking downtown in my hometown. Suddenly like a flash I said, 'Even if I die now, I have found what I was looking for. I don't need to look for anything else.' I felt this so strongly: no matter what happens, I know I am on the right path. It is incredible, because there is nothing more than this that you can wish for anyone. Rinpoche saved my life."

The elephants

"That same year I started to travel a lot with Rinpoche, to Nepal and Tibet and since then I have been to Borobudur many times. When we are there in this holy place with Rinpoche I feel that the stupa is alive, the stories on the panels are vivid, the animals are moving. It is just like that.

I like to speak to the panels of Lalitavistara. I like the elephants very much, so one day I was offering flowers, incense and mantras there. Moreover, the elephant was an important symbol for my grandmother and so it is special for me. Then on my last day, on my way down from the stupa, some real elephants came walking towards me! I took it really as a sign: this stupa is alive and talking to you. It was a big blessing.

I deeply thank my guru, all teachers and dharma friends. I rejoice in the positive karma created in the past. May I always develop the causes and conditions to have the merit to be guided by them until enlightenment."

Our heads were shaved like monks
Claudia Rapisarda (1964) Brazil
When Claudia Rapisarda heard the sound of the NgalSo Self-Healing for the first time on a CD, she had a special vision.

Sickness and healing

"My father was dying in Sao Paolo, while I was staying in New York, and was very sick with asthma. My sister Laura[12], who was taking

---
12 Read Laura Oliveira's story in Chapter 5.

care of my father, already knew Rinpoche and she sent me the NgalSo Self-Healing CD practice.

So I put the CD on, lay down on the sofa and then I had this vision:

We were walking around this massive stone together: my father, Laura, Rinpoche, an elephant and I. Our heads were shaved like the monks. Lama Gangchen was there, but at that point I didn't know it was Lama Gangchen because I had never met him! We were walking around this stone though I didn't know what it was. This place felt very comforting and very familiar.

Six months later, Rinpoche came to visit New York. Of course Laura had told me a lot about him so I called the place where he stayed. That time there were many obstacles in my life and I was still very sick. He picked up the phone himself and said, 'Hat!' while laughing. He was referring to my hat-making profession. He invited me to come to his hotel right away, so I went. I was so surprised to see him because I recognized him immediately: he was the one from my vision! When I told him this, he said, 'Yes, we know each other.' I stayed with him for several days. And he healed me, no doubt about it."

The stone of my vision

"After that Laura and I decided to go to Borobudur together, where we took our father's ashes. When I arrived at Borobudur, I immediately recognized the place. It was the stone of my vision, where I was with my father and my sister, and going around it together with Rinpoche!

This is the most important story to me, and Borobudur is the most important place on earth!"

The woman who prays for all of us
José Mutsaerts (1950) The Netherlands

José Mutsaerts' daily life was interwoven with Borobudur, even before she had ever been there. She couldn't imagine that she would ever travel to Indonesia. She considered it an impossibility for a long time that one day she would reach the top of the stupa. But reality proved otherwise.

José Mutsaerts

A building like Borobudur

"A year after Frans, whom I had been together with for fourteen years, died in 2005, I returned to Geldrop, the village where my daughter also lived. I got a job at a home for the elderly; a square building with four levels and a beautiful garden in the center. It is called Maison St. Cyr – the pure house.

To me this building was Borobudur. I only did the evening and night shifts, so in the evening I would walk around the galleries, checking every door to see if things were okay, while reciting the mantras of the Borobudur practice. In my own way, I worked for the residents. It was a beautiful place and the thought often came to me that I would like to live there myself.

My next occupational workplace was in a high nine-storey building. Here again, I did many mantras during my rounds. Sometimes I helped people going to bed by giving them a nice foot-massage, after which they could go to sleep completely relaxed. I truly felt blessed that, despite the cuts in the healthcare budgets, I was able to do so much for these people."

I could not even think

"Some years later, in 2009, I had many losses over a short period, but at the same time it was a beautiful phase. First my mother died. She had been ill for a while already when Lama Gangchen came to

The Netherlands for a few days. I was asked to visit a friend from the sangha who was dying. Lama Gangchen was also there and while we were doing our prayers, I received a phone call to tell me that my mother was in her dying process as well. Hence, Lama Gangchen prayed for her too.

On the eleventh of the eleventh of that same year I fell off my horse and suffered severe injuries. My wrist and my knees were broken, my ribs were bruised and I suffered from concussion. I had to lay flat for six weeks. That same week, a baby was born in our family who lived for only three days. This was the first time that I had a really hard time dealing with grief. Before, I had always handled death easily. Even standing next to my mother in her death process had been beautiful. But this time it was a little child who had died. And there were other people close to me who passed away as well.

Not much later, in 2010, I got a serious Transient Ischaemic Attack – a mini stroke. Then after that, they found out that I had also broken my back as a result of the fall from the horse. From that moment on, I couldn't do anything any longer, not even speak or think.

For six months I just lay on my bed. Slowly, slowly, I learned to walk again with a stick, but I had lost my balance completely. When I stood in front of a door, I didn't know if I had arrived or I was leaving."

Now people came to help me out

"Despite the fact that everything that had happened to me was pretty tough, I went through it rather calmly. I could let it happen and I knew why it happened: I had needed a break. In the period before, I had been helping lots of people. Now, suddenly others came to help me out.

So there I was: fully incapacitated and forced to move into a care home. There was a place for me in the nine-storey building, but of course I had a strong wish to go to the square 'Borobudur' home. Luckily that was possible. I got an apartment in the northeastern corner, and since then, I live among the elderly for whom I had worked in the years before. They call me: 'The woman who prays for all of us.' The apartment has the shape of a triangle, which is special for me because I worked with triangles and pyramids when

I gave healings to people for many years. For example, I sometimes place a pyramid on the picture of a person that needs help. In fact, Borobudur itself is also a pyramid.

One effect of the stroke and the fall from the horse was that I couldn't do my meditations in the same way as before. However, every day I played the CDs from Lama Gangchen. During the daytime, I lay in my relaxing chair and listened to the Guhyasamaja CD for hours and hours. At night, Self-Healing was continuously playing next to my bed, and in fact it still is. It really heals me and at the same time I dedicate to the people who need help or who simply come to my mind. I have inner conversations with the Buddhas – I tell them what I am working on in that moment."

'See you at Borobudur…'

"In the autumn of 2011, when I felt a little bit better, I managed to attend Lama Gangchen's NgalSo Reiki initiation in Holland. I was still walking with a stick and I wore a corset – I could hardly sit, but I really wanted to be there. It was lovely to meet Rinpoche again. When my taxi came I said goodbye to him and much to my surprise he said casually, 'See you at Borobudur.' I still remember how I was laughing inside, 'I don't think so!', I thought because it seemed truly impossible. Physically, I was hardly able to get into the taxi. And also financially, it didn't seem to be an option since I no longer had a job. My current apartment was more expensive than before, while at the same time I lived on government support. Besides, in the twenty years that I had been with Lama Gangchen, I had never joined a pilgrimage. During my meditations I had asked if I should, but I always got the answer that the teachers would come to me, so no need for traveling. I had only been to Albagnano once, after Frans had died.

Some months after the NgalSo Reiki initiation and the special words of farewell by Lama Gangchen, I visited my friends Nico[13] and Lidy[14] in Sappemeer. They both planned on going to Indonesia for the retreat and Nico said, 'We would like you to join us at Borobudur.' I said that I didn't have a clue how to realize that. 'We'll pay for everything, if you are willing to receive it,' he continued. 'We have

---

13 Read Nico Smith's story in Chapter 10.
14 Read Lidy Haarman's story in Chapter 2, Chapter 9 and Chapter 10.

the opportunity and want to do this for you.' It took a while before the impact of his words sank in. But then the penny dropped and I remembered Rinpoche's words. I was so happy and I laughed! When I told them, they also laughed. There was no doubt. Rinpoche's words became true. We booked immediately and in March 2012 I traveled to Borobudur."

The green Kuan Yin

"It was fantastic to participate in the vivid lessons together with the teacher and to see how he behaves with people. I was a bit anxious that I wouldn't be able to climb the stupa. Beforehand, I trained like a maniac on the stairs of my own 'Borobudur' at home, while ironically I had actually moved there to avoid stairs! With some effort, every day it went a little bit better. On the actual Borobudur it went really well; I felt I was just carried there. That time, Lama Gangchen gave me an important message: he told me I should walk more and start doing Tai Chi.

Back home, I had a vision of *Kuan Yin*,[15] the female Buddha of compassion. It was strange because she has not much to do with Tibetan Buddhism. In the vision I could also feel the presence of my late boyfriend Frans. 'Look,' I said to him, 'Kuan Yin. But it could also be Tara.'

Not much later, amongst her stuff, my daughter found an old leaflet of a Tai Chi course in my home town. I remembered Rinpoche's advice and went there. They had already been working for over a month on the *108 steps,* and despite my doubts, I joined them anyway. The number 108 that I know well from Tibetan Buddhism gave me the confidence to do so. Physically I improved a lot and progressively I could keep up with the exercises. One day, they took me to a big center for Taoist Tai Chi in Helmond.

We walked into the space and my mouth fell open. There stood a beautiful huge green statue of Kuan Yin, exactly as I had seen in my vision. Now everything fell into place. I spontaneously started to make prostrations, which was not exactly customary. However, I felt completely comfortable there.

---

15 The female Buddha known in China as the Buddha of Compassion. Equivalent of the male Buddha Avalokiteshvara in Mahayana and Vajrayana Buddhism. In Tibetan: Chenrezig.

Recently I attended a workshop with two hundred fifty people in that same place in Helmond. We stayed overnight and once again, I had a vision. I saw Kuan Yin wearing a white gown, and she had a black dot on her heart. I also saw a monk with a long beard. He wore a black gown and had a white dot on his heart. Slowly, Kuan Yin and the monk floated towards each other and together they formed a big ball in the shape of the Yin and Yang symbol. It gave me a feeling of great joy. For it validated to me that things are good as they are."

A flower for my dog
Renata Zincone (1969) Brazil
Renata Zincone's first visit to Borobudur was marked by her dog having an operation shortly before she went.

A good omen
"Shortly before I went to Borobudur for the first time I received a message from my mother about our dog, Lola. I live in Italy and my mother takes care of our dogs at home in Brazil. Then, I was told that my favorite dog, with whom I have a special connection, had cancer. At that time, Lama Gangchen and Lama Michel were both in Thailand. Dawn – who also lives in Albagnano – advised me to send a WhatsApp message with a picture of my sick dog to a friend who

was accompanying Lama Gangchen in Thailand. When this friend showed the picture to Lama Michel, he did a special dedication for Lola. Later, Lama Gangchen also saw the picture.

In the meantime in Brazil, the dog was operated on because her tumor was bleeding too much; they did not know what to do anymore. My mother couldn't tell me any more than that we had to wait and see how things developed. On the day of the surgery it was Buddha's full moon, I thought this was a very auspicious sign. So, all went well during the surgery, but we had to wait. She was fine for the moment so I decided to go to Borobudur."

Called back by Lama Gangchen

"Obviously, Lola's worrying situation was occupying my mind pretty much, and I dedicated my prayers to her. Then, on the fifth day, we gathered early in the morning as usual and, just like every morning, we were given a flower by Lama Gangchen to take with us to the stupa.

However this time, after I received my flower and continued to join the line-up along the path, Rinpoche called me back. He gave me a second flower and said, 'For your dog.' I hadn't spoken with Lama Gangchen about anything to do with my dog's situation. But he knew exactly what was going on and what this meant for me. I took Lola's flower with me to the top of the stupa and there I put it at one of the Vajrasattva Buddhas.

The following day my mother called. My dog was much better! Already a week later she was cured. The wound of the operation that didn't look good at first now was only a thin pink line. And the cancer had gone. It was very special. I am convinced that Lama Gangchen has healed my dog.

Almost one year later my dog fell ill again. I went to Brazil to be with her. This time she wouldn't make it. Everybody adviced me to put her down but instinctively I knew I shouldn't, so I decided to take care of her until the end. Later, I found out that in Buddhism it is considered better not to intervene in the dying process so that, in this way, the suffering will finish and the negativities be purified for a better rebirth. I was relieved that I decided to follow my intuition."

Chapter 8

The Way of Personal Growth

An elephant never forgets

In Holland during the 1990s a popular commercial appeared on TV: a little boy lingers near some elephants in a zoo holding a roll of 'Rolo' caramel candies in his hands. The boy calls a young elephant to come near the gate and reaches out to offer him his last sweet. When the elephant is about to take it with his trunk, the boy quickly withdraws his hand and puts the sweet in his own mouth. Then he rubs it in by wickedly shouting at the elephant, "na na na-na na!" while showing the sweet between his teeth.

In the next shot we see the boy 25 years later. The young man is standing at a road watching a circus procession passing by. The now adult elephant is there as well; he recognizes the man and remembers what happened that time. He lifts his trunk, taps the man on the shoulder and when the man looks up, he gives him a brisk rap on the ear. Then the elephant trumpets triumphantly, "na na na-na na!", leaving the man aghast. Then we hear a voiceover, concluding the advertisement, "Beware of what you do with your last Rolo."

An elephant never forgets, so they say and in fact the same holds for karma. On Borobudur the law of karma is portrayed very explicitly on the faces of the lowest base-level. Here hundred sixty reliefs are found that depict the 'Mahakarmavibanga', an important discourse of the Buddha. The reliefs tell us how positive and negative deeds lead to positive and negative consequences, respectively, in the future. For example, those who kill will have a short life. Those who protect others will be happy and earn respect. Also is depicted how sentient beings find themselves in the world of desire, how they are sometimes apparently in heaven and then suddenly in hell.

This is called samsara. Samsara is not a place or environment; It is a state of the mind where we are constantly driven by our desire for things which we think will make us happy and an aversion to things which we think will make us unhappy.

Lama Gangchen compares the message of the panels around the base of Borobudur with the cost of cellphone use. "The Mahakarmavibanga is showing clearly that some actions are too expensive, like killing, violence, depriving others of resources, lying, pride, sexual misconduct, imprisoning others, speaking maliciously – it is like when we use our mobile phones, some places are much more expensive to call than others. But if, out of ignorance, we don't know – then sooner or later when the bill comes we get a huge shock!"[1]

Exposed corner of Mahakarmavibangha

Hidden behind stone

For unknown reasons the reliefs of the Mahakarmavibanga are not visible to visitors to the stupa; since their construction twelve hundred years ago they have been hidden behind a stonewall several meters thick. Scholars give various explanations for this mystery of Borobudur. One of them is the assumption that religious convictions altered during the long period of construction, and that, as a result, the revelation of the reality of the law of karma was hidden from an audience.

---

[1] *Seeds for Peace – Homage to Borobudur: Ocean of Mandalas* (2011), contribution by Lama Gangchen: '*The Hidden Meaning of Candi Borobudur*', p. 344, Lama Gangchen Peace Publications

Others suspect that the risk of subsidence is the reason for the stone platform that was subsequently laid against the carved base. Lama Gangchen and Lama Caroline suggest an interesting third possibility: The adjustment was needed in order to correct the measurements of the mandala so that they are fully coherent with the mandala principles of Vajrayana Buddhism. Lama Caroline suggests that Borobudur was built by the first Sailendra king, Raja Indra, as a Mahayana stupa. Later, when highest yoga tantra was introduced to Java, his son and successor Samaratunga adjusted the design of the stupa for it to fulfill the 108-units schedule of a Vajrayana mandala. Possibly, this coincided with the need to strengthen the construction.[2]

When the Dutchman IJzerman discovered the hidden panels in 1885, they were exposed one by one, to be recorded for posterity by photographer Kasian Cephas, and then covered up again. Due to these efforts, the images on the reliefs of the Mahakarmavibanga are available for everyone to see after all.

The difference between Buddhism and psychology

Spiritual development means to develop one's qualities. When we speak of developing qualities, what we actually mean is personal growth. In Vajrayana Buddhism this is an important aspect. But how can we define the difference with psychology?

Lama Michel says the following: in psychology one works on *mental defilements*[3] like anger, dissatisfaction and fear in order to achieve emotional balance. This state of emotional balance is the ultimate goal. In Buddhism however, emotional balance is not a final goal but a starting point – because from here we can progress; we want to develop ourselves to the maximum potential. This means we develop great stability, love, compassion, patience, generosity, equanimity and wisdom, so that we can help not only ourselves but also others in the best possible way. A Buddha is someone who has

---

2 *Seeds for Peace IV – Homage to Borobudur: Ocean of Mandalas* (2011), contribution of Lama Gangchen, 'The Hidden Meaning of Candi Borobudur', p. 344 and Lama Caroline, 'A Short Exploration of T.Y.S. Lama Gangchen's Theories about the Meaning of the Sacred Geometry and Mandala Symbolism of Candi Borobudur in the Light of Academic Scholarship on the Subject', p. 373
3 Any aspect of the mind that – once it is activated – perturbs our inner peace. The most significant mental defilements are ignorance, close-mindedness, attachment, desire, anger, hatred, miserliness, pride and fear.

developed his or her qualities to the utmost possible degree.[4]

Hence, we have to achieve a state of balance first by eliminating our obstructions. Some people suffer their whole life from anger and irritation; others have fears that block their development. There are people who are dissatisfied, unhappy, stingy, proud, or who judge others out of feelings of superiority or inferiority.

This is where the concept of karma from the Mahakarmavibanga pops up again: with each and every unfriendly remark, every fit of anger or selfish action, one creates damaging karma, which forms an energetic imprint on the subtle consciousness.

Sooner or later, when the time is ripe, or more exactly, when causes and conditions come together, the seed ripens in the form of a similar experience. A negative action always leads to a negative result, a neutral action leads to a neutral result and a positive action always brings something positive. So it is important, not just for the present moment, but also for the future, to do something about our negative habits and to start collecting positive karma.

The way out

Karma – which literally means 'action'– is not a fatalistic fact of life in the sense that there is some kind of predetermined destiny, as some people may think. When you believe in the law of karma – or in the saying, 'what goes around comes around,' it offers a way to liberation, because you can break through the pattern of negative habits: we have a choice. For example by not getting angry but by accepting when something bad or difficult is happening to us, and by acknowledging that sometime in the past we ourselves created the causes for this to happen.

In Buddhism, emotions are connected to certain energy chakras in the body. Lama Gangchen teaches, "A strong negative emotion such as anger affects the corresponding heart chakra by blocking the energy, which in turn energetically disturbs all the organs that are linked to the chakra by the channels. ... Instead of continuing to blame outer circumstances and other people when something we do not like happens to us, we should analyze and try to fully understand

---

[4] Lama Michel, October 10th 2015, Teaching: *Guru Puja Commentary*, 4th weekend - day 1, AHMC, Albagnano, Italy

the negative effects of the mental poisons on our health. If we do not resolve and eliminate the negative karmic causes of our own emotional problems, no medicine – no matter how good it is, no surgical operation, no therapy or therapist can completely heal us. By healing the underlying mental and energetic disturbances, even what is considered to be a terminal illness can sometimes be healed."[5]

The Buddha has followed this path before us, and he shows us the way to enlightenment. To be successful on this path we need – besides qualities like love and compassion – a lot of wisdom. We need to be aware of the true nature of reality.

The Buddha became aware of the true nature of reality. He discovered that everything is interdependent and nothing exists from its own side. This concept is called *emptiness*,[6] but it is far from being empty. Those who become aware of emptiness discover the infinite interconnectedness of every single aspect of the universe. This brings a feeling of great space and joy. The fact that nothing exists from its own side and that nothing is permanent gives hope. Everything is moving and changing constantly. The philosophy of emptiness is vast and deep. Lama Michel can teach on this theme for days in a row. But even if you only understand a little part of it, it can already help you to experience more space in the events that you find difficult in your life.

No preaching

Lama Gangchen says that the historical Buddha transmitted the Mahakarmavibanga as an answer to the many questions of ordinary people. The Buddha never preached, but only responded to the needs that people expressed.

"... the Mahakarmavibanga speaks to the majority of people, ordinary people with normal aspirations. Many people, even scholars, misunderstand the concept of 'renunciation', thinking it means they have to give up their comfortable lifestyles; they don't understand that the only things they have to give up are suffering, violence and

---

5 Lama Gangchen, T.Y.S. (2004) *Great Wheel Vajrapani NgalSo Self-Healing Practice,* p. 14, Lama Gangchen Peace Publications

6 The concept that everything is empty of inherent existence. This is the absolute nature of all phenomena. In Tibetan Buddhist philosophy, developing insight into emptiness – by study and through experience in meditation – is a method to eliminate suffering.

the dependently arising causes and conditions of those."⁷ Hence one doesn't have to sit and meditate in a cave to eliminate suffering.

Within Vajrayana Buddhism there are several methods and rituals to diminish suffering and to develop oneself. In one of his Self-Healing books Lama Gangchen says, "We are all responsible for our own karmic debt, but instead of feeling guilty or behaving like a victim we should use one of the many methods available to heal ourselves."⁸ At Borobudur these methods are also displayed, for example in the symbolism of the six perfections, in the tales depicted on the reliefs and in the ten stages of the Mahayana path.

The five Buddhas and their qualities

Now we will look at the five Dhyani Buddhas, who are positioned on the four sides of the stupa, and who are described in the NgalSo Self-Healing practice. How can they help us develop our qualities?

Each of the five Dhyani Buddhas or Meditational Buddhas has specific characteristics and qualities that can help us overcome various emotional obstacles so that we can then develop ourselves further.

In the Self-Healing practice these Buddhas are connected with the five most important chakras in our energy body. We will now name and describe these five Buddhas in turn. Note that this description is far from comprehensive and not intended for practice. For that, we should refer to Lama Gangchen's Self-Healing books where we can find the correct instructions and more extensive explanations of the qualities and aspects of these Buddhas.⁹

---

7 *Seeds for Peace IV - Homage to Borobudur: Ocean of Mandalas* (2011), contribution by Lama Gangchen, '*Uncovering the Meaning of the Hidden Base of Borobudur*', p. 345
8 Lama Gangchen, T.Y.S. (2004) *Great Wheel Vajrapani NgalSo Self-Healing Practice,* p. 15, Lama Gangchen Peace Publications
9 Lama Gangchen, T.Y.S. (1993) *Self-Healing II,* Lama Gangchen Peace Publications,
Lama Gangchen, T.Y.S. (1999) *NgalSo Tantric Self-Healing Commentary,* Lama Gangchen Peace Publications

● Amoghasiddhi is the green Buddha found on the northern side of the stupa. Those who suffer from fears and jealousy can turn to Amoghasiddhi for refuge. His hand gesture offers protection and strength. Amoghasiddhi is connected to the base chakra.

● Ratnasambhava is the yellow Buddha on the southern side of the stupa with the hand gesture of generosity. Ratnasambhava helps us to develop generosity and be less arrogant, proud and miserly. Ratnasambhava is connected to the navel chakra.

● Akshobya is blue on the eastern side. His hand gesture – touching the earth with his fingertips – symbolizes stability. This Buddha is related to love and compassion, the antidote for hatred and anger. Akshobya is connected to the heart chakra.

● Amitabha, red, is found on the western side. His hands are folded together in meditation posture. His meditative concentration helps to resist impulses of desire and attachment. Amitabha is connected to the throat chakra.

● Vairochana is positioned in the center, on all four sides on the fifth gallery. This white Buddha radiates *omniscience*. He helps to banish ignorance and closed-mindedness, and to develop wisdom. Vairochana is connected to the crown chakra.

In the following stories, disciples of Lama Gangchen tell us how they developed themselves and overcame obstacles on their spiritual path. Roberto Mori's and Lotte Janssen's stories illustrate how negative emotions like anger and fear can be tackled. Kersten Dohmen realized a deeper awareness of the law of karma. Loes Thijssen had an experience directly related to the Buddhist concept of emptiness and interconnectedness. And Maurice Bosman managed to get closer to his own feelings. Finally Claudia Sobrevilla shows how one sometimes has to tackle many obstacles before reaching the ultimate goal.

Even if you don't want to change, you change
Roberto Mori (1968) Italy

Roberto Mori works as a cook in the kitchen of Lama Gangchen's center in Albagnano. He tells us how he ended up there. It all started with an intense near-death experience.

A serious car accident

"When I was 25 years old something happened that changed my life completely. Until then, I didn't want to hear anything about Lama Gangchen and meditation. I had started working at age fifteen, in hotels and restaurants as a bartender. While I loved going out, going to nightclubs and drinking, I never did drugs. In those days I also had big problems. A large sum of money had been 'stolen' from me. It had to do with a restaurant and the money actually belonged to the bank. I had to repay everything myself. Practically my whole salary went to the bank. I was full of anger and considered revenge, like burning down the restaurant that belonged to the people who had ripped me off. My sister knew Rinpoche already and she asked me from time to time to join her. But I just laughed at her, 'That stupid business is not for me.' In the meantime, I remained stuck with my problem.

Then something happened. In October 1992, I was involved in a serious car accident that left me in a coma. For three days I remained unconscious and during that period I experienced only tremendous bliss. It was an extraordinary experience! Also, there was someone with me while I was in that other dimension, though I wasn't quite sure who it was. When I woke up I was not happy at all. It was terrible. I wanted to go back. After that, I spent another fifteen days in the hospital. I was a mess. All over my body, things were broken or bruised, and the nerves in my face were cut so that half of my face was paralyzed.

While in hospital, I mentioned the name Dario from time to time. I asked when he would come by to visit. They answered me then that Dario would come later. I repeatedly mentioned his name. A month after the accident, three people who had also been in the car came to visit me. They were unharmed. And then they told me that Dario had died in that same crash. It was only then that I understood what was going on. He was the person who had accompanied me during the blissful experience in that other dimension, during my coma. 'Oh, lucky him!', was my first reaction, because Dario had stayed there, while I had to return."

Death is not horrible

"The weird thing was that I didn't know Dario at all before the accident. He was the fifth person in the car, but I didn't know his name or who he was. We were simply a group of young people on our way somewhere, and he also happened to be in the car. I knew him only from the days I was unconscious… After that, I asked for him time after time, ever repeating his name.

I wanted to tell everybody, 'Death is not horrible.' I spoke about my experience with friends, my parents and family, but they thought I had gone mad due to the blow to my head. So I had had this great experience, but I couldn't share it. It was impossible to talk about it."

Food

"In the period after this, I eventually joined my sister for a meeting with Lama Gangchen and I started to practice the Self-Healing. I did it for a year without knowing what I was actually doing. But it worked! In 1999, I joined the Borobudur retreat for the first time. That was a beautiful experience, I felt really close to Rinpoche. I remember him hugging me strongly. And that time something special happened, but I only realized the impact later.

Lama Gangchen was walking through the galleries and I was right behind him. At a certain moment Rinpoche pointed at a panel that depicts the Buddha with various offerings. Rinpoche turned, looked at me and said, 'Food'. I didn't know what to make of it. Those days I worked in hotels as a bartender, but never as a cook. I only prepared food for myself; there was no special interest in cooking. But in 2007, I understood the message. That year Rinpoche asked me to work as a cook in his center in Albagnano, and that is what I do to this day."

Roberto, Isthar and Dawn with Teresa

Teresa and Dawn

"Since then, I have been to Borobudur three more times. Always together with Dawn, who also works in the center, and Teresa. Teresa is a very old and very special lady who lives in Albagnano. Rinpoche wished for her to come to Borobudur but she needs accompanying. That's why Dawn and I took her with us. We were together day and night, also sharing a hotel room between the three of us, because Teresa said, 'We came together, so we stay together!' From the first time I met her in the center, years before I came to work there, I felt a strong connection with Teresa. Nowadays, I take care of her. But in fact it is also the other way around. On a spiritual level, she cares for me! She teaches me to be patient, caring and to give assistance.

Borobudur is magic for me. Going there with Rinpoche can change your life, though it might take a while. When Rinpoche showed me the stone panel with the offerings, he implied that I should work with food, but it took seven years for this to actually happen. It is a nice and pleasant job, but how you perform it is more important: how you deal with your emotions. In the beginning, I was not so relaxed as I am nowadays. My character was much more hot-tempered. But coming to work in the center, and wanting to change, will bring change for sure.

Even if you don't want to change, you change. That is how things work with Rinpoche; it is the reason why he established the center. It is very important." *(Teresa passed away in the summer of 2015 in Albagnano. Roberto and Dawn took care of her until she passed.)*

A journey through volcanic ashes
Lotte Janssen (1981) The Netherlands

Upon arrival in Indonesia, where she traveled despite her huge fear of flying, Lotte Janssen was confronted with an even bigger fear – a volcanic eruption occurred in the region.

Help from Lama Gangchen

"Since I was young I have had many fears and I have felt unsafe frequently. This has stopped me from doing what I really wanted to in many ways. I always made up a reason not to do something or I created an obstacle. In this way, I also hesitated to go to Borobudur with Lama Gangchen. In the first place, I had a fear of flying and besides that I had a phobic anxiety of natural disasters like earthquakes and volcanic eruptions. And Indonesia is full of volcanoes...

When he visited Holland, I asked Lama Gangchen to help me to overcome these fears. Not much later, I found myself actually on the plane to Java. The long flight wasn't as bad as I had expected; it felt good. I have conquered that one, I thought. I did it!

However when we landed in Jakarta, we were informed that we couldn't continue to Yogyakarta because there had been a volcanic eruption elsewhere on Java! Oh what to do now?, I thought. This was exactly what I had been so afraid of. Now my fear came really close.

Mother stupa wrapped in plastic after volcanic eruption

We went to stay in a hotel that night and were in doubt about what to do next. Eventually our group of twelve pilgrims decided that we would travel to Borobudur by ourselves by taxi the next morning, aware of the fact that a layer of ashes had settled over the land there. But later that night, a fellow traveler said that, according to his family in Holland who were following the news, it wasn't safe out there. I was happy when he expressed this, as it was exactly what I felt. He also looked scared.

Not much later, he came to my room again with two women. They said they had been in touch with Lama Gangchen who was still in Thailand. I assumed they had phoned him. Lama Gangchen had given his blessings to continue our journey they said. What struck me was the change in the face of the man who had been so scared earlier. His expression showed so much confidence now! All his fear had vanished."

Letting go of my fears

"For me it was different, I hadn't yet made up my mind what to do – my fear was still there and I didn't have that kind of faith. I felt pressurized to join the group, but also felt I couldn't handle it. I know myself to be rather compliant when it comes to decisions made by others, and I also know that I tend to lose myself in situations like that. I decided to wait until the next morning before deciding whether to join the group or stay in Jakarta. I wanted to allow myself the time to feel what was good for me.

That night, I was sobbing so much. I cried my heart out. It was as if, with all these tears, I let go of many, many of my fears. Slowly, slowly I sensed a feeling of faith coming over me, faith in something bigger than me. The fear of all things that were also bigger than me – like eruptions and other disasters – was no longer present and suddenly I felt safe!

It was not until the next morning, when they came to ask if I would join them, that I understood that Lama Gangchen had phoned us himself, in person, to inform himself about our wellbeing. It moved me deeply that he was so concerned, that he takes such care of us. The night before, I had missed that point completely. They had told me, but I hadn't heard.

Later, when we left Jakarta in our taxis, I saw a huge signboard along the road that said: LOTTE, my name. Right after, I saw a board picturing a rainbow. For me this was a wink, a confirmation that it was okay to follow this way!

That day, I experienced a beautiful journey over Java Island. I also enjoyed nice conversations with our driver about how it is to live among volcanoes. He taught me that, on one hand, you can fear an eruption and, on the other hand, you can live your life full of confidence."

Elephant's karma
Kersten Dohmen (1964) Germany

Feeding the elephants is a daily ritual during the retreat. While with the elephants, Kersten Dohmen received a clear insight about how the law of karma works.

The guards of the sanctuary
"Thinking about when this story began, to be honest, I don't know.

Did the story start when it actually happened or had it already begun earlier? It may even have begun in a previous life of my mental continuum.

At the doors of a sanctuary you will usually find guards; the protectors that have the power to repel evil, the ones that watch over the building and that make sure that no-one with wrong intentions may enter. When you go to the entrance of Borobudur, you find that the stairs are adorned with sculptures, shaped like an elephant trunk. They are not trunks but they look like it, they remind me of the elephants.

My story is about the elephants. The elephants that live in the park at the foot of the stupa, the elephants that are chained to prevent them from escaping, the elephants that we always visit while doing the kora around the stupa, before we actually climb Borobudur. To me the elephants are the guards of Borobudur. We feed them with coconuts and carrots while reciting the Six Mantras and Six Mudras, which is a prayer for making peace with the environment."

Cleaning the ears

"I arrived some days before the actual retreat started and I decided not to put my feet on the Borobudur before Lama Gangchen arrived. However, I did a kora around the stupa in the park every morning and I also stopped every day at the elephant house, as we usually do with the group. I had quite a good contact with one of the elephants; in my imagination he was looking at me all the time. He was the one standing up front in the middle. I felt a wish to get closer to him and do something to connect more, so I decided to clean his ears from possible insects and other things bothering him. He was very calm, I was not afraid and even the guy working there saw it was okay and left after a few minutes. So there I was, alone, touching first his neck, then his trunk, his cheek and after a while I took his ear. I had never seen an elephant's ear from inside before. I expected it to be full of insects and dirt but it was pretty clean. The elephant was completely relaxed while I did my investigation; he was only flapping his ears a bit when I first touched them. All in all, it was a nice experience.

Some days later, we started to do the kora together with Lama Gangchen and one day, somehow everybody moved very close to the elephants. Some people gave them bananas, others coconuts and somebody gave me some carrots to give to them. It was quite crowded so I went to the side where there was more space. It must have been the biggest elephant that was standing there. I offered him some carrots and he was taking them with his trunk and then eating them. One carrot fell on the ground, so I decided to pick it up and give it again. I was quite confident due to my previous experience with the other elephant. My motivation was to help him, but apparently he had another idea of what I was doing there."

A big and gentle punch

"When I bent over to pick up the carrot, the elephant gave me a big punch with his trunk! For the elephant it must have been quite a gentle punch, considering the fact that he has the strength to pull trees out of the ground with his trunk. But for me it was a really hard one. I lost consciousness while flying through the air. When I landed on the concrete, two meters away, I was aware again. It was a perfect boxer's punch because he touched me right under the nose, on the mouth. If you touch the nose itself, it breaks, but underneath is quite a stable point. I had some pain on my elbow from falling, but the nose did not hurt so much."

Lama Gangchen's facial expression

"I stood up, looked at the elephant and I will not forget the moment; it was a wonderful impression. I was not angry for even one second. This was between us. Immediately, I found Lama Gangchen standing next to me, taking out his water and cream pills and smearing some on my elbow. His facial expression struck me. No anger, no pity, nothing. As if he said, 'Okay, this is done now.' Following, we did our prayers and then we left the elephants to move on to the stupa.

This story brought me a very nice thought. I realized the confrontation was simply due to my karma, which may even have started between the elephant and me in another life. Since then, whenever something unpleasant happens to me, even banging my head against a door, or losing some money from my pocket, most of the time I am able to say, 'Okay, now this karma is finished!' I don't get angry or fight against it like I used to. I have learnt to accept obstacles as karmic results that ripen in that moment. The experience with the elephant and seeing the face of Lama Gangchen afterwards brought me a deeper understanding of the law of cause and effect."

Sweet rice with raisins
Loes Thijssen (1980) The Netherlands

Loes Thijssen became aware of the power of her own thoughts and intentions while reciting the mantra of emptiness.

Wishes come true

"I have been to Borobudur three times and what strikes me most is how everything there happens and works directly. I experience a kind of instant mode of how things work in Borobudur. If you wish something or think something, it might occur and come true on the spot.

For instance, during the retreat of 2012 it happened that I was reciting the mantra of emptiness while walking in the car park, while others were preparing for a fire puja. I also saw that they were serving sweet rice with raisins. And I heard myself thinking, 'No one is giving me any...' In the meantime I was still doing the mantra of emptiness, of interdependence: 'All phenomena depend on causes and conditions. Nothing exists inherently...' And I realized I could turn the situation myself. Immediately after this thought, somebody came to me and gave me a portion of rice! For me this was a clear example of how one can influence the things that happen.

In 2014 I had a similar experience. Sometimes I find it hard to make contact with the lamas. At the time, I was really keen to talk to Lama Michel, but I felt anxious and hesitant to go see him. When I shared this with a fellow pilgrim, she said, 'The only thing you need to do is to wish for it to happen. I made a wish myself and an hour later it became true.'

Later that day in the gompa, I still had doubts but I also realized that it was me myself who created the distance and obstacles that I felt. As soon as I realized this, they were gone... Without hesitation, I walked towards Lama Michel and talked to him. Again the solution, or the insight, manifested immediately.

How is this possible? I think it is because the energy at Borobudur is so clear and also you are there together with your teacher. You resonate along with the immensely powerful and pure energy of Borobudur. I have never felt energy as strong as at that place on the earth."

Family feeling

"It was also helpful that Lama Michel had advised us to focus on one aspect of ourselves to work on during the retreat. This made me so happy, because I had hundreds of things that I was dealing with at that time. He listed several things that you could pick. Anger, fear, dissatisfaction... The latter stood out for me, and with this thought I could feel relaxation right away. It helped me to be able to go more inside myself during meditation, and to feel more peaceful.

The next day I read in Lama Gangchen's book *Choose Peace* the following quote, 'With inner peace you will be more successful in everything you do. All that you need will come to you automatically when you develop inner peace.'[10] This pushed me even further to relax, to find peace within myself and to have faith that everything will be alright.

With the security that insights and realizations will come, and that external conditions will be okay, it is possible to help others and myself. All in all, the visits to Borobudur bring me more and more insight into the dharma and into myself. It is furthermore an increasingly joyful feeling to be part of this family."

---

10 Lama Gangchen, T.Y.S. (2013) *Choose Peace – A Gift of Wisdom for a Less Expensive Life*, p. 9, Lama Gangchen Peace Publications

I only saw a heap of stones
Maurice Bosman (1984) The Netherlands

During his first visit to Borobudur, Maurice Bosman was rather bothered by his rational mind. He didn't manage to experience the place as being holy. But gradually something changed inside.

High expectations

"After I broke up with my girlfriend and returned to living by myself again, it became easier for me to organize a trip to Borobudur. The journey had been on my wishlist for a couple of years, but I had not managed to realize it, no matter how hard I tried to create the conditions, partially because my girlfriend did not feel for it.

Now that I was on my own again, I made the decision to go. I managed to find the time and I had sufficient money. I was looking forward to it tremendously and my expectations were high, for I had heard so many stories about how special it was to be at this holy place with Lama Gangchen. Some people had mystical experiences, others saw beautiful rainbows and halos, so it was all very promising. I wished to experience this for myself once in my lifetime.

But when I arrived at Borobudur, I only saw a heap of stones! I felt so disillusioned. For the first days I felt rather ill, had difficulties with getting up early, was suffering from the tropical climate and during the circumambulations I did not feel comfortable in the crowd. In brief, I was disappointed, frustrated and even a bit pissed off.

Fortunately, I realized soon enough that this was typical of me, the fact that I did not manage to see Borobudur as a holy place.

I remembered the philosophy teaching by Lama Michel in which he explained that what is experienced is determined by the observer. So I knew that what I saw was due to myself."

A disapproving voice

"Sometimes, during the walk around the stupa, I stayed behind to be alone a little, while doing mantras and mudras of the Borobudur practice. At times when I met tourists looking at me in the galleries, I heard a disapproving voice in my mind, 'What are you doing?!' In those moments, I felt rather embarrassed about my performance.

And this was actually the same for my life at home; in my family and during my technical studies in university, I was not taught how to take care of my inner self. I noticed that whenever I tried to share my spiritual experiences with people outside the sangha, I did not feel understood. Sometimes, people even reacted with disapproval or denial. Therefore I started to keep my experiences secret. Hence, it was quite some job to learn to trust my own experience and not to be led by other people's opinions.

Slowly my observations changed during that first retreat. That first day, maybe I was ten per cent convinced about my experience. After a week, it had already become sixty per cent. For the remaining forty per cent, I still found that we were doing very daft things, but I did not allow these thoughts to control me."

Headache and dizziness

"About halfway through the retreat, I woke up with a severe headache. While we were seated at the foot of the stupa doing prayers, the pain became worse; it was pounding in my head. After a while, Lama Gangchen got up to start the circumambulations. I stayed behind for a while because I felt dizzy. Lama Gangchen came in my direction and I wanted to step aside to make space, but he placed his hand on my head to push off making the step over the edge of the gallery.

I was still quite dizzy when I followed the group. Barely twenty meters along, I suddenly started to cry. I did not know why but it came out anyway. Then I started to feel more relaxed and joyful.

From that moment, I began to help prepare the offerings in the gompa and to clean. Sometimes during the Self-Healing on Borobudur,

I carried the megaphone that was amplifying Lama Michel's voice. This was all very satisfying to me."

Glued to the spot

"A year later, when I arrived at Borobudur for the second time, once again I saw a heap of stones. But this time, it was a fifty-fifty experience and soon I could feel more connected. This time, it felt truly wonderful to be there and I could sense the loving energy around the place.

But it was not until the third time that it really hit me. That time, when I arrived and first saw Borobudur, it was like being glued to the spot, almost frozen. It touched me; I felt a deep relationship with myself and with the place. It was like coming home – a connection to a holy place. This was something from deep inside; it came from my mind and not from my eyes. At that moment I cried.

Now at home, I can recall that energy again and again. I establish a connection with the love and compassion of Borobudur and Lama Gangchen. It has become clear to me that it is up to me to realize that. The energy of love and compassion is always there, but I am the one who is able to access it."

A journey with obstacles
Claudia Sobrevila (1954) Venezuela

Claudia Sobrevila had to conquer several obstacles before arriving at Borobudur. When she finally got there Lama Gangchen explained the meaning of these challenges to her.

A preparing dream

"I scheduled my first trip to Borobudur in 2007. Some weeks before, I had a dream where I was in a pilgrimage with Lama Gangchen. In the dream, he was sitting high up on a throne. It looked like a pyramid and he was on the upper part of the pyramid. He started making some prayers. I was among the public. While he was reciting these prayers, I saw how Lama Gangchen's body turned into a rainbow. When I woke up, I had this clear understanding that Lama

Gangchen had attained the highest realization of clear light. After going to Borobudur and learning about the deep connection of Lama Gangchen to the stupa, I feel that the dream was preparing me for the experience of Borobudur.

On March 5, we all arrived at Bangkok airport to catch the flight with Thai Airways directly to Jakarta. The group was not very large. There were around eighteen pilgrims joining Lama Gangchen's pilgrimage to Borobudur. At the airport, everybody was excited about traveling to Borobudur with our great master, Lama Gangchen Rinpoche. Cosy, Lama Gangchen's secretary was busy getting everyone's boarding pass. However, she came back with seventeen boarding passes. Mine had not been issued. The reason was that my Venezuelan passport, out of at least thirteen or fourteen nationalities, required a visa prior to boarding the plane and landing in Jakarta. All the other pilgrims could get their visa upon arrival in Jakarta.

I was so disappointed and sad, but Lama Gangchen approached me and he said with a big smile in his face, 'You do everything possible to come.' His loving presence and words gave me confidence and hope. After I waved goodbye to them, I took a taxi and went straight to the Indonesian consulate. They told me that it would take three days to get a visa, because the next day was a holiday. I begged them to do it in one day, but they refused. I did not know what to do next, but it occurred to me that I should call other airlines to ask them what the visa requirements and exceptions were to travel to Indonesia. Garuda Airlines told me that if I had a corporate credit card they might let me board. I had no idea what this was but I decided to arm myself with all the possible tools to fly out as soon as possible and get admitted.

I also called the Jakarta office of my employer, and asked if they could write a letter to customs officials asking for their help in allowing me to enter the country to join the Peace Pilgrimage to Borobudur organized by the Lama Gangchen World Peace Foundation and attended by many people from around the world. One kind person did not see any harm in writing such a letter and I received the letter by fax at the hotel. I printed it and went late that night to Bangkok airport to catch a flight to Jakarta with Garuda Airlines. At the check-in counter, I gave them my passport and after a while they said that

I could not go. I explained that another employee had told me that there were some exceptions such as, for example, if I possessed a corporate card. I showed them my card and also handed them the letter explaining the reason for the trip. After examining these documents they looked at me as if I was crazy, and told me that there was nothing official in what I was presenting to them but that they would allow me to go if I signed a waver saying that I would pay three thousand dollars in fines if the Indonesia government deported me. I said that I was willing to take my chances."

I got scared

"Was I foolish? Why did I care so much to reach Borobudur? Between the dream that I had and all the reports coming from friends about the effects that experiencing Borobudur with Lama Gangchen has on your karma and path to enlightenment, I really wanted to go. I boarded the plane and felt somewhat relieved that I was on my way to Jakarta. I was about to take a nap as the trip was about three hours long, when the pilot announced through the speaker that there was a very bad storm ahead of us and that the airport traffic control could not change the plane's route so they had ordered the pilot to return to Bangkok. We had already been flying for one and a half hours! I got scared. I thought that so many obstacles kept arising to prevent me reaching Borobudur. I had racing thoughts that said to me that I was not good enough to deserve to travel to Borobudur. Sadness invaded me, but again I remembered the dream and remembered the face of Lama Gangchen at the airport saying, 'You come'. I really wanted to reach Borobudur and be with him. I prayed. The plane turned around and landed in Bangkok."

An important trip

"We had to wait about five hours until they allowed us to board the plane again. This time we reached our destination. While going through Customs in Jakarta, an official stopped me and sent me to a special room. There was a desk with two chairs and another official asked me to hand him my passport. He examined it and said to me that he could not let me enter the country. I told him that I was on an important trip and that they were expecting me in Borobudur for a Peace Pilgrimage and I handed him the letter and the credit card. He looked at them and said that he could not help me. I begged him to allow me in for only two days, that he could keep my passport until I returned to his office. He asked me if he could call someone from my employer in Jakarta. I gave him a number and he rang it. The person on the other line was friendly and said that they knew about the letter and that they had done it to help me out so that I could join the Peace Pilgrimage. Everything was very honest and open. In the end, the man agreed to let me in, but asked that when I leave the country I go through a similar process of going through a special desk like his. I promised I would do that."

Don't let yourself be distracted from your focus

"Now, I was in... My joy was immense and all my worries were gone. I took another plane and a taxi and in another four hours I finally reached the Borobudur Temple. Lama Gangchen was very happy to see me. He said as he embraced me, 'There were many obstacles for you, but the most important thing is that you overcame them all. When one is so set to reach enlightenment, strong obstacles will come, but it is very important not to be disturbed by them and not to allow them to move you away from your focus. You did very well. It is this kind of determination and stable mind that can help you reach enlightenment. Congratulations. Now you are here with me.'

My first experience at Borobudur was very strong. I was in an elevated spiritual state for the two short days that I spent there. Walking around all the levels of the Borobudur stupa with an enlightened master like Lama Gangchen clears away many impurities. I noticed that Lama Gangchen operates in many other subtle dimensions that I cannot dream of really understanding. He observes the inner and outer environments in a masterful way and the pace or sequence of the prayers, rituals or silence seem to be synchronized to an invisible clock that knows everything. It is hard to describe how he manages all the pilgrims, the locals, the symbols, the statues, the rain, the clouds, the whole environment and let's not forget the elephants that he nourishes on a daily basis. Through his movements, intentions, prayers, and loving heart, he allows each of us to have a glimpse of the purest states of our minds. It is such a gift!"

Lama Gangchen in the 'Borobudur' temple in Albagnano, Italy

Chapter 9

In the Mandala of the Guru

Crazy wisdom

Toet de Best[1] met Lama Gangchen for the first time in The Netherlands in 1987. She already knew some Tibetan lamas when she made an appointment with this lama healer. A quote from the book about her life: "They invited her to enter his room. There she saw a small man sitting. He wore a shiny yellow jacket, a black pointed beard and a bald head. It was mainly the setting that confused her. This lama was sitting there, with a friendly smile, relaxed in his chair. It was all unbelievably informal. Other people were present in the room, like a couple of beautiful Italian ladies. One of these women was massaging his bare feet! And she simply continued that when Toet arrived. What to think of all this! This picture didn't fit the image she had of Tibetan lamas and teachers."[2]

The unconventional style of Lama Gangchen is sometimes called *yogi* style. The way in which he works is called crazy wisdom. The crazy wisdom lama has a spontaneous and unrestrained attitude, free from conventions and ego. Crazy wisdom masters are known for the fact they go off the beaten track, and sometimes use shock methods to take people away from their culturally and historically-based concepts and ideas.[3]

Lama Gangchen often surprises people with unexpected actions. Sometimes he puts things on his head like a singing bowl, flowers, or a present he has received. He can suddenly change the timetable and

---

[1] Read Toet de Best's story in Chapter 3 and Chapter 4.
[2] Best, Toet de & Zwaan, Karin (2013), *De Magie van het Tibetaans Boeddhisme - Over een Lama Healer en de Zoektocht van een Limburgs Meisje*, p. 121, Aspekt, The Netherlands
[3] Lama Gangchen, T.Y.S. (2013) *Choose Peace - A Gift of Wisdom for a Less Expensive Life*, p. 10, Lama Gangchen Peace Publications

the program. Every now and then during teachings, he summons his students to rearrange all the furniture and decorations in the gompa.

Lama Gangchen may be seen as unconventional, but at the same time he is extremely traditional. Lama Michel explains that 'tradition' in Tibetan Buddhism means that the method with which the teachings are transmitted by the teachers is adjusted to the mentality and capacity of the disciples of that time and context. That is exactly what Lama Gangchen has done; in NgalSo Self-Healing he has adjusted the original methods to the mind and abilities of modern people. Nothing of the original content is lost in the new manner of practicing. This makes him an extraordinary traditional teacher according to Lama Michel.[4]

Whether one has a crazy wisdom lama or a more conventional teacher, both are there to offer help on one's spiritual path. That is the only reason why you need a guru. In the same way as you need a surgeon to perform an operation, or a language teacher to learn a new language, you can seek guidance from a guru for spiritual growth. He doesn't need to be your friend, you don't even have to like him; the only thing he should be good at is to show you the way in your spiritual development. Originally it was advised to take twelve years to investigate whether a teacher is fit to be your guru before you take official refuge in his or her guidance.

All the same, Lama Gangchen is an extraordinary lama. He works day and night with great compassion and love for anyone that he meets and all sentient beings around. He travels ten thousands of miles yearly and works tirelessly in different places over the world on peace projects, books, environmental conservation, helping people, healing people, offering advice, praying, giving teachings and so on. Meanwhile, everything that occurs around Lama Gangchen can be taken as a method to learn and to grow. The most important thing of all is our experience. He teaches his disciples to remain balanced no matter what situation arises, and not to judge out of convention or cultural background.

---

4 Lama Michel, March 20th 2016, Teaching: *NgalSo Self-Healing*, AHMC, Albagnano, Italy

Cultural influence

Kiran KC[5] from Nepal had already been living in The Netherlands for some years when he decided to look for a guru; a spiritual guide who could give him direction in life and where he could find refuge. Kiran grew up in a Hindu family. In his surroundings it was very normal to follow a guru. "They used to tell us in school; without a guru there cannot be wisdom. A guru teaches you to develop your own wisdom." Due to a combination of coincidences and circumstances he met the Buddhist Lama Gangchen in Amsterdam. Soon he realized that this was the teacher he had been looking for, even though Lama Gangchen was not Hindu. In Asian countries it is very common to look for spiritual refuge with someone who has the wisdom and realizations for this purpose. However, in the West, following a guru is often considered eccentric and incoherent with our autonomous and individualistic lifestyle. When Westerners do decide to follow a guru, they enter a world they are unfamiliar with. They lack a frame of reference of what this guru-disciple relationship should be like.

It may be helpful to understand how these kinds of reactions and thoughts come about. In Buddhism two parts of the mind are distinguished. One part of our mind is formed by external influences, like culture, religion and family education. According to Lama Michel the main influences for Westerners come from monotheism, capitalism and the rational technical-scientific worldview. This constructed mind colors the way you look at the world around you, like the example of Toet who got upset when she saw the lama's feet being massaged.

Then everybody has a spontaneous mind. This is the part of the mind that continues from life to life, says Lama Michel. And this part is similar regardless of one's culture: wherever in the world, people have the same emotions and feelings like love, joy, jealousy and anger. The spontaneous part of the mind is the part we work with on the spiritual path; to develop qualities like love, compassion, patience, satisfaction, wisdom *etc*. In Tibetan Buddhism it is the guru who shows you the way on your spiritual path. However, you have to walk the path yourself.[6]

---

5 Read Kiran KC's story in Chapter 10.
6 Lama Michel, May 3rd 2016, Lecture: 'Aspects of the Mind', Keizersgrachtkerk, Amsterdam,

Panel from Gandavyuha: The magical tower of Vairochana

A magical pilgrimage

Borobudur also shows how spiritual guides can help you on your path. The rich Indian merchant's son, Sudhana, meets fifty-two gurus during his search for ultimate truth. This famous story from the Mahayana text *Gandavyuha*[7] is depicted in four hundred sixty panels on the second, third and fourth galleries of Borobudur. The young Sudhana has a deep wish to reach enlightenment for the benefit of all sentient beings. At the insistence of Manjushri, the Buddha of Wisdom, he undertakes a pilgrimage. It turns into a magical quest; he meets philosophers, gods, Buddhas and bodhisattvas. Each guide teaches him another aspect of the path and then sends him on to the next teacher.

Among his masters are 'ordinary' people like a banker, a prostitute, a nun, a sea-captain, a slave, a housewife and a writer. The highlight of the pilgrimage is his meeting with the future Buddha *Maitreya*, who opens the magical tower of Vairochana for him by snapping his fingers. In this tower Sudhana experiences a series of surprising

---

7 Translation from Sanskrit: *Sutra of the Entry into the Realm of Reality*

visions about the ultimate truth, *dharmadatu*. For example, he sees billions of universes full of worlds and as many reflections of himself and he obtains insight into the nature of reality. But the journey doesn't finish here. The last master he meets on his travels is Buddha Samantabhadra, who teaches him that wisdom only exists in order to be applied with the objective of helping others.

Women

Among Sudhana's fifty-two guides are twenty-five women. It is remarkable that these female teachers are not mentioned in the Tibetan translation of the Gandavyuha. In the same way as guru devotion is a sensitive issue in modern Western society, in Tibetan culture at the time of translation it was apparently not appropriate to mention female teachers. However in the early years of Tibetan Buddhism, women did have high positions, according to Lama Caroline. She sees the sculptures of Borobudur as a snapshot of what Buddhism was like back in the eighth century. From this image we can tell that at least until the time of the construction of Borobudur enlightened women occupied equally high positions in Buddhism.[8]

Many stories in this book show how Lama Gangchen takes care of his friends and disciples and how he helps them with their spiritual development. People particularly feel the impact of being connected within the mandala of the guru during significant life events. Being in the guru's mandala also implies that you are there for each other when needed, that you offer help to one another as a spiritual family.

The following stories about sickness, birth, marriage and death show the importance of the guru in the lives of these sangha members. Florence Roulleau speaks about her marriage and the wish for a child. For Petrus Linnemann, who died in 2015, Borobudur referred to something external, as well as to an internal state. The story of Anouk de Best is about relying upon the guru. Anneke Tabak shares with us what happened when her daughter became seriously ill and died. Betty Voon connects different worlds in various manners. And finally, Lidy Haarman tells us about the dying process of her friend Pia.

---

8 LINKS VI *'Borobudur 2014' World Congress - An Education for the Third Millennium*, p. 88, Lama Gangchen Peace Publications

Mathias Nguyen Tat and Florence Roulleau on their wedding day

Child of the sun and the moon
Florence Roulleau (1969) France

What do you do if the man you love chooses to live with his guru? Florence Roulleau decided to give up everything that was important to her to join him.

Giving up dreams

"When I first met Mathias[9] around twenty years ago, he was very clear about two things: he didn't want to marry and he didn't want children. He was quite serious about this. His sister even showed me a jotting he had made when he was only six years old, where he had written that he would never ever have children. It was a deep conviction, much deeper than I could have presumed. But I was in my early twenties, and I fell in love with the man, not with the family man he was to become, so I didn't bother so much. Some years later, when we were in our early thirties, Mathias met Lama Gangchen

---

9 Read Mathias Nguyen Tat's story in Chapter 10.

through his sister Annabel[10], and soon he decided he wanted to follow Rinpoche and live with him in Albagnano.

Again, for me, there were only two options: either I stayed behind and we would split, or I would follow him to live with his guru. This was all very difficult for me. My autonomy, which I projected in my car, my flat and my job as a social worker, was very important to me. Previously, I had given up the dream of getting married and having children. Now, I also had to sacrifice these anchors in my life. And not just that: to follow the love of my life, I had to leave my family and friends behind in France. It was almost too much. But I loved him, so I decided to join him and in June 2005 we settled in the small village of Albagnano, up in the mountains near Lago Maggiore where Rinpoche had established his center."

A wedding in Tibet

"At first, it was difficult, but fortunately, Rinpoche helped me out and he somehow 'persuaded' Mathias to marry me during a pilgrimage in August that same year. 'You travel by road from Kathmandu to Lhasa,' he said, 'and then, you will get married in Tibet!' Mathias agreed, and to me, this was a very important statement. So we made this beautiful trip, passing by many important holy places. I had bought a Tibetan dress for the wedding in Tibet, and from the moment we had arrived, every day I asked Rinpoche: 'Should I wear my wedding dress?' For several days in a row he would look at me, seemingly thinking it over, and say, 'No, not today...' But one day he took us to this small Borobudur temple in Tibet, which looks similar to the stupa in Indonesia, and that day he said: 'Today you will get married.' I picked flowers from the field around this sanctuary for the wedding ceremony, wore my dress and Rinpoche married us during a small but beautiful ceremony. I was extremely happy and grateful for this and it much strengthened our relationship; we became a strong couple. But still there was this other issue.

Sometimes I expressed my wish to have a child, and also his sister Annabel mentioned this every now and then to Mathias in an airy way, but he was determined. No baby for him! Then Rinpoche

---

10 Read Annabel Nguyen Tat's story in Chapter 1.

started to work on this part, 'Why not have a baby!' he said to us, and slowly, slowly Mathias changed his mind until one day the decision was made. It was the year 2007; we had been married for two years.

I remember it well: Before, my periods were always extremely painful and I often even fainted because of the severe cramps in my body. But from the moment that Mathias decided we would try for a baby, the pains were gone! As if my body had been suffering from not being allowed to bear a child. Anyway, it didn't go easily after that. I became pregnant three times in two years, and three times I lost the baby within the first twelve weeks. It was devastating. The way I was treated in the hospital the first time was traumatic. I was there for a regular ultrasound scan, had my legs still spread, clothes not yet on, when the doctor said coldly that he couldn't hear the heartbeat and he walked out of the room while leaving me behind in agony.

That day, Rinpoche came to the house and felt my belly. He said that according to Tibetan medicine, the doctor had spoken too early; we should have faith and give it a chance. But I was already in shock and lost the baby anyway three weeks later. After the third pregnancy, in late 2009, the grief was too much and my body was worn out. We decided to stop trying for a while, also based on the horoscope that Rinpoche's student Francesco[11] had made. He said there was still a chance that I would conceive a child, but not that coming year, so we would take a break in 2010."

The eleventh Tara

"Annabel, who was very much concerned, told me about a dream she had in between my second and third miscarriage. She saw me walking in the fields, in a medieval environment, carrying a baby in my arms. I was crying, screaming even, because the child was dying of hunger. 'I will never ever have a child again!' I shouted. In the dream, Rinpoche told Annabel to recite the 21 Tara Prayers, so she did and she woke up with the eleventh Tara in her mind. When she looked up the meaning of this verse, she found that it was about hunger and poverty. To me, this dream showed me a possible karmic cause for my childless life and the difficulties in getting pregnant. It was somehow comforting and hopeful, because now that I was

---

11 Read Francesco Prevosti's story in Chapter 1.

with Rinpoche this karma could maybe be solved in a quick manner. In 2011 we decided to give it another try. In February, we joined the Borobudur pilgrimage once again, and every day when I reached the top, I touched the mother stupa with my head and I prayed deeply to become pregnant. This was the right time. This was the right place.

One day, at the top, Lama Caroline surprised me suddenly by giving me a pregnancy test kit while laughing in her typical way. We were ready for it. It couldn't go wrong anymore. After Borobudur, Mathias continued with Rinpoche to Nepal and I went with some friends to Bali for a couple of days. I was convinced I had conceived, but to my disappointment, on the 8th of March, International Women's Day, on the flight back home, I started to menstruate. I moved on to Marseille, to visit some friends and family, but I knew my cycle and I knew when Mathias was to come home. Though my friends tried to persuade me to stay a bit longer, I had to be there that very moment. Mathias came straight from the journey with Rinpoche, so he was fully in bliss and harmony when we met. It couldn't have been a better timing. And indeed, that very day I became pregnant."

In the mandala of Lama Gangchen

"This time the pregnancy was nice and smooth, and nine months later our daughter was born, at a very auspicious moment when the sun and the moon were in a perfectly harmonious position. It was not easy: her heartbeat was not reacting as it should in correspondence with the contractions and the doctors decided she had to be delivered by caesarean section. I panicked, but Mathias told me to do Tara mantras, and that somehow calmed me down.

As soon as she was born, Mathias started to do the Guru Puja. Fortunately she was fine, a healthy yellow-skinned baby with a thick mop of black hair. We called her Yoko, which means: girl of the sun. In Tibetan Buddhism, the sun symbolizes the female energy. Rinpoche gave her the name Nimda: Child of the sun and the moon. Tibetans believe that if you are to be born as a girl, you choose the father, not the mother. Yoko Nimda chose Mathias to be her father. But actually she has two fathers, because she was lucky to be born in Albagnano, inside the mandala of Lama Gangchen Rinpoche."

Lama Gangchen with Daniel Calmanowitz, Petrus Linnemann and Liana Casagrande on their day of ordination

Absolutely in heaven
Petrus Linnemann – Sangye Chöpel (1949 – 2015) England

For Petrus (Pete) Linnemann, Borobudur was an internal state and he was intensely grateful to Lama Gangchen for this experience. Less than a year before he passed away on August 25th 2015, he told his story.

My heart opened in Dharamsala

"Around 35 years ago I left England. I didn't really have a plan but just followed my intuition. I had a deep inner certainty that I didn't want the security of a job or a career. I couldn't hold one down. So first I travelled overland to Greece, Turkey, Iran and then Afghanistan. I already felt more at home there. Then I moved on to Pakistan and India. 'What the heck am I doing here?!', I thought. 'Let's study Sanskrit. That may be good for my inner development.' But it was too hot.

Somebody advised me to go to Dharamsala, because there was a nice Tibetan community there to experience and explore. So I went there and I was delighted to find that every experience and every memory I could catch, suddenly fell into place. My heart opened there, it was a big homecoming. I stayed for almost a year. I worked, smoked, partied, and did my first retreat with Lama Zopa. That was my first Gelug experience. From there I went back to England and joined in the building of a Buddhist college where I stayed and moved around for 35 years. I met my two wives there, my children grew up there, my oldest friends live there and still I go back there."

Something grave

"Meanwhile, in 1996, I met Lama Gangchen, and later moved to Albagnano. I first joined the journey to Borobudur in 2009. With this great and exciting adventure ahead of me, I was quite busy with all kinds of things. By then I had already moved to Italy, and I went back to England for a health check and some family business. Then back to Italy. When I took off for Borobudur a couple of days later, I had a bit of a cold. On the way, and during the stopover in Bangkok I watched a couple of movies, ate a big meal, had a massage and felt pretty miserable. But arriving in Borobudur felt like coming to a place that was so safe, welcoming, familiar and secure that I was able to relax completely. This 'relaxing' took the form of a total collapse of my immune system; I contracted pneumonia and had to lie down for a week outside the conference room, our gompa. Physically, I was in a bad state, had difficulty breathing, a high fever and couldn't move, but mentally I was happy as Larry! Absolutely in heaven!

I had experienced this before, in India: my body falling apart but mentally being happy. This state had lasted for around two years, and it appeared to have been a good preparation for what was happening to me now, because this was nearly terminal. Rinpoche said, 'We try not to leave you here.' This is something grave, I thought. It indicates the grave...

Rinpoche told the group: if you are a healer, a doctor, or anything else useful, please feel free to give Pete a hand in this situation. So I was lying there outside the gompa, on a mattress – Dawn protecting my head, Manuela sitting at my feet, while around twenty people very enthusiastically came to give me Reiki, Shiatsu, homeopathic things. Somehow it was quite forceful.

So that is how time passed. Weak like a baby, I couldn't breathe, couldn't walk, but I had no fear. Dying or not dying: it was unimportant. I have had plenty of dying experiences before, and now it was the same. But I was very aware that Rinpoche was taking care of me and that it was a delicate situation."

From better to better

"Rinpoche told Dawn to ask me to write a will. But she was afraid it would make me scared, so she said that Rinpoche had asked me to write something. So I thought Rinpoche wanted me to write something about my experiences, but obviously I was not in a position to write anything at that moment. When Dawn told me later what Rinpoche had really meant, I said: 'Dawn! For heavens' sake!' But of course they protected me, taking any possible fear away. Good old them!

Anyway, it wasn't my time yet because, by the end of the retreat, I was strong enough to travel on to Kathmandu with Rinpoche. In Kathmandu I recovered further and later I flew back to Albagnano.

It was a good experience; the internal experience got from better to better. It was sickness with great meaning, a great purification."

Becoming a monk

"In 2011, I received another opportunity to go to Borobudur. This time I was no longer Pete; I was Sangye Chöpel. Talking about making the decision to become a monk, it sounds very interesting. An old friend of mine once said, 'If you are on a journey and you reach a point where you cannot see clearly where you are heading – if you are kind of in the dark – you have to make a plan. The more information you have, the more difficult the decision. But if you have the whole panorama in front of you, you don't need to take decisions, you just put one foot in front of the other and you won't fall into the bog.

One day I was speaking to Rinpoche about my life as a child, my religious life as a Roman Catholic, my relationship with the church. And we talked about my lack of ability to engage in religious practices. I remember explaining that even having been a Buddhist half of my life, with many lamas, teachers, pujas and sangha, it didn't change anything regarding my reluctance towards sadhanas, practices and temples. At this point Rinpoche indicated, 'monkhood.' This was the greatest gift I could receive.

Becoming a monk changed every aspect of my life. When I arrived in Borobudur, I had already received the name, the blessings and the robes from Rinpoche in his house at Albagnano, in the presence of several monks from Shar Gaden Monastery in India. It was on Shakyamuni Buddha's birthday. In Borobudur, Khyen Rinpoche from Shar Gaden Monastery gave us our vows. I was ordained at the same time as Liana and Daniel, Lama Michel's father. It was a moving event.

For me Borobudur felt like a natural ground for my spirit. It was not something secondary. I remember I went up to the top of the stupa alone. It was not my intention, but somehow I didn't catch up with the group at the right time. I expected to meet up with them on my way down because apparently I was early, but even that didn't work out. However, it was a very gentle experience making this kora by myself."

Borobudur is inside

"A third visit never happened because, ever since that visit, my Borobudur is in Albagnano. Borobudur is more inside than outside. For me it is like a landing, an arrival, an accomplishment. Before I went to Borobudur the first time, I was offered a piece of land in England where I would have been able to grow my own food. I never got it because I decided to move to Albagnano. But Borobudur has a similar resonance. It is a place where you can grow something, where we can share some kind of fruits. In fact, I relate it to a feeling in the mist of my memory, of something that was there even before Borobudur was built.

I came from a very secure background, but I never owned a home, I was homeless but Rinpoche offered me Borobudur. Borobudur is home. That is quite a good thing to say. Home is safety, family, food... A place where you can shut the door. That is what I feel."

An ordeal
Anouk de Best (1989) The Netherlands

Anouk the Best was born into a family that follows Lama Gangchen. In April 2010 she travelled with her guru to Borobudur because he told her this was important. However, she had to overcome something and the journey took an unexpected turn.

The last chance

"My first journey to Borobudur was a kind of ordeal. I was challenged to step out of my comfort zone, to give up my safety nets and to have faith.

It all started in Albagnano, February 2010, I was nineteen. Lama Gangchen told me that he would make an extra trip to Borobudur with a small group of people, separate from the main retreat. I should join him, he explained, because this could be the last chance to experience this. Lama Gangchen finds it important that his adepts come to Borobudur at least once in their lifetime. Well, I hadn't yet been there ...

One or two weeks before the journey, my aunt Toet[12] who lives in Albagnano, called me about the dates and itinerary. She said that Rinpoche wanted me to join him and the group on the plane that would leave from Italy to Indonesia and not from Holland where I live. After I hung up, I looked at my school schedule. It appeared that I would have exams precisely during that week and that I would also miss the first week of the last trimester. It was the year before my final year in university for my Bachelor's degree.

This was, by itself, a great effort of practice, because for me it was simply not done to miss out on school. I have been quite an academic fanatic since I was young. Never had I even missed a test. I had always earned good grades, I was always well prepared and followed the rules, being a good girl. To follow my guru and join him travelling to Borobudur implied that I had to skip three exams! These were three exams I could catch up with by the end of the school year, but then I would have only one chance to succeed. If I failed them, my whole planning for the following academic year would be messed up and

---

12 Read Toet de Best's stories in Chapter 3 and Chapter 4.

my regular visit to Albagnano during the summer holidays would be at stake. In brief, thinking over this situation, I was stuck.

It took me so much effort, I had to think it over again and again, but I conquered my fears and myself and came along. Jan de Ruiter sponsored me, because I couldn't afford the trip myself. By itself, Borobudur didn't really appeal to me, as I felt more of a connection with Nepal and India, where I had been as a child. If Rinpoche had not told me to go, my interest wouldn't have been aroused. However, by then I was quite happy that I had been given the opportunity.

We travelled in a small group from Italy to Indonesia. I enjoyed the first ten days. The group was nice, the people were pleasant; it was intimate and we had the chance to spend a lot of time together with Rinpoche. The *United Peace Voices* vocalists were also present for filming, which was special. But it was not until the last two days that Borobudur really got me. As we walked through the stone galleries, I looked around at the images on the panels and suddenly I was overwhelmed with a strong sense of joy and happiness. This was really special. It had taken some time for it to happen."

An ash cloud covering Europe

"Then the time arrived for me to travel back home. I would land in Milan on Saturday and continue to Holland the next day; then I would go back to university on Monday. It was important to arrive in time, because I had already missed one week of lessons and was only allowed to skip one more hour. Otherwise I would have to repeat the whole trimester the following year. My college was very strict about this.

We flew from Yogyakarta to Jakarta. I remember that I was walking hand in hand with Rinpoche when Lama Caroline told us that she had heard about a volcanic eruption in Iceland and that this had had quite some impact on the air traffic. It seemed okay, as Iceland was a long way away. We took note of the information and checked in for our flight to Dubai. All went well but when we arrived in Dubai, we found out about the actual turmoil that the ash cloud had caused. We heard that practically all air traffic to Germany, Holland and France was shut down. Heaps of people were stranded all over the place. It wasn't certain at all that we could continue from Dubai to Milan. The ash cloud was slowly moving towards Southern

Europe. Eventually we were allowed to take off, but it was a close call. We were on the last flight that was allowed to land in Milan.

Hence our journey was flawless, whereas others who had been heading from Borobudur to Europe before and after us were almost all stranded in Singapore or Jakarta. My aunt even had to wait ten days before she could move on from Yogyakarta. So far I had been lucky. However, I still had to find my way to Holland from Milan. Obviously my flight the next day had been cancelled. It was a tense moment, as I really had to make it home in time. There was a lot at stake. But whatever I tried – bus tickets, a train journey – there was no other itinerary to be found. Everything was fully booked because air traffic was impossible. I was increasingly worried but Lama Gangchen remained calm and relaxed. Although, he did say, 'You need to get to the university. That is very important, otherwise you get a problem.'

Well, what to do next? There was nobody in Albagnano who could drive me, because they were stuck elsewhere in the world. One of the few who had stayed behind in Albagnano was Kris,[13] a German. I went to see him there to let off some steam. When I told him of my problem he said, 'Oh, well, you can take a ride with me; I am heading to Germany by car tomorrow.' Well, that was a surprise! And that is how we went. Kris took me to the station in Munich. Fortunately I asked him to join me, because I had a gut feeling I should not enter the station by myself. And what happened? My bankcard didn't work when I tried to pay for my ticket. He took his credit card and paid for me. That night I was home in Venray around three o'clock and I was in class that same morning, in time, at eight thirty without having missed a single class!"

Experience what is possible

"This journey to Borobudur enhanced my faith in the guru for sure. It made me even more aware of how important it is to follow the guru. Before this trip, I had faith and I followed, but with great doubt. When you follow, you increasingly experience the possibilities that it brings along. Even though you may not see that on the spot. Someone else might say things all happened merely by chance.

---

13 Read Kersten (Kris) Dohmen's story in Chapter 8.

Like the fact that I was able to get a lift with Kris. Or the fact that our flight still went ahead while everyone else in our group was left stranded. However, for me it was an important experience. For example, if I had not listened and had flown from The Netherlands and not from Italy, I would never have made it back in time. Eventually, everything fell into place. Later that year I caught up with the exams I had missed, and I didn't have to repeat any classes during the following academic year."

The other end of the rainbow
Anneke Tabak (1959) The Netherlands
When her daughter became seriously ill, tough times began for Anneke Tabak. Hence, her retreat at Borobudur was completely devoted to her daughter Kim.

The Buddha museum

"Early in November 2013, I received a phone call from my daughter Kim. She had received the results of a medical examination: melanoma cancer with metastases in the thorax, pleura and brain. I had a kind of vision. I saw a brown plain faraway, just brown. For me it was clear; it will be short, she won't survive this. But she herself kept up hope.

Some weeks later, we were with Lama Gangchen and a group of people in the Buddha Museum in Traben-Trarbach, Germany. I asked Rinpoche whether I should go to Borobudur in February 2014. First of all, the money that I had reserved for the journey was consumed by the costs of my divorce. And now on top of that, my daughter was also ill. Rinpoche said, 'Yes, you go. And I will take care of her.'

We did Guru Puja in the museum. There were chocolate coins being put in a big bowl for offering. I remember Rinpoche saying, 'More, more, more', while someone was filling the bowl. It was a special moment and I was crying.

While leaving the museum, a German man from our group came to me. 'Anneke, I want to pay for your ticket to Borobudur. When I entered here this morning, I saw you standing there and this was the first thought that came to my mind. The idea occupied my mind during the whole day and I really want to do it.'"

A heavy burden

"Some months later the moment arrived. My retreat in Borobudur was fully dedicated to Kim. I went there to help her. Every day I climbed the stupa with the puja text and a picture of Kim in my rucksack. But that rucksack felt so heavy. It was as if I carried her in person on my shoulders up the stairs. After a few days I went to Rinpoche with her picture. I thought maybe he needed it. Rinpoche looked at it, blew over it and whispered some prayers. He called Lama Michel and Lama Caroline and they did the same. Afterwards, I got the picture back while he said; 'Now it is okay.'

When I called Kim later that day, she said, 'Mom, I went upstairs alone and showered all by myself!' This was indeed special, because she was pretty much exhausted by all the cancer in her body and the insults this caused her. For weeks she hadn't been able to climb the stairs and cope by herself in the bathroom. She slept downstairs and washed in the kitchen. Also my rucksack felt lighter now: it was as if the burden was shared.

Another morning I came down from the stupa, and I wasn't able to move; I simply couldn't leave the place. I started crying, almost hysterically. I felt so lonely and abandoned. Then Daniel came to me, Lama Michel's father. Apparently he had also stayed behind. He held me for as long as it took for me to calm down and until all my tears were shed.

Later, during a Rabne-Chenmo ritual with the monks, I had a similar experience. I cried and cried; all the tension of the preceding months came out in that moment."

Carry together

"In the months afterwards, Kim's situation was getting worse. Rinpoche and the sangha were very supportive. Rinpoche said I shouldn't carry this all by myself. He also said I should stay close with two friends from the sangha who live near my town. I am not sure whether he talked to them as well, but from then on they were there for me all the time!

When Lama Caroline came to Holland for a workshop she

dedicated the weekend to Kim and me. She also helped me a lot together with her partner Eleanor. They both told me about all kinds of things one could do when people are sick or dying.

Kim was not a Buddhist. When I was with her, I did the Self-Healing and the mantra 'Om Mani Peme Hung' in silence. But when during the final stage, she was very much in pain and the morphine wasn't sufficient any more, I was allowed to use my voice and sing for her. That made her calm and relaxed, and in that way she could bear the pain.

Some weeks before she died Kim said, 'Mom, when I am gone I hope to see my pets that have died again at the other end of the rainbow.' One of her pets, a cat, had only recently passed away. I said, 'You might see your cat, but the others won't be there anymore. But you can see an emanation and that is Rinpoche. Listen very carefully to what he tells you because he will show you the way.

She died on June 11th, 2014, at thirty years old. That evening we had been doing the Self-Healing with the Northern Dutch sangha in our friend Jany's house. During meditation there was intense silence, the energy was equal, stable. Afterwards we drove home and there was a double rainbow in the sky. Immediately I knew: the moment has arrived. At home I grabbed some things, lingered a bit, and then drove off. She passed away just before I arrived, while her boyfriend was taking a nap, around one in the morning. I phoned the nurse and asked if they could leave her alone until I arrived, because I wanted to do a ritual. I recited all the preliminary prayers aloud in her room. Every now and then the nurse peaked around the corner and asked, 'Are you okay?' 'Yes,' I replied. 'Am I making too much noise?' She said, 'It has never been quieter in this ward and nobody is screaming with pain, so please continue.'

When I finished all the prayers I looked at Kim and thought, Hey, you are already gone! You are no longer in your body.

Two days later we dressed her and put on her make up. I did this together with Marjolijn, who is also in our sangha. In the meantime, we sang the *bardo*[14] prayer about twenty-five times I guess. While we were busy, the big light in the room switched on by itself and got

---

14 Intermediate state. This starts when the mind finally separates from the body (death) and ends at the moment that the consciousness enters the next life body (rebirth).

brighter and brighter. Then when we were finished, it switched off again and there was only the light of two table lamps like before."

A halo around the sun

"Rinpoche had said from the start that he couldn't cure Kim, but we could help to make it all a little easier for her, and that is how it went. She was so positive up to the moment shortly before she died. Five days before she left us we barbecued together, and she even sat at the table for a minute.

In February 2015 I went to Borobudur again. I had taken some of Kim's ashes with me, in a Tupperware container wrapped in a khata. Rinpoche told me precisely which day I should bring them to scatter at the stupa. Exactly on that day, a halo appeared around the sun. And that is how we experienced many special events.

In May 2015 Lama Michel gave extensive teachings about Self-Healing in The Netherlands. It was a four-day course and on the last day I cried and cried the whole day long. It was because only then did I fully realize the power of Self-Healing, and the power of what I had been able to give to Kim thanks to Rinpoche and Buddhism."

Connecting worlds, feeling togetherness
Betty Voon (1971) Malaysia

When Betty Voon is at Borobudur she experiences her mind as calm and clear. She sees clearly how to tackle her problems and getting up early is no problem at all. Since 2010 she has been increasingly involved in working for Lama Gangchen.

A large Buddha at the top

"The first time I came to Borobudur was in 1992. I was 21 years old. There were only about twenty pilgrims that time. Later, I found out it was the year that Lama Gangchen got the inspiration for Self-Healing. At that time I had no clue; I was simply there, being awed by the stupa and trying to understand more about Lama Gangchen's teachings and practice. We were only doing preliminary practices, we didn't start very early and we climbed the stupa for no longer than one hour a day, though sometimes we would go back up again in the late afternoon just before it closed. That was it. I remember that it was a nice experience because the stupa seemed to change all the time; the silhouette, the colors. I could imagine a big Buddha on the top.

The second time I came with my mother in 1995. There were already many more people by then. I was quite in shock, because I hadn't expected it. After that and up to the present time, I have come many times, always skipping two or three years. In the beginning things were easy, you could come and go whenever you wanted and the program wasn't so full."

Scientists and intellectuals

"But from around the year 2000 things changed. The retreat became more intense; we focused more on the practice. Nowadays we leave very early in the morning to climb the stupa, and in the afternoon we have teachings and conferences. We need to create something positive together, and we also need to hear from people on an intellectual and scientific level. Meanwhile, they also need some spiritual input. It is amazing to see how Rinpoche manages all these things. Borobudur seems an excuse, but things happen there. The energy is there, our minds are busy and we open up many things.

Whenever I am at Borobudur, I always become aware of the things that occupy my mind, and I want to deal with them. This problem, that problem; I am very much aware of what I need to get rid of. In the early years, I was still an infant somehow. But my mind always became very clear, even when I was tired. When I close my eyes there, my mind seems extremely bright. I have interesting dreams there that make me feel calm and relaxed. And I never have a problem getting up early. All that is only the case at Borobudur."

Travelling with Rinpoche's brother

"In 2010 I started to become more active helping out with different things for Rinpoche. First, Rinpoche asked me to escort his brother from China to Borobudur. He is a monk from Tashi Lhunpo monastery and he doesn't speak any Chinese or English. Though I had long since been trying to study Tibetan, I had never really taken off with it except for a few basic words. I was informed what Rinpoche's brother's likes and dislikes were for food and drink, which was really helpful. The journey started with a slight glitch; we could not leave on the scheduled day and I had to call Rinpoche to inform him about the change in our itinerary. At first he thought I was joking when I told him the news.

We had to wait another three days before we could depart. I felt bad that we could not travel smoothly so I did Guru Pujas daily, hoping to purify whatever obstacles were there or yet to come, and to ask for the Gurus' blessings.

Finally a solution came, and we were able to move on to Borobudur. We travelled without any other problems; even the stopover at Bangkok was smooth. Lama Michel came to receive Rinpoche's brother at Yogyakarta airport and I was relieved to have accomplished the task successfully."

My mother got lost all the time

"Coincidentally that year, I had planned to meet my mother at Borobudur so I could spend some time with her as I was living in China then and she was alone in Malaysia. Due to my delay, my mother had arrived before me at Borobudur, and every day she would ask Rinpoche's secretary Cosy if I had arrived yet. Later, upon my arrival I was informed that she couldn't find her way around the hotel and got lost all the time. When I saw her, I realized something was wrong with her. But I was also occupied with other things and I could not understand why she was behaving like that. When it was time for her to return to Malaysia, I sent her to the airport and was hoping that she could manage the journey. What I didn't know then was that she was exhibiting the first signs of Alzheimer's. It took me two years to accept her disease, and even now I still tend to see her as she was before, even though she has changed. Right now I am back in Malaysia looking after her."

Karma yoga

"In 2011, they asked me to take care of the gompa in the Manohara hotel at Borobudur. I agreed, but it was all very new for me. You have to take care of the flowers, the offerings, the food and drink. Suddenly

I was the gompa coordinator and it felt like a big responsibility, so to avoid making any mistakes I did a lot of work there. I did not know how to delegate. Our friend from Italy, Ariella, helped me a lot in this, as well as many other kind and wonderful vajra-brothers and sisters from around the world. I felt a strong bond with our group and I was really overwhelmed by the closeness that we share despite the distance between continents and cultures. In Borobudur we are all one.

Lama Gangchen helping the workers at the stupa

In 2014, I was also supposed to help out in the gompa, but then a Chinese group came and they needed help with interpretation. As I could speak Chinese, I translated for them. It was very busy and chaotic, but also satisfying to be able to help them.

Whenever Rinpoche travels to Tibet with a group, I try my best to join them. Then, I also help the Westerners to communicate with him. Usually, only Lama Michel speaks Tibetan, but when I am there we don't have to bother him with all minor issues because many Tibetans also speak Chinese.

It brings me joy to help people communicate with each other. You help them interact, not only between different languages, but also between different cultures. It feels good that I am given the chance to help create a connection between people. Also to translate for Rinpoche and our group gives me the opportunity to watch closely how he communicates with his friends, disciples and other people. By translating I get to see how he works. I stay a little bit to one side and at the same time I have to be very precise and careful about how I translate, so that they really and deeply understand each other. So it is nice but also scary, because if I were to make a mistake, I would feel terrible.

I don't feel that I am specifically a translator, or that I am specialized in any kind of job. I feel more like a gap filler: wherever there is some work that needs to be done, I can step in to help out, as long as it is something that I am able to do."

Pia's ashes
Lidy Haarman (1956) The Netherlands
Lama Gangchen played an important role over the last two years of Pia's life. Her friend Lidy Haarman tells us about it.

Contact with Rinpoche

"In 2010 we had a special mission. A good friend, Pia, had passed away after a long illness with cancer after undergoing a double transplant. Two years before she died, she met Lama Gangchen and she visited him twice in Italy. She was also practicing Self-Healing.

This gave her much strength to cope with her disease and with the coming of the end of her life. On her deathbed, she had a lot of contact with Rinpoche on an energetic level. She communicated with him through a picture that she kept with her all the time.

Nico and I guided her and cared for her very much during her dying process. In that period, she asked Lama Gangchen through us whether to be cremated or to be buried. Her husband had died some years earlier and he had been buried. Lama Gangchen's advice was the following: 'The advantage of cremation is that you can do various things with the ashes, like making *tsatsas*[15] or taking small amounts to holy places.' Her wish was to follow Rinpoche's advice and this is what happened.

We brought a small portion of her ashes to Borobudur and sprinkled them on the stupa. Rinpoche told us to put very small amounts in many different places. While we were doing this during the Self-Healing, he blessed the ashes, sprinkled them with water, and blew on them. This was also a deeply moving experience. I could sense Pia's presence very close to us at that moment. I admired her total surrender in the last phase of her life. Later, we took some of her ashes to Tibet and her daughters took some to Nepal."

Nico and Lidy with Pia's ashes

---

15 Votive clay tablets, usually with an image of a Buddha.

Photo by O. Kurkdjian (ca 1895-1915)
collection Rijksmuseum, The Netherlands

Chapter 10

Ocean of

Mandalas

Meditating at home

Rinjun Dorje (1972) from The Netherlands is a disciple of Lama Gangchen and a practitioner of NgalSo Self-Healing. He explains, "Early in the morning I sit on my meditation cushion. I close my eyes and imagine being at Borobudur, at the place where we usually gather. I make prostrations, do purification mantras and preliminary prayers. I concentrate on Lama Gangchen and visualize that an emanation of the guru comes and sits on a lotus in my heart. The lotus petals close around him. At the same time I visualize that the guru – as a person – holds my hand and takes me with him around the stupa.

While he is guiding me, I perform the NgalSo Self-Healing practice. At the base of the stupa we open the lotuses in our chakras, and at the first level we visualize the seed syllables and elements in the lotuses. This happens inside me, but it also happens on the stupa. I see the 92 male and 92 female Buddhas on each side of the mandala. I see their colors and their hand gestures. On the highest gallery I see the 64 Vairochanas with their female consorts. And Lama Gangchen accompanies me all the time in this meditation, taking me with him, up the stairs, each time to a higher level. I endeavor to do the complete visualization of NgalSo Self-Healing in this way, until we reach the tenth level, the mother stupa, symbol of enlightenment.

Some years ago, we did the practice of the *Great Mothers* together with the male Dhyani Buddhas at Borobudur. Ever since, I do this integrated practice daily at home. In one way or another, the visualizations of the Borobudur practices are easier for me than any other practice."

Inner science

Lama Gangchen often compares the Buddha with a scientist. He calls him the 'inner scientist'. The Buddha shows us how you yourself can be a laboratory where you can perform alchemy – where you transform poison into medicine and where you can develop love, compassion, wisdom and inner peace.

In recent years, Western science increasingly acknowledges the effects of meditation on human beings. Studies have been conducted that show results like people being able to concentrate better or become less stressed. Those studies focus mainly on mindfulness-meditation, or *samatha* – calm abiding. Lama Michel is happy that meditation in the West is becoming increasingly accepted and applied. However, he also notices the emergence of a misconception. According to him meditation is one of the most powerful methods to eliminate our negative aspects and to develop our qualities to their maximum potential. "But most of the time we use meditation only as a method to relax. This is wonderful in itself, but it is only a small part of what we can achieve with meditation!" Lama Michel explains that the most important objective of meditation is to familiarize ourselves with positive states of mind like love and compassion, in a way that these feelings become deeper and stronger.[1]

In the Vajrayana practices the techniques of mindfulness are also used, but numerous other techniques are also applied like various forms of analytical meditation, Vipassana, visualization, mantra, mudra and special breathing techniques.

What do we do when we practice NgalSo Self-Healing?

When we do the practice, either at home or at Borobudur, we loosen the knots that constrain our chakras, dissolve blockages, throw negative energy away from us and receive the healing energy of the Buddhas in our chakras. NgalSo Self-Healing is extraordinary because, at first sight, it seems simple and practicing it is easy for anyone.

Often Lama Gangchen makes his disciples do meditations or mantras without any explanation beforehand. This prevents us from

---

[1] Lama Michel, December 13th 2015, Teaching: *Noble Minded Answers to Wholesome Questions*, part 21, AHMC, Albagnano, Italy

Lama Gangchen performing mudra of union

using our rational and intellectual mind too much. We can simply experience something by singing along and making the mudras.

Children usually also like the practice very much. Even though we don't understand much in the beginning, we can sense there is something positive happening internally. When we look further and steadily start discovering the deeper meanings, we find that NgalSo Self-Healing comprises an ocean of ancient Buddhist wisdom and meditation techniques from Tibetan Vajrayana Buddhism.

Channels, winds and drops in the mandala

The Tibetan Vajrayana practices assume that we have a gross as well as a subtle body and mind. The subtle body and mind consist of tens of thousands of channels, drops and winds. The chakras are the energy centers from which these channels radiate out. The winds and drops have different functions and move through the channels.

Lama Michel teaches us that this channel system resembles our nervous system and the winds match with the energy impulses that flow through the system.[2] He suspects that the drops are related with the hormones in our body.[3]

When we do the Self-Healing meditation, we visualize that we have a central channel that starts at our crown and descends to the base of our spine, with two thin parallel side channels. Many channels go out from the chakras at our crown, throat, heart, navel and perineum. These channels divide first into 72 branches, then into the 72,000 channels in our whole body.

As shown in the example of Rinjun Dorje, the outer mandala - in this case Borobudur - helps us to experience our inner mandala. In this way, the five Dhyani Buddhas are connected to the five

---

[2] Lama Michel, March 17th 2015, Teaching on Borobudur stupa mandala, Indonesia
[3] Lama Michel, May 14th - 17th 2015, Teaching: *NgalSo Tantric Self-Healing Commentary,* Diessen, The Netherlands

main chakras in our body and the 72 Buddhas in the stupas on the higher part of Borobudur represent our 72,000 channels. Like us, Borobudur has a central channel that culminates at the top of the mother stupa; the place where we can experience enlightenment on a very subtle level.

Through intense training in various techniques from Vajrayana Buddhism, guided by a qualified teacher, it is possible to control and navigate the winds and drops in our channels. This is important because our emotions 'ride' on the winds that flow through the channels. So if we could manage to absorb the winds into our central channel, we would no longer be driven by attachment and aversion. In that case, we could experience great bliss and emptiness. This is exactly what occurs during the dying process. When we die, the winds and drops are all absorbed in the central channel. In this sense the top of the Borobudur stupa mandala also represents the dying process, where the winds and drops come together into the central channel.

Lama Gangchen explains, "The stupa mandala can be read as a very detailed map of the human mind. From its grossest and most impulsive state ... until we eventually achieve the highest level of human development; complete enlightenment and the awakened Buddha nature, a crystal clear state of mind."[4]

Multi mandala

Lama Gangchen sees Borobudur as an ocean of mandalas; the stupa mandala is suitable for every Vajrayana practice, including the extensive *Kalachakra* practice.[5] Lama Gangchen states that the Buddha gave the Kalachakra transmission for the first time on the exact spot where Borobudur was later built. Moreover, he is not the only Tibetan who takes this view. According to Lama Gangchen, in ancient texts many of the Tibetan great masters already referred to Borobudur as the place where the Kalachakra Tantra was transmitted: "In fact, Borobudur has been cited at different moments by a great master called Tubwang Lobsang Trinley. He wrote a very important

---

[4] Lama Gangchen, T.Y.S. (1997) *The Borobudur Stupa Mandala NgalSo Self-Healing*, p. 5, Lama Gangchen Peace Publications

[5] Lama Gangchen, T.Y.S. (2012) *Seeds for Peace V - Lalitavistara Mahayana Sutra*, p. 361, Lama Gangchen Peace Publications (This publication includes an extensive list with practices that can be performed on the Borobudur stupa mandala.)

Buddhist dictionary which talks about Sri Danakot – the place where Buddha gave Kalachakra teachings for the first time; it is also described as being like Borobudur here – Palden Drepung. Many other lamas: Lhunpo Lama Rinpoche, and even Pabongka Rinpoche in his texts, also commented on Borobudur."[6]

Hence Borobudur as a whole forms a three dimensional Kalachakra mandala – Lama Gangchen and Lama Caroline are currently investigating its precise meaning – but it is also suitable for less complex practices. Lama Gangchen interprets the three round tiers on top of Borobudur with the 32, 24 and 16 stupas plus the mother stupa, as representing the practice of Guhyasamaja with its 32 deities, Heruka with 24 deities and Yamantaka with 17 deities (16 plus 1) respectively.

Meanwhile, we have been introduced to the NgalSo Self-Healing when we meditate on the male Dhyani Buddhas that are positioned on the four sides of the stupa.

A second NgalSo Self-Healing practice exists, which is connected to the female Buddhas. On Borobudur, these Great Mothers are found in the alcoves next to each of the male Buddhas. They are connected to the elements earth, fire, water, wind and space. The space mother Akashdevi is related to Vairochana, the fire mother Pandaravasini is related to Amitabha, the water mother Mamaki is related to Akshobya, the earth mother Lochana is related to Ratnasambhava and the wind mother Arya Tara is related to Amoghasiddhi.

While we meditate on the mothers, we purify our inner elements as well as the elements of the surrounding environment: from Borobudur we focus on all directions and the center of the earth.

Once in your life to Borobudur

One can perform NgalSo Self-Healing without ever visiting Borobudur. One can even do the practice without knowing anything about Borobudur. However, Rinjun Dorje's story in the beginning of this chapter illustrates how helpful it can be to actually practice Self-Healing on the Borobudur stupa mandala, even just once. He shows how you can bring everything together at home in your

---

6 *LINKS VII 'Borobudur 2015' World Congress - An Education for the Third Millennium*, p. 20, Lama Gangchen Peace Publications

Self-Healing on the stupa

meditation place: the Self-Healing, the Guru and Borobudur. By knowing the outer mandala it is easier to open the inner mandala. Borobudur shows you the way. Lama Gangchen urges his disciples to visit Borobudur at least once in their lifetime. Many people claim that joining the Borobudur retreat has made their practice at home stronger, clearer and more effective.

World Peace Stupa

Lama Gangchen sometimes calls Borobudur the World Peace Stupa. One of the effects of practicing NgalSo Self-Healing is to develop greater inner peace, which in the words of Lama Gangchen "is the most solid foundation for world peace". He summarizes the complete process of Vajrayana practices as follows: "The main point in Indo-Tibetan Vajrayana is purifying one's *five aggregates*[7] (one's body and mind) and transforming one's five principal mental energies of ignorance, hatred, desire, pride and fear into five pure minds of wisdom, stability, equanimity, discrimination, plus the ability to accomplish whatever positive project one wishes. These are represented by the five Dhyani Buddhas: Vairochana, Amitabha, Akshobya, Ratnasambhava and Amoghasiddhi. This is yoga, an inner scientific view and a method for human development. ... With

---

7 A person consists of five aggregates: form, consciousness, feeling, discernment and compositional factors. Each of the five Dhyani Buddhas is connected with one of the five aggregates in its pure state.

positive thinking, mudras, mantras, breathing and so on we try to heal our bodies and minds and imagine that world peace increases."[8]

The following stories are about the meditation practice. First, Professor Paola Muti speaks about her preparation for scientific research into NgalSo Self-Healing. Following her account, other sangha members with different ways of practicing tell their stories. Mathias Nguyen Tat meditates on a daily basis and couldn't consider living without it anymore. Lidy Haarman explains how the outer mandala helped her in her meditations. Nico Smith shows how he combined studying the philosophy with the Borobudur retreat and practice. Kiran KC experienced a series of hefty hospital admissions – Buddha, dharma and sangha helped him during his illness. Dharma singer Tiziana Ciasullo shares how Lama Gangchen taught her the first mantras and the first mudras of NgalSo Self-Healing.

Scientific research into NgalSo Self-Healing
Paola Muti (1956) Italy

We introduced medical scientist Paola Muti earlier on in Chapter 7. Together with some other scientists she is preparing an international scientific research project into the effects of NgalSo Self-Healing on physical health. She visited Borobudur for the first time in 2016.

A different approach

"Borobudur allowed me to think more about the NgalSo Self-Healing research project that I am involved in with some colleagues in the sangha. The experience made me truly believe that we should have a different approach towards the causes of disease. We will do scientific research on Self-Healing with breast cancer patients who are not undergoing treatment.

From a scientific point of view we have very few instruments to investigate the influence of the mind on physical health, so we

---

[8] *Seeds for Peace IV – Homage to Borobudur: Ocean of Mandalas* (2011), contribution by Lama Gangchen: *Discovering the Meaning of Candi Borobudur,* p. 351, Lama Gangchen Peace Publications.

are looking carefully at that. NgalSo Self-Healing is a complex meditation method.

We do not know exactly how it will go, but I am expecting that it will at least follow a similar path to what I have seen in my research into environmental factors in relation to inflammation."

Effect on inflammation

"We will look at inflammation, which is a cause of many diseases. We know that the causes of chronic inflammation are very much connected to negative lifestyles. Due to the relationship between mind and health, NgalSo meditation may correct these causes.

So we will investigate if NgalSo Self-Healing has an impact on inflammation in the sense that the inflammation diminishes. That is our hypothesis, though this is only one aspect. There are a thousand ways to look at the impact of NgalSo meditation on physical health.

If the predicted effect of NgalSo Self-Healing is demonstrated regarding inflammation and the chronic diseases that come from inflammation, then we can assume that other diseases will follow the same pattern, the same impact. That is what I expect. So in this way we look at the association between the mind and health, or the mind and body."

An appointment with the five Dhyani Buddhas
Mathias Nguyen Tat (1967) France

The life of Mathias Nguyen Tat is completely interwoven with meditation. In Albagnano he also feels the power of Borobudur.

Psychotherapy wasn't sufficient

"The first time I met Lama Gangchen there was a Rabne Chenmo puja. This is an extensive ritual that lasts for at least three days, during which all the holy statues, objects and places are blessed by the monks. While I was present there, many negative thoughts and anger came up about this puja. I was ashamed and told Lama Gangchen. 'No problem,' he said. 'You put the thoughts and anger into space and you do Self-Healing.' That is how I started the Self-Healing practice.

Mathias Nguyen Tat 'The meditator'

Once a week, on Monday morning in my house in Marseille, I had a kind of appointment with the five Dhyani Buddhas. And every time I felt better and more relaxed afterwards. Prior to that, I had followed traditional psychotherapy. That therapy was more conceptual: What was my story? Why was I how I was? And so on. After an hour talking, I felt somehow better and happier, but something was missing. I failed to get in touch with my deeper emotions. I couldn't manage to transform them.

From that time on, I gradually started to do more meditation. Soon after, I moved to Albagnano with my girlfriend Florence[9]. And then I went to Borobudur for the first time, alone, without Rinpoche, to visit my sister Annabel[10] who was there. Lama Gangchen instructed me how to perform Self-Healing on the stupa. At that time, I didn't know much about it and thought it might be difficult. But eventually it turned out to be rather easy; it is all quite clear. When you are on the stupa, you can tell that it is the source that everything comes from. It all makes sense, with the ten levels, the four corners, the various Buddhas and deities. Borobudur *is* Self-Healing with the five Dhyani Buddhas."

---

9 Read Florence Roulleau's story in Chapter 9.
10 Read Annabel Nguyen Tat's story in Chapter 1.

The lights are fully on all the time

"But it was not until I did the practice in Albagnano again, after returning from the journey, that I discovered the deep effect of Self-Healing! I need to do Self-Healing more or less daily to calm my mind and my negative emotions. Besides that you can also experience effects that are not described so distinctly in the books. Self-Healing really works on your subtle body: the three channels, the five chakras, the drops and winds. It is possible to gradually discover and shape the subtle body within the gross body. And it is due to this experience that I value the meaning of Borobudur and the NgalSo Self-Healing.

So this all happens in Albagnano and I personally believe that Borobudur is also there. Of course I like to go to Borobudur in Indonesia with Lama Gangchen. In my opinion, he truly switches on the lights when he gets there. And when he is gone, the lights don't go out, but for sure the energy changes. However, in Albagnano all the lights are fully on all the time! The energy remains the same, twenty-four seven, whether Rinpoche is there or not. In the temple there I feel much more, there is full energy. In my view, Rinpoche has transported the mandala from Indonesia to Albagnano.

I started to meditate because I wasn't able to deal with my inner suffering. I longed for healing on a deep level. For years, I did half an hour of Self-Healing with the five Dhyani Buddhas and fifteen minutes of Self-Healing for the environment with the Great Mothers every morning. And each day before lunch, I chose one of the other practices, which then took me another hour to do – for example, Singhamukha, Medicine Buddha, Tara, Kalachakra, Maritse, *etc*. Finally, I discovered that Self-Healing is contained within all these practices, and in fact you are performing Self-Healing all the time when you practice these sadhanas."

Opening the channels

"With practice, you can open your central channel, discover the other channels and gradually start to sense the chakras, drops and winds in your subtle energy body. This is important because by arousing the drops and winds, you can experience a sensation of deep peace.

It is a feeling that is impossible to compare with anything I know. Not even with what I experience after an hour of running, during yoga, when having a meaningful conversation or any other kind of positive experience. It is an incredible experience of concentrated peace in parts of your body. When you perform Guhyasamaja or Kalachakra, for example, you can have this special feeling in different points of your body that are within the practice. It feels as if something peaceful enters the body from outside, peaceful radiation like a healthy kind of x-ray. It is true what Lama Gangchen sometimes says, 'I am only a small lama, but you can have great experiences with me.' To me, these experiences indicate the value and meaning of Borobudur. To me, Borobudur is more than a holy place by itself. It is a holy place thanks to the Guru. He gives you the blessings in the right parts of your body. We need the Guru and the lineage to be able to experience this."

Western yogis

"When Lama Gangchen says that we are the NgalSo lineage, I feel very happy and fortunate. It means that we Westerners are creating our own lineage, through this NgalSo Self-Healing. That is why we can all be researchers! We are capable of looking with a scientific eye, simply because of our cultural background. This NgalSo lineage has still to be established, and we all carry a kind of laboratory inside us. My hope is that in the future, we may all become 'researchers'; modern Western yogis."

Lidy Haarman

An intense sensation of warmth
Lidy Haarman (1956) The Netherlands

When she went to Borobudur for the first time, Lidy Haarman never expected to experience anything special like the others around her did. Then something happened to her that she didn't see coming.

Not really my path

"The first time I met Lama Gangchen was in 2001, in The Netherlands. My husband Nico[11] has known him longer, and he had already visited him in Italy. My first impression was positive; however it remained kind of distant. I didn't feel immediately that this would be the path for me to follow. However, from that moment on I started to meditate and recite certain mantras. Also in the beginning, I asked an inner question during a workshop with Lama Gangchen about whether I should quit my job. Time was passing by and it took until the end of the weekend for the answer to come. 'Don't quit but take a sabbatical!' I arranged that immediately the next day and it worked out really well.

In the following years, Nico became a serious practitioner and

---

11 Read Nico Smith's story further on in this chapter.

spent quite some time in Italy. That was not always easy for me. Sometimes I had my doubts, but I didn't want to quit because in that case I was quite sure I would lose Nico. On one hand our relationship influenced my spiritual path, but on the other hand Nico's spiritual path influenced our relationship.

After a couple of years things calmed down and, slowly, my connection to Lama Gangchen and Buddhism became stronger. When we went to Borobudur for the first time in 2009, I had already been practicing the Five Great Mothers – the Self-Healing for the environment – every day for several years.

Then something completely unexpected happened, because I never had these mystical experiences as you sometimes hear about from other people. At the airport in Yogyakarta we were picked up by a taxi, and after about forty minutes we approached the stupa. The taxi took a turn and in the distance I suddenly saw the top of Borobudur peeking out above the trees.

This moment I will never forget; it was as if Borobudur energy flew straight into my heart from up to down – an overwhelming, intense feeling of warmth around my heart. The closer we got, the stronger the feeling became.

Finally, when you are really close, you see a part of the stupa once again. Then the sensation increased and got even more intense, and this continued for the whole retreat. Every morning when we made the circumambulations on Borobudur, a new very subtle layer was added to this feeling. This first meeting touched something essential; a basic feeling that is usually not so easy to connect with. Even when thinking about it now, the feeling starts coming back. It was mainly an experience of great respect, but it was also touching and a great feeling of gratitude."

Being part of the mandala

"My subsequent visits to Borobudur always made me feel sheltered, secure, like coming home, and I experienced a deepening in my practice. I come from a traditional Catholic family with eleven children. Somehow, I never really managed to comprehend the Buddhist practice. It remained like something alien but thanks to my Borobudur experience this has changed.

Usually we practice the Self-Healing with the five Dhyani Buddhas – the male Healers, while making the circumambulations at Borobudur. But one day we combined this with the practice of the five Great Mothers. To me, this was an important experience. Suddenly everything fell into place, and I felt part of the mandala. The practice is more settled in my body now, instead of it being something external.

The pilgrimages to Borobudur have brought me more inner strength. It contributed much to my personal development. My self-esteem has not always been very high, but the Borobudur energy has made my self-confidence grow.

Lama Gangchen blessed our wedding vows once again in 2012 at Borobudur, and to me this was like the crowning of Nico, me and the thirty-years of our relationship. We both went through very different processes and we still do, but now we are able to share our experiences, which is beautiful."

Emptiness is something so beautiful!
Nico Smith (1958) Netherlands

Nico Smith has Multiple Sclerosis (MS) and it seems as if this disease only motivates him to meditate more, to deepen his study of dharma and to help others. He tells us about his experiences studying emptiness and about his unconventional path.

Intense fatigue

"In 2009 I visited Borobudur for the first time. The physical aspect was intense. Sometimes I was so tired that my only concern was how to put my left leg in front of the right. Being in this special place, I had to learn how to deal with intense fatigue. And, as is often the case with Lama Gangchen, I had to find my way in this all by myself. Eventually I started doing my Vajrayogini[12] practice. I asked Lama Gangchen and he told me to sit on the western side of the second square level, because there it is most shady. During the practice there I had all kinds of realizations, but in fact it was not so very different

---

12 A female Buddha from the highest yoga-tantra.

Nico Smith

from practicing at home, where I also do many meditations. It was a continuation of my daily practice and because I was in a different environment without any distractions, there was a strong focus."

Study

"During a subsequent visit, I intensely studied a book about emptiness for three days; *Ocean of Nectar - the true nature of all things* by Geshe Kelsang Gyatso.[13] I knew I had to bring this voluminous book to Borobudur, as well as a thin booklet by Zen teacher Thich Nhat Hanh,[14] *Form is emptiness, emptiness is form;* a commentary on the *Heart Sutra*.

I started at five in the morning in my hotel room and didn't stop until late at night when everybody was back home. I almost got sores from sitting for hours and hours. After I finished the six hundred pages, I read the thin book of 56 pages by Thich Nhat Hanh. I realized the content was exactly the same. But I also realized that I couldn't have drawn this conclusion if I hadn't read both. Hence, one cannot say, 'skip the *Ocean of Nectar*, to read the small book is enough.'

For me the practice always goes together with study. It is a com-

---

13 This is an important commentary on Chandrakirti's *Guide to the Middle Way,* which explains the aspect of emptiness according to Nagarjuna. Chandrakirti was an Indian Buddhist scholar from the seventh century. Nagarjuna lived between 150 and 250 AD in India and was one of the founders of the Madhyamaka school - the middle way - of Mahayana Buddhism.
14 Vietnamese Buddhist Zen-master and peace activist who is known worldwide for his powerful lessons and publications about mindfulness and peace.

bination. By practicing one can attain a certain realization, 'a flash of the mind' as Lama Gangchen calls it. But to truly penetrate the meaning of that insight requires time and study. The point is to recognize what manifests in the mind. For example, if you have never read anything about *tummo-fire*,[15] it may appear in your body but you won't know how to use it. Within the tummo-fire one can burn any negative aspect of the mind. This causes a sensation of bliss, which is short-lived however. In the realization of emptiness, the experience of bliss goes much deeper. So reading *Ocean of Nectar*, having the discipline to take the time and space to study emptiness, brought so many fruits in the years that followed. Through this effort the experience of bliss may be less spectacular, though it becomes much deeper.

Emptiness is something so beautiful, it is such a wonderful concept, but it can also be a tough one when studied along the lines of the philosophical schools. In our meditation group, I sometimes meet people who have great difficulty with it. Then I like to play with forms; so that I can also recommend them a small booklet like Thich Nhat Hanh's."

To the top with a urinary infection

"One of my most important experiences in relation to Borobudur – which also has to do with emptiness – was as follows: One can feel like, 'Pfff, no way am I able to make the climb up there.' The other extreme is, 'Well, let's see about that, whether I can make it or not.' But with an attitude like, 'Let's give it a try,' emptiness can manifest. Then miracles can occur, things that one never expected to happen. So for me, the fact that I reached the top in spite of a urinary infection, even though I had to pay several visits to the toilets downstairs in between. Or the fact that while I was exhausted after a long flight, long days, short nights, all of a sudden a large group of Tibetan monks manifested around me, while I was in deep meditation."

Swimming against the tide

"When I was diagnosed with MS during the 1990s, I knew there was something deeper beneath and I started my search. In 1999 this led

---

15 The inner fire energy of the body that is located around the navel chakra.

me to Lama Gangchen and I felt I had come home again. I had been searching for such a long time, even already in previous lives. So I was thrilled, but it hasn't always been easy. In the meditation center in Italy, I was often called up because of my unconventional behavior that accompanied my meditation. For example, sometimes I had an odd body position or made strange noises. But I always follow the instructions that I receive internally from Lama Gangchen.

Sometimes I feel – not lonely, but – as though I am swimming against the tide. Like when Rinpoche was in Holland with the Buddha's relics and we all had to step forward to receive the blessings. I was in deep meditation and couldn't do anything else but stay where I was. I followed the internal instructions that were given to me as usual. After everybody had been to Rinpoche, he came to me and gave me the blessings on my head. For me this proved that it was okay.

A German man came to me afterwards. He cried and said, 'I need to apologize because I was so angry that you didn't get on your feet. But later I heard you are ill.' In that moment we were interrupted. A couple of years later I talked to him again and I was able to tell him how things really are and how things work for me."

In the mandala of the Medicine Buddha
Kiran KC (1965) Nepal

Kiran KC received a second life within this lifetime due to a liver transplant. He tells us about his illness and how the practices, Lama Gangchen and the sangha have helped him in this process.

The guru's advice

"In December 2011, I lost my voice for a while. I was in Italy in Lama Gangchen's center and people there gave me all kinds of advice, pills and creams. There was so much help but nothing really worked. Eventually I went to Rinpoche and asked him for advice. He told me to go see a doctor at home in The Netherlands where I live, to check my blood. That didn't sound logical to me, but I went to see my general practitioner and asked for a blood test. He wasn't very keen. 'What needs to be tested then?' he asked. I didn't have a

clue, so I told him it was my guru's advice and that my wish was to follow this. The blood test took place and showed some abnormal liver values. Another test was required but that would take a while, because in the meantime I would be travelling for two months in Indonesia with my partner Karin Zwaan.[16] At the end of this journey we were going to get married at Borobudur, during the retreat with Lama Gangchen. Rinpoche had told us this was the best place for a marriage ceremony. The wedding was very special. To be honest, I was quite anxious about it, the two of us in front of this big group of people. But in the end, much to my surprise, we were with eight other couples in front of Lama Gangchen. It was a beautiful and festive ceremony.

Liver cirrhosis and a tumor

"Back at home the medical exams continued and finally they discovered I had severe liver cirrhosis caused by the hepatitis C virus. Though I didn't feel sick yet, the doctors were quite concerned about the situation. And so they should have been, because they later discovered a tumor in my liver. By then I had started to notice some effects of liver failure. Because we were in time, the tumor could

---

16 Read Karin Zwaan's experience in Chapter 6.

be removed quite easily. In July 2013 I went to the hospital thinking I would be back home after three days.

But things turned out completely differently. A part of the tumor had remained behind so I immediately received a second treatment with local chemo. That was too much for my weak liver and I was poisoned. I developed a severe delirium of which I remember very little. What they told me is that I refused to eat or drink, that I was confused and aggressive, that I spoke only Nepalese and didn't allow them to insert a drip.

This awful situation lasted for days and all that time Karin, Nico, Lidy[17] and some other friends from the sangha did mantras and meditations by my bedside. My room in the hospital was decorated like a sort of gompa; they showed me pictures of Lama Gangchen and told me to accept everything that happened. Each night Karin stayed with me in my room."

Lama Tsongkhapa

"When my brother-in-law Henk managed to get me to drink some orange juice, I suddenly came back to my senses in a miraculous way. Everybody was so happy and relieved and we had ice-cream immediately! They asked me what I had experienced and I told them I had heard singing and I had seen Lama Tsongkhapa. Now I don't remember that anymore.

After this intense experience I started doing much more Self-Healing and mantras than I used to before: the mantra of the Medicine Buddha, the Vajrasattva mantra, guru yoga. I started doing the mantra of Buddha Shakyamuni while I visualized golden light and nectar flowing through all my organs, as well as to the viruses and bacteria in my body. Meanwhile I was on a waiting list for a donor liver.

Six months later, January 9th 2014, something completely unexpected happened. I had a brain stroke. The aneurism in my head could be closed during an operation and again I found myself admitted to the hospital, for three weeks this time. Some days after the operation Lama Michel came to visit unexpectedly; he happened to be in Holland. I was still in intensive care and I was so happy when

---

[17] The stories of Nico Smith and Lidy Haarman are found in this chapter as well.

I saw him. This visit gave me so much support and strength to recover. Fortunately the brain stroke didn't leave any negative effect. All my functions remained intact."

'Doctor Blokzijl speaking...'

"Some months later, on April 10th 2014, early in the morning at five o'clock, the telephone rang. 'This is Doctor Blokzijl speaking. We have a donor liver for you. Please come to the hospital – but don't rush, take it easy.' This phone call is etched on my memory. My suitcase had been packed ready for months. Within a few minutes we were in the car and drove the hundred kilometers to the hospital. On the way we did mantras, also for the donor. In the hospital, just before I went into surgery, I called Lama Gangchen. He gave me some mantras and his blessings. He helped me to be completely relaxed and calm for the operation.

I saw the operating room as the center of the Medicine Buddha mandala. The doctors, anesthetists, assistants and nurses formed the family of the Medicine Buddha. This was how I had imagined the hospital during my previous admissions and now I saw it like this again. While I went into the nine-hour operation, Karin and her sisters, Irene[18] and Inge, were given a family room in the hospital. There they did practices once again and they performed the Guru Puja."

Second life

"The operation went well and so did my recovery. In this way I received a second life within this lifetime. I am so grateful to Rinpoche, the sangha, family, friends and all the workers of the hospital for how they helped me during this illness. For me these three intense hospital admissions already seem like a long time ago, but I realize that it is part of a great transformation in my life. Since the transplant I haven't made it to Borobudur yet – I don't feel ready for it. But if I go again, it will be when Lama Gangchen is there as well, because he brings the monument to life. He opens your third eye when you are there. He makes you feel the spiritual truth."

---

18 Read Irene Zwaan's story in Chapter 5.

Dharma Singer
Tiziana Ciasullo (1968) Italy

Tiziana Ciasullo was one of the first to learn the NgalSo Self-Healing from Lama Gangchen. Ever since that time, she has been singing the mantras and transmitting them to others. Currently, she is president of United Peace Voices and she is working on a record label and a number of publications.

Joyfully singing, learning like children

"When I met Rinpoche, I was very young – in my early twenties. One of the first things he said to me was, 'You are a dharma singer and a dharma teacher.' Even though I was very musical, I had never sung before. But Rinpoche made me sing the 21 Taras and all kinds of traditional practices and prayers from the moment I met him. Strangely I had the capacity to memorize all the words and melodies easily in Tibetan, Italian and English. So in this way, wherever we travelled, mainly I and another disciple, Carmen, had to sing the practices and show the mudras to the people so they could join in.

Not long after I had joined Rinpoche, he started to teach us Self-Healing. He introduced this in a center in Velletri near Rome, shortly after he had met the holy Pope there, John Paul II. I took this as a sign that there was some kind of blessing in it, as if there was a connection.

We started learning Self-Healing without any explanation. First we were just singing and making the mudra of the lotus opening. Rinpoche gave us a melody. *O-om mani peme hung... O-om mani peme hung... Om ma-ani pe-eme hung... O-o-om mani peme hung... O-o-om mani peme hung.* Then, slowly, he added the mudras of the five Dhyani Buddhas. Then the words came, and everything with this same melody, which was catchy and helped us to learn. Purification of the elements: Eh Yam Ram Lam Bam. Seed Syllables... Lotus flowers... Colors... Buddhas... Every evening we sat together in the gompa in Milan where Rinpoche lived back then. We were like children, joyfully singing and slowly learning the practice.

It took quite some time before we started to get an explanation, for example, about the meaning of the five principal chakras. First he gave us the music, the mudras and the mantras and in this way

The young Lama Michel with Tiziana Ciasullo

he gave us the transmission. From the way I know Rinpoche, I think he didn't want us to use the intellectual mind, but he wanted to go straight to the essence. Then you can relax and receive the blessings. Later you can start to understand it."

"Lama Michel has arrived!"

"Not much later in 1993, I went to Borobudur for the first time, and it was the first time the group went there after Rinpoche had introduced the Self-Healing method to us. But before Borobudur we went to Brazil. I remember Daniel[19] and Bel[20] picking us up at the airport. Rinpoche introduced me to their son, a young boy of eleven years old, 'This is a lama incarnation', Rinpoche told me. That is

---

19 Read Daniel Calmanowitz's story in Chapter 6.
20 Read Bel Cesar's story in Chapter 6.

how I first met Lama Michel. I didn't know about his existence until then. But now, as soon as Rinpoche had said this, I felt a strong wish to help him. I stayed near him all the time. He showed me the tree house he had built in the garden and I showed him Self-Healing.

As for Lama Michel, after Borobudur, he would continue on to Sera Monastery in India. He had already been recognized when he was five, but Rinpoche had advised his parents to let him go to a normal school first. One day he would decide to go to the monastery, Rinpoche had told them, and now this moment had arrived.

So he also came to Borobudur and I was happy to see him again after having met in Brazil. Nobody called him Lama yet. I remember when he arrived, I received him with a khata, and I said loudly, so that everyone heard, 'Lama Michel has arrived!'

That time at Borobudur, Rinpoche traditionally cut a piece of his hair and gave him his monk's robes. Bel asked me if I would take care of her son and make sure he ate well while we were traveling together, and Daniel asked me to ensure that he took a regular shower. From then on, I started to take care of him in my Southern Italian women's way. In fact that is what I do to this day!

During that retreat, Rinpoche started to show us the Self-Healing on the stupa mandala. He showed us all that we had already learnt by heart. Now we saw the correspondence between the mudras and mantras. We saw the symbols, the lotus flowers and the Dhyani Buddhas. The Self-Healing came alive on the stupa. It was obvious that Rinpoche had not been inspired by the stupa; he already knew how to use the mandala as soon as he saw it. It is like driving a car: when you don't know how to drive, it is a bit difficult. But Rinpoche had been driving this car for thousands of years, so he was confident."

The real work is inside us

"In those days I wasn't very aware of the law of karma, the fact that causes and conditions come together, that actions have results. Twenty-five years ago I chose my life by intuition to serve Rinpoche and Lama Michel. There was something very strong, which was connection. Since then, it hasn't always been easy, because sometimes your body asks for a normal life, like having children or making a home for yourself, or being alone sometimes. This is normal: we are human beings, not enlightened yet. But I know that when I made the choice to live not only for this life but also to prepare for the next, I made the right decision.

Maybe it sounds easy to live so close to the gurus. But a strong connection with the lamas is not a guarantee that you are free from suffering. What you have to understand is that, in the end we are on our own. You have to make your decisions on your own. You have to grow on your own. You have to change your mind on your own. The truth is that we are alone, guided by our emotions and that is what we have to work on. That is why we need a guru.

Up until now I have been to Borobudur seventeen or eighteen times and I can say that something has started to grow. Being there in that amazing place is beautiful. Receiving the blessings, feeling the holy energy and even being able to keep that feeling in your mind, in your memory, is all very helpful, because we need to awaken our spiritual mind of love and compassion. But the real work is inside us."

Practicing Self-Healing

Thomas Nitzsche, holding the umbrella

Epilogue

The

rainbow picture

Thomas Nitzsche from Germany took the picture of the double rainbow above Borobudur in March 2013. It was early morning after the extensive Buddhist Rabne Chenmo ritual guided by Lama Gangchen had been finished. The sunrise around the equator is very brief; the morning sun broke through the dark and cloudy sky and a vivid rainbow suddenly appeared.

Thomas moved back a bit from the stupa entrance to a spot from where he could photograph the complete rainbow. Because of the wide angle, it took three shots, which were later put together. It was lucky that the visitors present at the stupa mandala had just moved out of sight – so the picture shows the sheer stupa mandala.

Thomas, "One can take a rainbow as an indication for an auspicious moment. Lama Gangchen Rinpoche told us to recall the situation prior to and at the appearance of a rainbow. This helps us to strengthen our faith through our own experience.

When a rainbow appears I see it always as a precious moment, especially in times of difficulties, because it reminds me to consciously choose a positive perspective. The light is extraordinary and one can sense harmony among the elements. It reminds me also of the constant presence of holy beings; it is as if they give us positive feedback."

Biographies

Lama Gangchen Rinpoche

T.Y.S. Lama Gangchen Rinpoche is the holder of an ancient and uninterrupted lineage of Tibetan masters that goes back to the time of Buddha Shakyamuni, more than 500 years before Christ. Based on Buddha's teachings and inspired by Borobudur, he developed the NgalSo Self-Healing meditation method especially designed for modern people. At present, he has over one hundred centers and study groups where Inner Peace Education and NgalSo Self-Healing are practiced and studied.

Lama Gangchen Rinpoche was born in Tibet in 1941. At a very young age, he was recognized as an incarnated Lama Healer. When he was five years old, he was ceremonially enthroned at Gangchen Chöpeling Monastery. At twelve, he received the *kachen*-degree, which is usually only granted after twenty years of study. From age thirteen to twenty, Lama Gangchen studied medicine, astrology, meditation and philosophy in the two most significant monastic universities of Tibet: Sera and Tashi Lhunpo. He also studied tantra and secret healing-methods guided by H.H. Trijang Rinpoche and Zong Rinpoche.

In 1963 he left Tibet due to the political situation and started studying at Varanasi Sanskrit University in Benares, India. In 1970 he received his *Geshe Rigram*-degree – comparable to a PhD – in Buddhist philosophy at Sera Me Monastic University in southern India.

Since finishing all his formal studies, Lama Gangchen has dedicated his life and activities to sharing this precious knowledge with everybody interested in inner development and healing. For a while he worked as a Lama Healer among the Tibetan community in Nepal, India and Sikkim, where he cured many people and saved many lives. For part of this period he served as private doctor to the royal family in Sikkim.

In 1981 he visited Europe for the first time and, in that same year, he established his first European center: Karuna Chötsok on Lesbos,

Greece, where he planted a *bodhi* tree in the 'Buddha Garden'. This marked the beginning of a long series of peace activities and initiatives in places all over the world.

Since 1982 Lama Gangchen has lived in Italy where he has been granted citizenship. From that time, he has traveled the world intensively to give teachings, to transmit his ideas on peace education and to give healing. He also conducts numerous pilgrimages to important holy places in Nepal, Tibet, Indonesia, Mongolia, *etc.*

Moreover, he advocates integration of Tibetan and Western medicine. In 1995, he initiated the *United Nations Spiritual Forum for World Peace – a solution for the third millennium* under whose auspices several congresses and activities are held.

Since 1998, the Albagnano Healing Meditation Center was established at his place of residence in Albagnano, Italy. Here as well is the Temple of Heaven on Earth, which is related to Borobudur, where daily meditations for world peace are performed and numerous Buddhist teachings and workshops are organized.

Lama Michel Rinpoche

Lama Michel was born in Brazil in 1981 to a family with Jewish and Christian backgrounds. When he was five years old, he was recognized by Lama Gangchen as a *tulku* – a reincarnation of a Tibetan Buddhist lama. Lama Gangchen had been invited by Lama Michel's mother Bel Cesar to visit and teach in Brazil, where she and Lama Michel's father Daniel Calmanowitz later established Lama Gangchen's first center in the country.

At the age of twelve, Lama Michel decided for himself to enter the monastic life. He moved to Southern India to live and study in the monastic university of Sera Me. During the twelve years that followed, he received formal education of Buddhist practice and philosophy according to the Gelugpa tradition of Tibetan Buddhism.

In 2004, he moved to Italy to live with his root guru Lama Gangchen. Since then, he continues his studies, traveling to Tashi Lhunpo

monastery in Shigatse, Tibet each year to visit his teachers there.

He oversees several Buddhist centers including Kunpen Lama Gangchen in Milan, Italy, Albagnano Healing Meditation Center, in Albagnano, Italy and Centro de Dharma da Paz in Sao Paolo, Brazil.

Lama Michel dedicates his life to transmitting the dharma; he teaches about Tibetan Buddhist practices and philosophy in many different places, contexts, and dharma centers all over the world. Lama Michel is known for his profound and crystal-clear teachings on Tibetan Buddhist philosophy. With his clarity, wisdom and a pragmatic mind, he imparts the deep ancient Tibetan knowledge in an extraordinary way that perfectly reveals its meaning and value for contemporary life.

Lama Michel is lineage holder of the NgalSo tradition.

Lama Caroline

Lama Caroline, Dorje Kanyen Lhamo, was born in England in 1965. As a child she was fascinated by science, astrology and space exploration. From 1986 to 1991 she studied Gelugpa Buddhism in Cumbria, England, with Geshe Kelsang Gyatso. In 1991 she met Lama Gangchen Rinpoche and, impressed by his open modern approach to spirituality, she began to collaborate and study with him.

Since then she has accompanied him on numerous journeys and pilgrimages worldwide, she has helped him with writing all his books and she teaches about Buddhist philosophy, tantra, medicine, yoga and astrology.

In 2000, Lama Caroline was recognized in Tibet by Lama Gangchen as Lama Dorje Khanyen Lhamo and since then she is - together with Lama Michel - lineage holder of the NgalSo tradition.

She has a diploma in Inter-Religious Studies from the Open University (UK), an MA (with merit) in Buddhist Studies from the University of Sunderland (UK) and currently studies Tibetan and Sanskrit.

Glossary

Bardo Intermediate state. This starts when the mind finally separates from the body (death) and ends at the moment that the consciousness enters the next-life body (rebirth).

Bhumi Literal meaning: 'ground' or 'stage'. The ten bhumis refer to the development stages a bodhisattva goes through on his or her way to enlightenment.

Blessing The energy of gurus, holy beings and holy places that helps sentient beings on their spiritual paths and creates the conditions to transform body, speech, mind, activities and qualities.

Bodhichitta Mind of enlightenment. The deep wish to reach enlightenment with the objective to help all sentient beings.

Bodhisattva A person who has the unchangeable, spontaneous mind of bodhichitta and is still in the process of perfecting his or her body, speech, mind, quality and actions. Bodhisattvas continuously work on their personal development in order to be able to help others in an optimum way.

Buddha A person who has reached enlightenment; this means that his or her body, speech, mind, qualities and actions are perfected, and that he or she is no longer led by mental defilements and their imprints.

Chenrezig Buddha of Compassion.

Deity A being considered holy, divine or sacred. Deities occur in various religions. In Buddhism, deities usually represent manifestations of Buddhas.

Dharma Spiritual 'medicine' that heals the suffering of body and mind. In Buddhism, it refers to the teachings and the inner realizations and experiences that are achieved.

Dharmadhatu Ultimate truth. The realm of experience where one perceives the true nature of phenomena.

Dhyana Meditative concentration.

Dorje See vajra.

Emptiness The concept that everything is empty of inherent existence. This is the absolute nature of all phenomena. In Tibetan Buddhist philosophy, developing insight into emptiness – by study and through experience in meditation – is a method to eliminate suffering.

Enlightenment Complete liberation. A state of the mind in which a person is all-knowing and has developed infinite wisdom, compassion and power.

Five aggregates A person consists of five aggregates: form, consciousness, feeling, discernment and compositional factors. Each of the five Dhyani Buddhas is connected with one of the five aggregates in its pure state. Vairochana is connected with form (the body), Akshobya with consciousness, Ratnasambhava with feeling, Amitabha with discernment and Amoghasiddhi with the aggregate of compositional factors (personality).

Five Dhyani Buddhas Archetypical meditation Buddhas who represent the five wisdoms in their perfected state. The position of the Dhyani Buddhas in the mandala of Borobudur is as follows: Akshobya in the East, Ratnasambhava in the South, Amitabha in the West, Amoghasiddhi in the North and Vairochana in the center.

Five great mothers The female Buddhas who are connected to the five elements. They are the consorts of the five Dhyani Buddhas. Mamaki is connected to water and to Akshobya. Lochana is connected to earth and to Ratnasambhava. Pandaravasini is connected to fire and to Amitabha. Tara is connected to wind and to Amoghasiddhi and Akashdevi is connected to space and to Vairochana.

Five wisdoms Each Dhyani Buddha represents one of the five wisdoms.

Akshobya has perfect *dharmadhatu* wisdom: the pure state of the mind, free of defilements.

Ratnasambhava has perfect wisdom of equality: the ability to recognize that all phenomena are the same: one taste in emptiness.

Amitabha has perfect wisdom of discernment: the ability to recognize differences.

Amoghasiddhi has perfect all-realizing wisdom: the state of mind free from doubt.

Vairochana has perfect mirror-like wisdom: the ability to perceive all phenomena at the same time.

Gandavyuha The Gandavyuha is part of the Avatamsaka Sutra and narrates the pilgrimage of the young merchant's son Sudhana who meets more than fifty spiritual guides – bodhisattvas – on his path to enlightenment. Among them are Maitreya, Manjushri and Samantabhadra. Literal meaning of Gandavyuha: Sutra of The Entry to the Realm of Reality.

Gelugpa One of the four traditions of Tibetan Buddhism. The Gelugpa lineage was founded by Lama Tsongkhapa (1357 – 1419). The NgalSo tradition belongs to this lineage.

Gompa Prayer hall, temple.

Guhyasamaja A highest yoga tantra practice to develop inner peace, in which 32 deities each have a place in the mandala.

Guru A spiritual teacher who conveys to his or her students the correct methods for going beyond suffering and for perfecting body, speech, mind, qualities and actions.

Guru Puja An extensive practice with recitation, visualization and meditation. This prayer ritual, which usually is performed frequently and commonly in monasteries and Buddhist centers, is important in the Gelugpa tradition. The text and melodies were written and composed in the seventeenth century. It is an overview of the teachings of the Theravada, Mahayana and Vajrayana traditions. The heart of the Guru Puja is formed by the 'tsog' offering to the assembly of all the holy beings to nurture our connection to them.

Heart Sutra One of Buddha's Mahayana sutras about emptiness, an essential concept in Buddhist philosophy.

Hinayana The small vehicle. This form of Buddhism focuses on the liberation of the individual.

Impermanence The constant transformation of phenomena.

Inherent existence The according to Buddhist philosophy wrong view of reality is to think that phenomena exist from their own side, independently of causes and conditions. The correct view of reality is that phenomena are empty of inherent existence. Everything exists in interdependence.

Jatakas and Avadanas Jatakas are stories of the earlier lives of Buddha Shakyamuni, sometimes as a human, sometimes as an animal. In each of these tales, he develops a specific quality. There exist hundreds of Jatakas, some of which are depicted on Borobudur.

Avadanas are similar stories in which the good deeds of the main character are related to events in subsequent lives.

Kalachakra Literal meaning: 'Wheel of Time'. A highest yoga tantra in which the microcosmos is related to the macrocosmos, this world is connected to Shambala and the possibility is offered to reach enlightenment in one lifetime.

Karma Literal meaning: 'activity'. Actions and their consequences. The process where actions of body, speech and mind with positive motivation bring positive results in the future. Actions that are performed with negative motivation lead to negative results. Actions done with neutral motivation lead to neutral results.

Karma yoga Those practicing karma yoga follow the path of unselfish actions and servitude. Karma yoga offers the possibility to turn all kinds of daily activities into meaningful practice.

Khata A traditional silk scarf with interwoven Tibetan Buddhist symbols, offered at various religious and social occasions.

Kora Ritual or ceremonial circumambulation around a holy place or temple. Buddhists usually make their koras clockwise.

Kuan Yin The female Buddha known in China as the Buddha of Compassion. Equivalent to the male Buddha Avalokiteshvara in Mahayana and Vajrayana Buddhism. In Tibetan: Chenrezig.

Lalitavistara Description of the life of Buddha Shakyamuni: How he was born as prince Siddhartha Gautama, how he gave up his comfortable life in the palace and reached enlightenment, and how he transmitted his first teachings in the Deer Park at Varanasi (Northern India).

Lama See Guru

Lama Tsongkhapa (1357-1419) Founder of the Gelugpa tradition of Tibetan Buddhism.

Lineage The series of spiritual teachers since Buddha Shakyamuni, from guru to disciple through the centuries up to the present day, who have transmitted the teachings of the Buddha following their particular tradition.

Mahakarmavibanga A sutra about the law of karma or the law of cause and effect. This sutra is depicted in one hundred sixty reliefs at the base of the Borobudur stupa that are hidden behind a thick stone wall. After the discovery by IJzerman, all reliefs were uncovered, photographed by Kasian Cephas in 1890 and 1891 and covered again. Two reliefs remained visible. The photos can be viewed on www.geheugenvannederland.nl (search for *verborgen voet*) or via http://bit.ly/28Jfgi0

Mahayana The great vehicle. Buddha's teachings on how we can reach full enlightenment for the benefit of all sentient beings. This can be achieved by either completing the gradual Bodhisattva path or via the quick path of tantra. This form of Buddhism is mainly found in Tibet, Nepal, India, Mongolia, China, Japan and Korea.

Maitreya The future Buddha of Compassion.

Mala A string of 108 beads that is used as an aid to meditative concentration and to count the number of mantras recited.

Mandala In Vajrayana Buddhism, a mandala forms an energetically pure environment in which one or more Buddhas reside. Borobudur is a three dimensional mandala of the NgalSo Self-Healing practice, in which the Five Dhyani Buddhas and the Five Great Mothers reside. At the same time Borobudur is an ocean of mandalas, representing many different Buddhas and practices.

Manjushri Buddha of Wisdom.

Mantra Literal meaning: 'mind protector'. A mantra is a series of sacred syllables with a deep meaning. Different Buddhas each have their own mantra. Reciting a mantra helps you to concentrate, to relax and to be protected. It brings you closer to the specific quality of the Buddha concerned.

Mental defilement Any aspect of the mind that – once it is activated – perturbs our inner peace. The most significant mental defilements are ignorance, close-mindedness, attachment, desire, anger, hatred, miserliness, pride, jealousy and fear.

Mudra Powerful hand gesture that helps to navigate the inner energies.

NgalSo Literal meaning: 'relaxation'. *Ngal* refers to all problems, stress and pollution of body and mind. *So* refers to relaxation, recovery and purification of the life energy.

Nirvana State of being free from suffering.

Omniscience All-knowing. The ability to directly and spontaneously know all phenomena simultaneously. Only Buddhas possess this ability, therefore they are called 'All-Knowing Ones'.

Rinpoche Literal meaning: 'precious'. Rinpoche is a title of respect and the form to address high incarnated lamas.

Rabne Chenmo An extensive Tibetan Buddhist purification ritual that lasts several days. This ceremony purifies and restores the relationship with the environment by the power of mantras, concentration, visualization and offerings.

Sadhana Literal meaning: 'method to accomplish'. Sadhana usually refers to the guidelines for a religious practice. A sadhana comprises the instructions for meditation, recitation and visualization.

Samsara The infinite cycle of death and rebirth in which lives are determined by karma and mental defilements. The only way out of samsara is along the path to enlightenment.

Sangha The spiritual company, ranging from the highest realized beings to the ones who are at the beginning of the bodhisattva path.

Shakyamuni The historical Buddha who was born around 560 years B.C. as the king's son Siddhartha Gautama in Lumbini (currently in Nepal bordering India). When he discovered how much suffering there was in the world, he started looking for a way out of suffering. By inner research and meditation, he attained insight into reality and reached enlightenment. He had disciples and started teaching on request. The sutras and tantras of the various traditions in modern Buddhism can be traced back to Buddha Shakyamuni. He is the founder of Buddhism.

Shambala The pure land of inner peace and world peace.

Shri Yantra The Shri Yantra consists of an interweaving matrix of geometric figures. A yantra is a symbolic representation of various aspects of a god or deity.

Stupa Originally a tomb for a highly-realized person. A stupa often contains relics and sacred objects. The stupa also symbolizes the enlightened mind of a Buddha. The complete Borobudur is a stupa by itself. The 72 bell-shaped constructions on the three highest levels are separate stupas.

Sutra Literal meaning: 'thread'. All Buddha's publicly transmitted teachings and methods.

Tantra The esoteric or 'secret' teachings of the Buddha that are followed in Vajrayana Buddhism, besides the sutras. The tantras are special practices aimed at transformation of body, speech and mind using mantras, mudras and visualizations. Tantra makes use of subtle psycho-physical energies to develop 'bliss and emptiness' or 'compassion and wisdom'.

Tantra can also mean 'energetic continuum': the mental stream that continues from life to life.

Tara Female Buddha, occurring in different forms. The green and white Taras are best known. Green Tara is connected to the wind element and is the consort of Buddha Amoghasiddhi. She protects from fear. White Tara is connected to long life. The 21 Taras – described in a popular prayer consisting of 21 verses – each represent a different quality.

Terma Literal meaning: 'treasure'. Ancient knowledge or methods stored in the consciousness of a master or in one of the five elements, to be recovered by a 'terton': a treasure finder.

Thanka Tibetan Buddhist scroll painting. The images of Buddhas and symbols are depicted following specific procedures and are used in meditations and ceremonies.

Theravada Literally: School of the Elders. This form of Buddhism is similar to the Hinayana path and is mainly practiced in Thailand, Myanmar and Sri Lanka.

Thich Nhat Hanh Vietnamese Buddhist Zen-master and peace activist who is known worldwide for his powerful lessons and publications about mindfulness and peace.

Three Jewels Buddha, Dharma and Sangha are the Three Jewels in which one can take refuge: the spiritual teacher, the spiritual medicine or teachings and the spiritual company.

Tsatsa Votive clay tablet, usually with an image of a Buddha.

Tulku A reincarnation of an important Tibetan teacher.

Tummo The inner fire energy of the body that is located around the navel chakra. Normally this energy regulates digestion and body temperature. With special yogic meditation this energy can be used to purify the subtle body, open the central channel and let the white and red drops flow through this channel, which causes great bliss. This bliss can be used to meditate on emptiness – the quick path to enlightenment.

Vajra Literal meaning: 'diamond'. An indestructible scepter. This ritual object – held in the right hand and used together with the bell in practice – symbolizes method: the masculine aspect. The bell in the left hand symbolizes wisdom: the feminine aspect. Combined they symbolize the union of bliss and emptiness.

Vajrapani Buddha of spiritual power.

Vajrasattva A tantric Buddha who is connected to purification practices. For example, one purification method is to recite the one-hundred-syllable Vajrasattva mantra.

Vajrayana The fast vehicle or the tantric path, which is an esoteric form of Mahayana Buddhism.

Vajrayogini A female Buddha of highest yoga tantra practices.

Vesak The yearly commemoration of the birth, enlightenment and death of Buddha Shakyamuni. Since it is calculated according to the lunar calendar, its date in the western calendar varies for different countries and from year to year.

Vipassana Meditation method aimed at the development of clear insight into the nature of reality.

Yogi/yogini A man/woman performing regular, long-term meditation, practices and prayers in order to achieve union with reality.

Literature
and other sources

Publications by Lama Gangchen:

❀Lama Gangchen, T.Y.S., (1993), *Self-Healing II*, Lama Gangchen Peace Publications

❀Lama Gangchen, T.Y.S., (1994), *NgalSo Tantric Self-Healing III*, Lama Gangchen Peace Publications

❀Lama Gangchen, T.Y.S., (1995), *Zhing Kham Yong So – Making Peace with the Environment*, Lama Gangchen Peace Publications

❀Lama Gangchen, T.Y.S., (1997), *The Borobudur Stupa-Mandala NgalSo Self-Healing*, Lama Gangchen Peace Publications

❀Lama Gangchen, T.Y.S., (1999), *NgalSo Tantric Self-Healing Commentary*, Lama Gangchen Peace Publications

❀Lama Gangchen, T.Y.S., (2004), *Great Wheel Vajrapani NgalSo Self-Healing Practice*, Lama Gangchen Peace Publications

❀Lama Gangchen, T.Y.S., (2013), *Choose Peace, A Gift of Wisdom for a Less Expensive Life*, Lama Gangchen Peace Publications

From the series Seeds for Peace:

❀Lama Gangchen, T.Y.S., (2011), *Seeds for Peace IV - Homage to Borobudur: Ocean of Mandalas*, Lama Gangchen Peace Publications

❀Lama Gangchen, T.Y.S., (2012), *Seeds for Peace V - Lalitavistara Mahayana Sutra*, Lama Gangchen Peace Publications

From the series LINKS –

Reports from conferences at Borobudur, organized by Lama Gangchen World Peace Foundation, (Editor: Isthar D. Adler):

❀*LINKS V 'Borobudur 2013' World Congress - An Education for the*

Third Millennium, Lama Gangchen Peace Publications

⚫*LINKS VI 'Borobudur 2014' World Congress - An Education for the Third Millennium,* Lama Gangchen Peace Publications

⚫*LINKS VII 'Borobudur 2015' World Congress - An Education for the Third Millennium,* Lama Gangchen Peace Publications

Publications by other Buddhist teachers:

⚫Pabongka Rinpoche, (first English edition, 1991), *Liberation in the Palm of your Hand,* Wisdom Publications, US

⚫Lama Yeshe, (1998), *The Bliss of Inner Fire - Heart Practice of the Six Yogas of Naropa,* Wisdom Publications, US

⚫Lama Michel Rinpoche, (2015), *Compassion in (Mental) Health Care,* lecture transcript, Lama Gangchen Peace Publications

⚫Gammon, C. (Lama Caroline) & Back, C., (2013), *Gangchen, a Spiritual Heritage,* Lama Gangchen World Peace Foundation, CH

⚫Vessantara, (1993), *Meeting the Buddhas,* Windhorse Publications, UK

Other publications:

⚫Bernet Kempers, A.J., (1970), *Borobudur Mysteriegebeuren in Steen - Verval en Restauratie - Oudjavaans Volksleven,* Servire, The Netherlands

⚫Best, T. de & Zwaan, K., (2013), *De Magie van het Tibetaans Boeddhisme - Over een Lama Healer en de Zoektocht van een Limburgs Meisje,* Aspekt, The Netherlands

⚫Oostindie, G., (2015), *Soldaat in Indonesië 1945-1950 - Getuigenissen van een Oorlog aan de Verkeerde Kant van de Geschiedenis,* Prometheus, The Netherlands

⚫Soekmono, R., (1976), *Chandi Borobudur - A Monument of Mankind,* Van Gorkum, The Netherlands and Unesco Press, France

⚫(2005), *The Restoration of Borobudur,* UNESCO

⚫(2010), *Borobudur, Majestic Mysterious Magnificent,* Taman Wisata Candi Borobudur, Prambanan & Ratu Boko, Indonesia

Besides the above-mentioned publications we have drawn upon numerous teachings by Lama Gangchen, Lama Michel and Lama Caroline. Where possible, we mention a specific teaching in a footnote. Many of these teachings are recorded and published on the NgalSo channel: *youtube.com/ngalsovideo*.

For more information visit *ahmc.ngalso.net* and *kunpen.ngalso.org*

Acknowledgements

Together we can

We wish to express our gratitude to all who have played a part in the realization of this book. However before we start, we can already say that this list will not be complete. The causes and conditions that have contributed to the creation of this book are infinite. As Lama Michel often points out during teachings, "How many things have happened prior to the fact of you being here now? How many causes and conditions have led to this exact moment?" If his mother Bel Cesar hadn't gone to a certain birthday party and if she hadn't been asked there to organize a visit to Brazil by the Tibetan Lama Gangchen Rinpoche, the course of Lama Michel's life would have been completely different...

An infinite number of factors have contributed to this book. Huge factors, like Lama Gangchen coming to the West, and 'little' ones like the fact we have a desk and a computer. Essential factors like the availability of several capable editors and graphic designers in our circle, and 'trivial' ones like the yellow Post-its that we used to scribble our notes.

First of all, we thank Lama Gangchen Rinpoche. He came from Tibet via India to the West and opened the mandala of Borobudur in Indonesia for all of us. We are intensely grateful for his wisdom and compassion, for his blessings and support, and for the trust he placed in us.

We thank Lama Michel Rinpoche for his deep and clear teachings. Steadily, he brings us insight into the depth of Buddhist philosophy, and teaches us how we can apply this in our daily life. We have extensively drawn upon the accessible way that he conveys and formulates Buddha's lessons.

Lama Caroline helped us a great deal - it is thanks to her scientific work combined with a Buddhist view that we can understand Borobudur better in detail.

Over sixty people have directly joined in the creation of this book. It has become a magnificent international collaboration between disciples and friends of Lama Gangchen. Around 55 people have shared their personal story or experience, for which we are very grateful. Together they paint the picture of Borobudur in relation to Lama Gangchen and the NgalSo Self-Healing.

In most cases we have interviewed them and written their stories. Many interviews took place in Indonesia, during a retreat at Borobudur. The stories of Lola Hernandez, Claudia Sobrevila and the late Dominique Detchen Bock Nayir were written by themselves. With their permission, we reproduced them and edited lightly. Sarah Steines wrote a touching poem that was granted a place as a prologue at the beginning of the book.

We thank Professor Lokesh Chandra and Professor Nirmala Sharma - both from India - for their presence and very interesting contributions during the conference held at the Borobudur retreat in 2013. We have gratefully made use of the information and experiences they brought and that was recorded in the conference report LINKS V.

Thanks to Isthar Adler, for her enthusiastic collaboration at various stages of the project, and for her tireless efforts to publish the LINKS series. These conference reports with many transcriptions, documentation and stories formed an invaluable source of information.

This book has been written more or less simultaneously in two languages. Karin mainly wrote in Dutch and Irene mostly took care of the English. We translated each other's texts. A result of publishing in the two languages was the fact that there was a large group of proofreaders and editors involved. Four people joined in the production of the Dutch version.

Lidy Haarman was asked to give feedback at an early stage. Her enthusiasm motivated us to continue the course we had set.

Our sister Inge Zwaan came with necessary corrections, and advised us where to clarify for the uninitiated readers.

Trudi Geugjes appeared to have been to Borobudur even before the restoration. Due to her enthusiasm about the magnificent building, she joined the club and her view on Borobudur gave us surprising insights.

Finally, Hanneke van der Woude took care of editing the complete manuscript. She convinced us that difficult or unfamiliar terms deserve an explanation in a footnote, in addition to the glossary, for readers' convenience.

Petrus Linnemann from England, who passed away in 2015, helped with translating and editing some stories in an early stage. After his death, Sharon Dawson edited his personal story and Lama Caroline read it at his funeral ceremony.

Laura Lau from Singapore corrected and edited the English texts, and helped by being vigilant regarding the content. Moreover, she brought an Asian reader's perspective, which made us aware of our sometimes-ethnocentric Western view that resounded in the text. This led to important insights and some adjustments.

Sarah Steines from England also helped with correcting and improving the English manuscript. She advised on content as well as on 'styling', and patiently helped to find the right tone, an adequate word or correct definition.

Both are not just editors; they are editors with dharma knowledge, which has been extremely helpful. Without their professional, passionate and encouraging involvement, an English version of the book would not have been realized.

We thank Thomas Nitzsche from Germany, for giving us the permission to use the magical picture for the cover. Thomas took the picture in three parts. The process of creating one complete image required some precise retouching, which was performed by Renata Reis, Jairo da Rocha and Denis Michael Lazaro whom we also thank.

The Brazilian graphic designers Renata Reis and Renata Zincone took care of the cover design, the layout of the text and the selection of suitable images. Without their creative minds, their eager and enthusiastic collaboration and talent to sense what is needed, this artistic result would not have been possible.

Matteo Calautti from Italy drew the beautiful Borobudur-inspired flower decorations that are used throughout the book.

For translations and corrections of additional texts in the second edition we thank Lama Michel Rinpoche, Cosy Back, Rocio Blanco Rubio, Kersten Dohmen, Carlotta Segre, Shi Yang Shi, family Nguyen Tat, Kiran KC, Renata Zincone and Alex Cooley.

We also thank:

Lama Gangchen Peace Publications, for allowing us to use their stock of images and office facilities.

Our Dutch publisher Perry Pierik from Aspekt, for embracing this bilingual project.

The protestant vicar August Ouw (from Indonesia) who planted some seeds in our childhood. He has contributed by translating some texts from Bahasa Indonesia into Dutch. Moreover, he urged us to reflect deeper upon Dutch colonial history.

Kiran KC for his boundless patience during our frequent and endless Skype sessions.

Our parents, for all they have done for us and for what they mean to us.

Without all the persons mentioned, including the international group of people who shared their personal stories, this book would not be here. Every contribution – big or small, direct or indirect – has been equally important for the result. One of Lama Gangchen's mottos is "Together we can." This slogan has been very much applicable to this Borobudur project. We did it together! Thank you all!

June 21st 2016

Stavoren, The Netherlands – Albagnano, Italy

Karin and Irene